ONE WEEK LOAN

MANCHESTER
UNIVERSITY PRESS

STUDIES IN
POPULAR
CULTURE

General editor: Professor Jeffrey Richards

Already published

Spiritualism and British society between the wars
Jenny Hazelgrove

Smoking in British popular culture 1800–2000
Matthew Hilton

Films and British national identity: from Dickens to *Dad's Army*
Jeffrey Richards

The car in British society: class, gender and motoring 1896–1939
Sean O'Connell

Forthcoming titles

Cultures of drinking in Britain since 1750
David Gutzke

**Capital entertainment: the transformation of
popular culture in London 1890–1960**
Andrew Horrall

Women's leisure in England 1920–60
Claire Langhamer

Music for the middle classes: a cultural history of amateur operatics
John Lowerson

Science and technology in popular culture
Simon Nightingale

Coming together: sex and popular culture in Britain 1800–1999
Tim O'Neill

The North in the national imagination: England 1850–2000
David Russell

The British seaside

Holidays and resorts in the twentieth century

JOHN K. WALTON

Manchester University Press

Manchester and New York

distributed exclusively in the USA by St. Martin's Press

Published by Manchester University Press
Oxford Road, Manchester M13 9NR, UK
and Room 400, 175 Fifth Avenue, New York, NY 10010, USA
http://www.man.ac.uk/mup

Distributed exclusively in the USA by
St. Martin's Press, Inc., 175 Fifth Avenue, New York,
NY 10010, USA

Distributed exclusively in Canada by
UBC Press, University of British Columbia, 2029 West Mall,
Vancouver, BC, Canada V6T 1Z2

British Library Cataloguing-in-Publication Data
A catalogue record for this book is available from the British Library

Library of Congress Cataloging-in-Publication Data applied for

ISBN   0 7190 5169 X   hardback
        0 7190 5170 3   paperback

First published 2000

07 06 05 04 03 02 01 00   10 9 8 7 6 5 4 3 2 1

Typeset in Hong Kong
by Graphicraft Limited
Printed in Great Britain
by Biddles Ltd, Guildford and King's Lynn

STUDIES IN POPULAR CULTURE

General editor's introduction

There has in recent years been an explosion of interest in culture and cultural studies. The impetus has come from two directions and out of two different traditions. On the one hand, cultural history has grown out of social history to become a distinct and identifiable school of historical investigation. On the other hand, cultural studies has grown out of English literature and has concerned itself to a large extent with contemporary issues. Nevertheless, there is a shared project, its aim, to elucidate the meanings and values implicit and explicit in the art, literature, learning, institutions and everyday behaviour within a given society. Both the cultural historian and the cultural studies scholar seek to explore the ways in which a culture is imagined, represented and received, how it interacts with social processes, how it contributes to individual and collective identities and world views, to stability and change, to social, political and economic activities and programmes. This series aims to provide an arena for the cross-fertilisation of the discipline, so that the work of the cultural historian can take advantage of the most useful and illuminating of the theoretical developments and the cultural studies scholars can extend the purely historical underpinnings of their investigations. The ultimate objective of the series is to provide a range of books which will explain in a readable and accessible way where we are now socially and culturally and how we got to where we are. This should enable people to be better informed, promote an interdisciplinary approach to cultural issues and encourage deeper thought about the issues, attitudes and institutions of popular culture.

Jeffrey Richards

General editor's foreword

John K. Walton is the doyen of seaside historians. In his definitive history of the eighteenth- and nineteenth-century seaside holiday, *The English seaside resort: a social history 1750–1914* (1983), his history of the premier British resort, *Blackpool* (1998) and his classic account of a legendary seaside institution, *The Blackpool landlady* (1978), he has made a major contribution to our understanding of that much-loved and much-mocked phenomenon, the British seaside holiday. He now turns his attention to the seaside resort in the twentieth century and brings to the subject his formidable intelligence, his unrivalled knowledge and his enviable ability to produce fluently readable prose.

Previous accounts of the seaside resort in this century have concentrated on the idea of decline. This is a view that Walton persuasively challenges. While acknowledging that there was a decline in the 1970s and 1980s due to a combination of economic recession and competition from cheap foreign holidays, he lays greater stress on the resorts' survival and incipient revival. Drawing on the work of sociologists, anthropologists and geographers as well as historians, he establishes the changing patterns of land ownership, consumption, transportation, provision and expectation. He explores the areas of planning, investment, regulation and redevelopment. Nothing escapes his eagle eye, from coastal erosion and sewage pollution to pier destruction and bungaloid growth. He vividly captures the subtle gradations in the hierarchy of resorts, the social distinctions within and between the different classes of holidaymakers, the variety and evolution of seaside pleasures and pastimes, and the kaleidoscopic cultural image of the seaside holiday. With his combination of scholarship and readability, he has produced a major interpretative work which enables us to view the British seaside resort with new understanding.

Jeffrey Richards

Contents

Preface

This book depends heavily on source material acquired through half a lifetime of research in second-hand bookshops, although the British Library has also played an important part (especially since the move to St Pancras, with the wonders of the word-search facilities in the new catalogue). Library staff in Blackpool and Scarborough, and archive staff at the Lancashire Record Office in Preston, also deserve grateful acknowledgement. So do several of my former students, most directly Julian Demetriadi and Nora Essafi, and the authors of the other research dissertations I have consulted (especially Nigel Morgan, Dawn Crouch and Laura Chase). Nigel Morgan and Annette Pritchard brought out their book, *Power and politics at the seaside: the development of Devon's resorts in the twentieth century* (University of Exeter Press, 1999) slightly too late for me to make proper use of it here: it should be read in conjunction with the present work. Colleagues at the University of Central Lancashire have been very helpful, especially Mike Paris, whose advice on films (and generosity in loaning them) has been invaluable, and Susan Burnett, whose comments have improved the Introduction. Jeffrey Richards has been an exemplary series editor. Sue Wright has continued to encourage me to be a cultural as well as a social historian (and to think about the distinctions and overlaps involved), and I hope that what follows will match up to her exacting requirements. If it does not do so, it will at least provoke domestic debate. I have enjoyed the writing of this book, and I hope that this sense of enjoyment will communicate itself to the reader. I am sure that this will still not be my last word on the British seaside, but I also have designs on more distant climes. We shall see.

Accrington
J.W.

Introduction:
representations and debates

The travel writer Bill Bryson tells us that,[1]

> Once many years ago, in anticipation of the children we would one day have, a relative of my wife's gave us a box of Ladybird Books from the 1950s and 60s. They all had titles like *Out in the Sun* and *Sunny Days at the Seaside*, and contained meticulously drafted, richly coloured illustrations of a prosperous, contented, litter-free Britain in which the sun always shone . . . My favourite . . . portrayed an island of rocky coves and long views that was recognizably British, but with a Mediterranean climate and a tidy absence of pay-and-display car parks, bingo parlours, and the tackier sort of amusement arcades . . . I was strangely influenced by this book and for some years agreed to take our family holidays at the British seaside on the assumption that one day we would find this magic place where summer days were forever sunny, the water as warm as a sitz-bath, and commercial blight unknown.

Children's literature is as good a starting point as any from which to introduce the enduring importance of the British seaside. At the end of the twentieth century as at the beginning, little books with themes based on an idealised version of the seaside holiday were indispensable to any self-respecting series of publications aimed at small children (and, of course, their parents). Few better indicators can be imagined, in outline, of the perceived importance of the seaside as basic cultural capital, as something every child can and should recognise, respond to and enjoy; although we need to know more about the role of television in all this. By the 1980s and 1990s, at least, the seaside was enshrined in media which were designed to foster the literacy of print rather than in the realms of the electronic. But a trawl through the British Library catalogue of post-1975 publications in the Humanities, following the key-word 'seaside', shows the pervasiveness of seaside themes in books for young children. Among the characters who 'went to the seaside' and had adventures there were Paddington Bear, Sooty, Basil Brush, Worzel Gummidge, Smudger, Noddy,

Topsy and Tim, Victoria Plum, Rupert, Orlando the Marmalade Cat, Cap'n Birds Eye, the Ghost Family Robinson, Roland Rat, Mr Happy, the Munch Bunch and the Naughty Shadows. There were nearly fifty such entries, including an extensive array of teddy bears, a seaside train in the Thomas the Tank Engine series, and Little Dracula. It seemed unlikely that literacy could be attained in the pre-school and infant school years without coming into contact with the images of seaside environments and seaside fun which these books provided. Twenty-eight of the publications listed by the British Library came from the 1980s, but the genre seemed to be holding up well in the last decade of the millennium, and further along the line there were also books on seaside maths, seaside science and the discovery of the Holy Spirit at the seaside, as well as the inevitable volume in the revived I-Spy series, originated by the *News Chronicle* newspaper, which sought to encourage children to be observant by awarding them points on a sliding scale for 'spotting' objects in particular kinds of place.

Books for slightly older juvenile readers, like Enid Blyton's *The Rub-a-dub Mystery* in the Famous Five series, might be more likely to be hidden from this kind of literal-minded electronic search. Frank Richards's *Billy Bunter at Butlin's* (1961) would be equally elusive, depriving the researcher of an interesting comparison between the Skegness holiday camp and a public school house system, and of a sycophantic panegyric on the camps themselves, celebrating their noisy gregariousness in a way that contrives to emphasise classless mingling while at the same time locating Butlinland as somewhere beyond the normal ken of a public school family. At least it rescued the equally anomalous Bunter from washing-up duties at his uncle's boarding-house in Folkestone, a perceptive recognition by Richards of the realities of seaside domestic economies (in both senses) among the submerged middle classes. More generally, the place of the seaside in juvenile literature was part of a tradition with roots before the Victorians: the seaside had long been thought to be an attractive way of capturing children's attention, as witness (for example) *The Walrus and the Carpenter*, and a necessary part of their socialisation and acculturation into a wider world of pleasures and experiences. It was also a plausible and attractive location for adventure beyond the supervision of adults, with props which might include caves, smugglers, rocks and whirlpools. By the late twentieth century, when the British seaside as a main holiday destination was in sharp decline, this preoccupation may say more about the nostalgic values of parents and publishers than about the notional preferences of the children themselves; but that does not make it less arresting. Related attitudes were still enshrined in (for example) the themes of jigsaw puzzles and greetings cards, in souvenirs and above all in reminiscence. Nostalgia was a growing force here. But even in the 1990s, at least half of all British holidays were still taken in seaside resorts, as the British Resorts Association was anxious to proclaim. The nature of the experience had changed a great deal over the century, as we shall see; but its power to command allegiance had waned without being altogether spent. And there was still scope for revival.[2]

The children's books highlight a seaside world which was already endangered, if not on nostalgia-fuelled life support systems, by the later twentieth century. They celebrate sea and sand, bucket and spade, crabs and starfish, rock-pools and coves, old salts and rowing-boats, ice-cream, Punch and Judy and other ostensibly innocent forms of beach entertainment, piers, bandstands, deck-chairs and cups of tea in faded but friendly sea-front cafes. This is the innocent and timeless vision of the seaside which the post-war generation embroidered from its own memories of childhood holidays, at resorts which were just beginning to pass into the time-warp from which it was to prove so difficult to rescue them, after the traumatic changes of the 1970s and 1980s which form an important theme of this book. There have been, of course, alternative versions of seaside experience, focusing on different stages of the life cycle, which emphasise (for example) the loneliness and isolation of seaside retirement; the threat posed by erosion and flood to life, property and security in vulnerable areas; the rootlessness of the young seasonal worker in arcade, boarding-house or bar; the sexual fears and opportunities engendered by the transitory and complicit aspects of the resort environment, for residents and visitors alike; the earthy seediness of the less glamorous levels of the entertainment industry; the violence of gangs and protection rackets in places where a high throughput of visitors seeking services on or beyond the fringes of legality has established lucrative and tempting markets for the providers; the poverty amidst plenty endured by those for whom seaside employment is intermittent, unorganised, patronage-dependent and ill-paid; and more generally the conjunctions of defensive gentility, precarious respectability, chromium-plated glamour, earthy humour and raw sexuality which make up some of the distinctively seaside-flavoured cocktails of British popular culture, and which will be pursued in later chapters.

All this is seasoned by the consensually liminal nature of the seaside as 'place on the margin', where land and sea meet, the pleasure principle is given freer rein, the certainties of authority are diluted, and the usual constraints on behaviour are suspended, however provisionally, to give a broader acceptability to, or at least tolerance of, variety of sexual partners and practices, or unscheduled bodily exposure, or drink-fuelled raucousness, ribaldry or indelicacy, or the consumption of greasy food with the fingers in the public street. The seaside puts the 'civilising process' temporarily into reverse (although the participants understand that they are defying its conventions) and conjures up the spirit of carnival, in the sense of upturning the social order and celebrating the rude, the excessive, the anarchic, the hidden and the gross, in ways which generate tension and put respectability on the defensive, generating culture wars in settings where the prim and the Rabelaisian sides of British character come into maritime confrontation, and where the genteel, controlled, symmetrical front of the resort finds itself invaded by the disorder, untidiness and misrule of the back.[3] These themes, which are as old in this setting as the seaside holiday itself, found their way into (for example) the grotesque prurience of the comic postcard, the nudging innuendo of the down-market music-hall and some kinds of end-of-the-pier show, the humorous sketches about landladies and lodgers, the stories of foreshore foreplay and sexual promiscuity which were current in pubs and workplaces and alluded to in other media, the self-conscious vulgarity of some kinds of commercial souvenir; and in more up-market vein, the knowing allusions of the *Punch* cartoon and its related commentaries, and the pervasiveness of the seaside as locale for the holiday romance and other kinds of popular story. The seaside holiday was a particularly strong theme in the metropolitan music-hall of the turn of the century. Peter Bailey lists it alongside 'booze, romantic adventure, marriage and mothers-in-law, [and] dear old pals', all of which were capable of being highlighted in a seaside setting anyway. The first two were often associated with the notion of a seaside holiday as liberating people from the leaden constraints of day-to-day identity, which is a recurrent theme in popular literature, and at least as old in principle as environments like eighteenth-century Bath, where in the absence of deeper knowledge of people's antecendents in a temporary community of strangers, appearance, manners and plausibility might be everything. Thus:[4]

> Tibbins the city clerk blooms into Captain Tickleby, habitue of Pall Mall and Monte Carlo, as he steps off the train for his week in Folkestone. Miss Becky Solomons from the fried fish shop becomes the beautiful Rebecca on the promenade at Margate . . .

The pages of *Ally Sloper's Half-Holiday* and similar late Victorian publications for a popular (and not just working-class) market both mocked such aspirations and sympathetically endorsed them. This was a view from the metropolis, and even in its anonymous orbit come-uppance for holiday role-play fantasists was likely to come from people who knew them at home. This was much more likely in settings like Blackpool, where whole northern towns went on holiday at once and pretensions were especially likely to be punctured by sardonic public comment, while excessive behaviour became the subject of adverse report; but even here it was possible to play at living beyond your station, especially when the rules were generally known, and getting away to the sea could mean more than simply suspending the daily drudgery of the work routine, especially for the young and unattached, although even that most basic temporary transformation was felt worthy of celebration in postcard and souvenir.[5] But even the liveliest and most popular seaside resorts were seldom places where constraints and conventions were cast to the winds: people brought their own internal controls and assumptions about proper behaviour with them, and still cared about what others thought of them; but the seaside provided a changed register of expectations, freer but still bounded by wider notions of respectability and propriety. Nevertheless, it was liberating in terms of recounted experience as well as myth, as Anthony Burgess's memories of inter-war Blackpool and Anglesey suggest. For Burgess in the late 1930s, 'The pleasure city of Blackpool, and even its refined annexes, seethed with sex, as it had to'; and here, but also a year later doing penance in an isolated farmhouse on the Welsh island, he enjoyed amorous encounters with the servants. He thus undermines the claim of Mass-Observation, the anthropological research organisation, that Blackpool's raunchiness at this time was more symbolism than substance, and given the (generally) middle-class observers' manifest inability to understand the languages of the culture they observed, he is the more credible witness.[6]

Such tensions ensured that the seaside featured in adult as well as children's literature. It was attractive to novelists, just as the social melting-pot of Bath, the first of Britain's large specialised resorts to pull in a national visiting public, had been present at the birth of the eighteenth-century novel.[7] Jane Austen identified its potential in her unfinished satirical novel *Sanditon*, and in the twentieth century the seaside resort continued to provide worlds in microcosm and opportunities for social comment for an extensive array of novelists. Arnold Bennett was particularly taken with the scope it offered for cheeky entrepreneurship, as Denry Machin in *The Card*, surrounded by fellow visitors from the Staffordshire Potteries, made a hat-box full of sovereigns out of his stay in Llandudno by providing sea trips in a lifeboat which he had helped to mythologise, and then capitalising on an accidentally discovered 'chocolate remedy', in a tale which might have been a parody of the well-rewarded opportunism of Blackpool's turn-of-the-century populist entrepreueurs. The same novel also presents the seaside as an arena of temptations to extravagance, in which the weaknesses of potential marriage partners are exposed, in a plot-line which points up both the suspension of everyday constraints and the dangers entailed by forgetting them altogether, which resonates effectively with notions of the seaside holiday as liminal and carnivalesque but not unbounded or consequence-free.[8] Graham Greene looked at the seamy side of Brighton life in the 1930s, with affectionate regard for the hard-won escapism of the holiday throng and due attention to the sharpness of class divisions in small areas. But his focus was on petty criminals and the violence of the gangs who battened on the race meetings, and he drew particular attention to the rootless and impoverished layers of poverty and insecurity which the larger resorts generated, worlds in which relationships were impermanent and instrumental, and the stable communities which mitigated the experience of poverty and unemployment in the industrial towns were not available to comfort, invigilate and restrain.[9] Related themes were taken up and developed more explicitly by Robert Tressell in *The ragged-trousered philanthropists*, an autobiographical novel which may lack the 'high culture' status even of Bennett or of Greene's 'entertainments', but has an enduringly enthusiastic following among those who appreciate its portrayal of the struggle for survival in Edwardian Hastings, thinly disguised as 'Mugsborough'. The author, who knew intimately whereof he spoke, presents us with building workers who are victims less of the rapid flux of migration and seasonal labour, than of the pressures towards deferential acceptance of authority in a stagnating town where access to work was regulated by reputation for tractability. On either model, the experience of working-class or small business life in seaside resorts entailed the construction of demanding survival strategies through dramas of daily living which provided compelling material for the observant novelist.[10] H.G. Wells preferred to by-pass this in *The history of Mr Polly*, moving briskly through his hero's fifteen years of stultifying dulness and dyspeptic respectability as a marginal small shopkeeper in 'Fishbourne', which resembled Herne Bay, while showing some empathy with his struggles. A little way along the coast, George Meek's autobiography confirmed the tone of Tressell's writings, as he narrated his precarious existence on the road to becoming the only socialist bath-chair man in Eastbourne (or, no doubt, anywhere else), earning a preface from Wells but little lasting fame.[11] Arthur Laycock's novel of Blackpool life, *Warren of Manchester*, likewise subsided into obscurity: this portrayal of the struggles of two landladies and their families, from contrasting backgrounds, carried a romantic socialist message in an improbable setting, though one which its author, a poet, dialect writer and Blackpool's first 'socialist' councillor, knew well; and he chose to celebrate the triumph of unpretentious neighbourliness and rough kindness over the spirits of snobbery and anonymous competition in a northern setting where the former virtues perhaps had more chance of survival.[12]

Such 'slice of life' novels in seaside resort settings remained unusual: the seaside was more likely to provide an episode or reflective interlude in the plot, as in Harry and Helen's brief holiday from Hanky Park after Harry's win on the horses (almost the only route to such an escape from working-class Salford in the inter-war depression, as portrayed by Walter Greenwood) in *Love on the dole*, or, in much more up-market vein, in Arnold Bennett's Edwardian portrayals of Brighton's great hotels in *Clayhanger* and *Hilda Lessways*, in which he contrasted Brighton's 'wealth and luxury' with 'the pleasure cities of the poor and middling such as Blackpool and Llandudno'.[13] There has not, in fact, been a great novel set primarily, or even to a large extent, at the twentieth-century British seaside: nothing to match Mann's *Buddenbrooks*, or the French seaside dimension to Proust's *A la recherche du temps perdu*, in their own century. The seaside has, perhaps, seemed too trivial, its denizens too petty bourgeois or retired from the world: although that has not deterred novelists from making such characters memorable in other settings. There have, however, been interesting vignettes, autobiographical or otherwise. Philip Norman's *The skater's waltz*, for example, re-created a childhood at Ryde (Isle of Wight) in the mid-1950s. Beyond the tortured family relationships at its core, the plot revolved around an attempt to revivify the pier through roller-skating, under insecure financial circumstances and against a backdrop of faded older glories (a Royal Hotel which had not coped with the motor age), and with a sub-text of furtive sexual adventure.[14] The social uncertainty, sexual unease and sense of full bloom and incipient decay which seemed to typify the Indian summer of the seaside in the 1950s had advanced into putrefaction by the time Matt Thorne produced *Tourist* in 1998. Set in a tacky, run-down Weston-super-Mare, among the flotsam of the fringes of the entertainment industry, the story links the rootless young who form the mainstay of the casual and seasonal labour force, with tolerant elders who have seen it all before, and febrile entrepreneurial activity against all the apparent odds. The rotting Grand Pier, the unemployable drunks who haunt the arcades, and the beach at night as an exciting accessible space for teenage sexual activity, are juxtaposed in the narrator's mind with memories of the banality of childhood seaside visits; but by this time the nostalgia has been displaced by something approaching nightmare. This is a telling imaginative reconstruction of the English seaside in calamitous trans-formative free-fall, with skeletons behind the net curtains of every outwardly respectable boarding-house.[15]

The seaside also found its way into British cinema, offering as it did an opportunity to depict people outside their usual social settings, advancing the plot with recourse to attractive surroundings connotative of pleasure (and to spliced-in newsreel film) while offering ample scope for the comedy of (cultural and sexual) embarrassment and the deflation of pretension and pomposity. The 1930s saw a string of films in which the seaside was at or close to the centre, including *The Good Companions* (1932), with its camaraderie among seekers after freedom and stardom through a touring pierrot troupe, *Bank Holiday* (1938) which circled uneasily around the idea of the dirty weekend while portraying (very successfully, to contemporary reviewers) a slice of life at a crowded resort, and the Gracie Fields vehicle *Sing As We Go* (1934). With its knowledgeable and sympathetic J.B. Priestley script, this was per-haps the most successful of all, depicting the petty tyranny of the Blackpool boarding-house proprietor, Blackpool's holiday industry from the Tower and open-air swimming-pool to the freak shows and song-pluggers of the 'Golden Mile', and Gracie's triumphant escape from servitude to bring consensus and humanity to management in the cotton industry from which she came.[16] These films largely celebrated the good humour and vitality of the 'common people' at leisure, especially at Blackpool, which was also one of the settings for *Hindle Wakes* (versions in 1918, 1927, 1931 and 1952), *The Three Kings* (1929), *No Lady* (1931) and *Cotton Queen* (1937, starring Stanley Holloway).[17] The popularity of *Hindle Wakes* was particularly striking, indicating that Stanley Houghton had hit a raw nerve with the original stage play of 1912, which affirmed a working-class woman's right to sexual enjoyment without marriage as a necessary expectation, and brought out the liminal nature of the seaside as a location for sexual encounters which crossed class boundaries, although this was a liaison between people from the same town facilitated by Blackpool's social melting-pot but consummated (in the play at least) in the more secure anonymity of Llandudno. The 1927 version of the film, the first to be set in Blackpool, did focus on the town itself, using the opportunities for sexual close-ness and excitement afforded by the Pleasure Beach and the Tower to advance the plot, and foregrounding Blackpool's distinctive version of seaside liminality.[18] Jeffrey Richards has suggested that the seaside films, and others which won lavish praise from critics, were 'concerned with areas, professions and aspects of life essentially peripheral to the everyday year-in, year-out concerns of the industrial proletariat'.[19] In the case of the seaside, this is overstated, especially as the holiday industry had, and has, its own proletariat; and the 'common people' theme in a seaside setting was also prominent (often with an air of condescension) in contemporary journalism, especially when supplied by the contemporary intelligentsia, as in Yvonne Cloud's celebratory compilation on popular resorts in 1934 which featured chapters by Malcolm Muggeridge and James Laver.[20]

Films with a similar outlook reappeared in the post-war domestic holiday boom, including *Holiday Camp* (1947), a 'seminal compendium comedy drama' which introduced the almost prototypical soap opera family, the Huggetts, making the point in the process that the crowds enjoying 'mass leisure', which the camera dwelt on through the grand-scale choreography of 'keep fit' sessions, swimming-pool action and the hokey-cokey, were composed of individuals with their own peculiarities and priorities. The seaside as a setting for romantic rule-breaking and card-sharping between strangers was a strong feature of the complex plot, with remarkable hints of the possibility of abortion. Seaside liminality was put in its place, literally, by the avuncular Jack Warner as Joe Huggett, who offered the homespun wisdom that pretty girls in 'pants and brasiers', as he pronounced it, were all very well at the seaside, but something plainer and more reliable was needed at home. There was also *Dick Barton Strikes Back* (1949), which featured a chase up Blackpool Tower, and *Forbidden* (1949), which had a Blackpool fairground setting and returned to the theme of Blackpool as hotbed of illicit seaside passions: here the 'common people' theme turns rather sour. Beyond this (but not for export far beyond Lancashire) lay the scabrous Frank Randle vehicle *Holidays with Pay* (1949), featuring Blackpool's most scandalous comedian on home territory, and in sombre vein the film version of Graham Greene's 'entertainment' *Brighton Rock* (1947). Interestingly, however, cinema interest in the seaside then disappears underground; and when it reappears in the late 1950s and early 1960s times and representations have changed. *Barnacle Bill* (1957), the last of the Ealing comedies, features the 'last of a long line of sailors' who suffers from seasickness and 'takes command of a decaying Victorian pier at an English seaside resort'. Leslie Halliwell thought it 'a little staid', and Jeffrey Richards argued that it occupied classic Ealing territory alongside, for example, *The Titfield Thunderbolt* 'a world that is essentially quaint, cosy, whimsical and backward-looking', celebrating the defenders of ramshackle old technology like paddle steamers and Heath Robinson steam trains.[21]

Significantly, this was to be an influential media perception of the seaside from this time on, and it was prominent in different but recognisable guise in *The Punch and Judy Man* (1962), which presents Tony Hancock as the itinerant showman of the title. He occupies theatrical lodgings for the season in a resort labelled Piltdown Bay, which looks like a miniature cross between Hastings and Bognor Regis. Here he provides alfresco children's entertainment while mixing socially with the presenter of a very decorous beach show about the life and death of Nelson (excluding Lady Hamilton), and an assertive promenade photographer. This way of life is presented as old-fashioned and under threat, with the Mayor and his smooth and corrupt cronies on the Council finding the showmen embarrassingly down-at-heel and atavistic, while the Mayoress goes further by booking Hancock (through his social-climbing wife and to his indignation) as an emblem of the seaside's traditions, a heritage entertainment, for the festivities to inaugurate the illuminations and commemorate the resort's sixtieth anniversary. Even more telling than the satire on local government, incompetent and ineffectually seeking promotional publicity, is the ruthless depiction of the deserted promenade in lashing rain, which makes the allusions to competition from foreign holidays all the more telling. The film conveys the sense that this kind of resort is at a crossroads, with shabby-genteel middle-aged visitors, the older entertainments going out of fashion, and nothing distinctive to replace them (hence, perhaps, the need for Hancock's booking). The Cliff Richard vehicle *Summer Holiday* (1962) picks up on these issues more directly (and also less subtly), as the star and friends take a London double-decker bus to the exciting technicolor delights of 'abroad' to escape from the monochrome dullness of the by-now traditional English seaside holiday, which here is straightforwardly both the butt of the humour and the kind of place no image-conscious teenager would be seen dead in. The Morecambe of *The Entertainer* (1960) conveys a similar impression, with its seedy impresario, grubby theatrical 'digs' and seedier theatre and bathing beauty contest. *The System* (1964) had a more up-market setting, but its focus on 'seaside layabouts', in Leslie Halliwell's phrase, formed part of the general disillusionment.[22] It may be significant that none of the bawdy but generously silly themed comedy series of the mid-1950s onwards, not even the 'Carry On' films with their infamously 'seaside postcard' humour and linkages to music-hall, had a British seaside resort setting, although *Carry on Abroad* visited package holiday territory in Spain in 1972, as did a cinematic spin-off of the department store sit-com *Are You Being Served?*, which was set on the 'Costa Plonka' in 1977.

After the clutch of films in the early 1960s, British cinema lost interest in the seaside: itself a telling development. *That'll be the Day* (1973) fuelled fantasies about sexual freedom in holiday camps, but as part of a picaresque account of a more wide-ranging journey through life; and it was not until *Wish You Were Here?* (1989) that a seaside resort setting returned to centre stage, in what Halliwell described as 'a film full of telling detail and compassion'.[23] In the meantime, the hit television comedy series *Hi-De-Hi* had evoked the seaside holiday camps of the immediate post-war years, which already seemed part of a distant past, and derived much of their humour from a recognizable outlandishness, which included, in early episodes, the new manager's anachronistic aspirations to educating the tastes and sensibilities of his customers. *Fawlty Towers*, John Cleese's lampoon of the pretentious and ignorant incompetence of a Torquay hotelier, likewise looked back towards an older style of holiday-making and holiday accommodation, and part of its appeal was nostalgic, although aspects of the experience were all too recognisable in seaside (and other) hotels of the 1970s and 1980s. These were, perhaps, straws in the wind: the slightly misleading overture to a new trend, along with *Angel Voices* (1988) which went back nostalgically to the relatively innocent social tensions of the transitional early 1960s.

During the 1990s British cinema has returned to the seaside, and especially to Blackpool, with a new agenda which contains a strong flavouring of affectionate nostalgia and a tendency to celebrate the camp or kitsch aspects of this setting with the hallmark ironic knowingness of post-modernism. *Bhaji on the Beach* (1993) brought new issues to the fore by chronicling (with surreal interludes) a West Midland Asian women's outing to Blackpool; *Funny Bones* (1995) revisited the seedier side of show business in a town where almost everyone seems to have an eye on possible stardom, but did so affectionately and with utterly convincing locations, as befitted the work of a locally born director; *Sista Dansen* focused on competitive ballroom dancing; and two utterly weird fantasy films, *Seaview Knights* (1994) and *Robinson in Space* (1996), again celebrated the peculiarities of Blackpool. Indeed, this end-of-millennium fixation on Blackpool, with its vulgar vigour and its combination of 'traditional' working-class, exotic night-life and ironic gay elements combining in a strong and distinctive identity, suggests that most aspects of the seaside's heyday remain on the fringes of popular culture, beached by the ebbing tides of the half-century since they were last at its heart.[24] This suggestion is reinforced by the predominance of Blackpool in television soap-opera or drama series representations of the seaside, whether in *Coronation Street* (reasonably enough, in 1989), or more surprisingly in *Eastenders* (1996), with a topical gay romance motif, or, also in sexually liminal vein, in *Oranges are not the only Fruit* (1990). And the Blackpool which recurs before these massive audiences is not so much a seaside resort on the older model, despite its willingness to be projected in this way when nostalgia seems appropriate: it is a pleasure town which, in itself, has little more to do with the sea than does Las Vegas.

The older incarnations of the seaside have practically disappeared from view in these true mass media of the electronic age. Where they have sometimes been celebrated in the mid- and late 1990s, again in an arch, kitsch and nostalgic vein, has been in more up-market settings, especially in the supplements of broadsheet newspapers. In this vein (some of the time) was the *Observer* supplement in July 1997 which was dedicated to 'the A–Z of the seaside' and featured piers, buckets and spades, oysters, beach huts, kiosks and holiday camps alongside the more explicit liminalities of 'sexy postcards', undressing on the beach, and casual and teenage holiday sex, spiced up with regular displays of the opulent model Sophie Dahl. A short piece on 'decorum' indicated awareness of this essential 'other', the reaction to seaside freedom, and there were affectionate depictions of a range of resorts from Abersoch to West Bay via Brighton, with the accent on idiosyncrasy and eccentricity. But the predominance, here and elsewhere, of this tone and emphasis again says much about the position of the seaside in media consciousness.[25] A less-forgiving treatment came in Martin Parr's 'Modern Times' BBC2 documentary in April 1999, which sought *vox pop* pronouncements on English identity but provided little germane or articulate comment from those who appeared on the screen. Its mission was to search for these views in what were regarded as 'traditionally English' locations, such as Henley Regatta and a village fete, with a brief incursion into the sort of trainspotters who frequent station platforms; and seaside resorts had a quite disproportionate share of the footage, especially Bridport, Weymouth and the inevitable Blackpool, with the accent on presenting older, socially conservative opinions from people who were deeply suspicious of 'abroad' without being able to articulate their Englishness. Charlotte Raven in the *Observer* described this tour as 'predictable', which is itself significant. Whether the film found its most suitable respondents and images at the seaside, or whether the predominance of seaside locations resulted from the prior expectations of the team, the result was to confirm the English seaside as the last bastion of those carried-over Victorian frames of mind which survived from the 1950s.[26]

Travel writers, whether British, American or Italian, have been increasingly bilious in their treatment of British seaside resorts, perhaps helping to justify the tourist boards' sustained unwillingness to market the seaside alongside other British tourist attractions from the 1960s onwards. Disenchantment with Blackpool has been particularly evident, as the celebrations of the gregarious virtues of the 'people' on holiday from the 1890s to the 1950s have given way in the 1980s and 1990s to revulsion at a perceived dominant combination of bloated bodies, alcohol abuse, junk food, litter and aggressive behaviour. In a tart but affectionate portrayal of the English at leisure, the Italian journalist Beppe Severgnini told his compatriots that the English working class have had no need to go to Spain to behave like beasts: they can do it perfectly well in Blackpool, which nourishes northern separatism and suspicion on a diet of fish and chips.[27]

Reactions to less strongly flavoured resorts might also be merciless. Paul Theroux, following the coastline round on foot and by public transport in 1982, was appalled by the extent of seaside suburbia, especially along the south coast: the proliferation of little bungalows in which, he suggested, small-minded people devoted their twilight lives to ironing antimacassars and the sterile manicuring of regimented garden plots. He also noted the ugly caravan sites, while trying to understand the culture that nourished them, just as he strove in vain to come to terms with the idea of visiting Morecambe for pleasure: 'Nothing is more bewildering to a foreigner than a nation's pleasures, and I never felt more alien in Britain than when I was watching people enjoying their sort of seaside vacation'. Or there was Mablethorpe, 'thronged with shivering vacationers', 'the coast of last resorts' for those whose dole would let them go no further, 'no more fun than a day out on the prison farm'. On the edge of Clacton, Jaywick Sands was 'crowded and cheap . . . and was awfully battered, like a seaside slum in Argentina or Mexico'. The English seaside regularly prompted Theroux to thoughts of Latin America, or indeed Africa. Or there was Weston-super-Mare, 'bleak and residential and rather funless . . . a large town with the soul of a suburb', prompting dark reflections on towns 'like river mouths where, mounting like silt, a century of pulverized civilization had been deposited, often floating from the darker interior of England'. Or Bexhill, where respectable elderly English people came to die quietly. Or Barry Island, where even the day-trippers had deserted the empty funfairs. Scarborough (especially), and Eastbourne, and Weymouth, and Tenby got a better press, but Theroux was happiest where the countryside met the sea: almost everything else was despoliation and, now, quiet despair.[28] A decade or so later Bill Bryson, despite his irritating attachment to imagined British quaintness, was hardly less forgiving, especially towards Blackpool. Weston-super-Mare and Llandudno were insufferably dull; Morecambe was in need of government funding to reverse its spectacular decline since the 1950s or perhaps the 1970s, and to restore it as a heritage resort; even Lulworth had lost its charms since the 1970s; and only Bournemouth, seen through the nostalgic haze of a remembered first job in journalism, and West Bay with an adventurous restaurant, came out with much credit. What is most interesting, however, is that this seeker after the quainter and more idiosyncratic aspects of Britishness should have devoted so much space in his valedictory tour of the country to its seaside resorts. This is now unusual.[29]

The eclipse of most of the seaside, for most purposes, is a recent development, and the decline of the British seaside resort, as a significant phenomenon, has been the subject of widespread media comment, with discussions on the crisis of the domestic holiday industry surfacing during every summer. This reached a climax in June 1999 with the release of an utterly damning Consumers' Association report (reported in the *Guardian*), which concluded that 'the overriding impression of our traditional resorts is one of ageing infrastructure, tired ideas and low quality accommodation', and sparked off a sequence of press commentaries which included a Rhyl hotelier's defence of his resort, couched in terms of the continuing popularity of its family amusements but also, and significantly, emphasising the countryside and heritage attractions around (just as a Victorian guide-book might have done).[30] These recurrent and almost obsessive debates on the theme of 'decline' reflect a widely shared perception of how important the seaside has been, and how the changes which are thus encapsulated have affected lives and cultures. Now is the time to return to the case for the historical importance of the seaside resort, as contributor to lived experience (a concept whose value is compromised but not destroyed by the impossibility of accessing it in any complete or literal-minded sense) as well as generator of representations, especially as most of the discussion hitherto generated in sociology, economics and cultural studies has been very present-minded, without the broader perspectives which the historical imagination can bring.

Historians have not been very actively engaged with the twentieth-century British seaside, leaving the field largely to sociologists, economists and geographers, who dominate the emergent and very present-minded sub-discipline of tourism studies (with its close relative, hospitality management, which is making its escape from the more down-market connotations of hotel and catering studies). There is plenty of work on the formative and maturing years before the First World War, but the flow dries up as the twentieth century proceeds, in common with many other historical themes. A roll-call of interpretations of the eighteenth and nineteenth centuries might begin with Corbin's evocation of the revolution in tastes and sensibilities which inverted existing perceptions

of the aesthetics of sea and shoreline and made the seaside thinkable as an attractive tourist destination. This is stronger on texts than contexts, and exhibits
an unwarranted confidence in the author's mastery of the literature beyond
his French home ground; but it is a creative, path-breaking and deservedly
influential contribution.[31] Hemingway's work on representations of the seaside in painting in early nineteenth-century Britain supplements this usefully,
but Thomas Richards's attempt to use advertisers' seaside motifs to support an
argument for the rise of a 'commodity culture' in Victorian England, saturated
with the images propagated by advertisers, suffers from failure to contextualise
and visible misreading of some of the advertisements themselves.[32] Much more
convincing is Pearson's depiction of the commercial leisure architecture of
the late Victorian and Edwardian seaside, the 'pleasure palaces' of the large
popular resorts and the uses to which they were put.[33]

The meat of this research has considered the relative importance of
changing demand patterns, landownership and local government in patterns
of nineteenth-century resort development, and it is here that the interesting
debates have emerged. There has been no dissent from the contention that
working-class demand first became an important influence on resorts close to
industrial population centres in the late nineteenth century (although 'excur-
sionists' and 'cheap trippers' made their presence felt on summer weekends
as soon as the railways arrived around mid-century). The notion that the seaside holiday as a widespread working-class experience was first enjoyed by
the Lancashire cotton workers, whose high family incomes, ability to save for
the enjoyment of unpaid holidays, and adaptation of the traditional 'Wakes'
holidays to seaside purposes, put them a generation ahead of industrial
workers elsewhere in this respect, has also commanded enduring assent. ('Wakes
weeks' were the traditional northern factory town holidays, which built on older
local religious observances and were secularised and converted into the bases
for seaside holidays.) Blackpool's readiness to welcome these working-class
visitors, to make room for them and cater for their tastes, was important here.
But there is room for argument about how far through the working class the
seaside holiday as an annual institution, as opposed to the occasional day-trip,
became the norm, especially for the casual workers and those with young
families in the trough of the poverty cycle. Early optimistic interpretations have
been challenged, and doubt has also been cast on the implications of the annual
holiday binge for living standards, and especially health, during the rest of the
year.[34] There is also some debate over the role of transport innovation in resort
development: no-one denies that the railways were essential to sustain the sheer

scale of resort growth between the early Victorian years and the First World War, but there are differences of emphasis as to whether they merely responded belatedly to demand flows whose main roots lay elsewhere, or took a more active role in encouraging demand.[35] Such demand-related issues retain their importance when we look at the twentieth century, with age, gender, ethnicity and cultural preferences taking their place in the equation alongside class, which was the main obsession of the Victorians. This raises the related, and likewise enduring, questions of respectability and 'social tone', and the conflicts which arose when contrasting holiday preferences came into contact and resort interests had to decide on which visiting publics to encourage and cater for, and how to promote a sense of security and relaxation for the mainstream or best-paying visitors without policing behaviour too intrusively. These tensions between freedom and restraint, in a situation where getting the balance right was central to resort identities and economic success, were again to remain important twentieth-century themes.[36]

There is also debate over the nature and relative importance of landownership and local government as influences on seaside resort development, although in practice the two were intertwined and the balance of power shifted between them as resorts grew in the nineteenth century. Harold Perkin argued that the central formative influence on resort 'social tone' was the original landownership pattern, with large estates offering opportunities for planning and control which tilted the balance towards catering for the 'better classes', while sub-divided landownership encouraged lowest-common-denominator development geared towards the less-demanding strata of the market.[37] David Cannadine posited, building on his case-study of Eastbourne, that the dominant motive forces behind resort growth in the crucial mid-Victorian years were aristocratic families developing their seaside estates on genteel lines, with careful planning and zoning; but this turned out to be one pattern among several, and some of the landed estate administrations were visibly driven by short-term profit-maximising rather than by long-term concerns to create and sustain desirable environments.[38] There is general agreement that the role of local government, emancipating itself where necessary from the tutelage of the large landed families and their estate managers, became particularly important in seaside resorts during the second half of the nineteenth century, as it took on an even wider range of responsibilities than was normal in this golden age of municipal autonomy and power. Over and above oversight of building plans and street layouts, provision of sewerage and public utilities like gas, water, electricity and tramways, resort local government increasingly became involved in providing promenades, sea defences, parks and amenities on a grander scale than in other kinds of town, as well as intervening in the entertainment industries where private enterprise feared to tread, regulating the beach and sustaining appropriate levels of public order through batteries of by-laws enforced by inspectors as well as police forces, and even dabbling in advertising. All this was driven by the need to make resorts as attractive as possible in the highly-competitive market-place of British seaside holiday provision, and it was, perhaps, municipal capitalism rather than municipal socialism in the sense envisaged by Sidney and Beatrice Webb, the Labour Party ideologues who were staunch advocates of municipal involvement in local economies. But it is a very strong theme indeed, and one which has been carried forward particularly powerfully into and through the twentieth century.[39]

More general surveys of nineteenth-century seaside holidaymaking and resort development have not been lacking, and some have followed through into the twentieth century. In many ways the most remarkable was Pimlott's *The Englishman's holiday: a social history*, first published in 1947, which in its brisk, commonsense, accessible, entertaining way picked up on all the themes which have remained important in the literature (including the peculiarities of seaside entertainment) and took them through to the author's own time, making good use of (among other things) the original Nuffield survey of the holiday trades by Elizabeth Brunner which had appeared two years earlier.[40] James Walvin's *Beside the seaside* took the story through the post-Second World War generation, incorporating some of the historiographical developments of the intervening thirty years, but without going into much depth in comparative local studies or primary sources.[41] There has been no historical overview of the twentieth-century British seaside since, perhaps reflecting the increasingly (but unjustly) unfashionable nature of the subject. The most exciting contributions to aspects of the seaside have been made by Colin Ward and Dennis Hardy, in their studies of the 'alternative' seaside resorts of the 'plotland' developments, a wonderful piece of detective work which also opens up an unorthodox aesthetic of the seaside, and of the rise of the holiday camp.[42] Most of the century is also spanned by Nigel Morgan's valuable study of the Devon resorts, incorporating an in-depth comparison between Torquay and Ilfracombe and offering particularly useful insights into local government and resort image and publicity.[43] My own book on Blackpool also comes right up to the late 1990s in its coverage.[44] Introductory overviews of the shorter periods between 1900 and 1950, and (a particularly neglected and important interlude) between 1950 and 1974, can be found in my chapter and that of

Julian Demetriadi in an interdisciplinary collection of essays edited by Shaw and Williams.[45] Demetriadi's thesis expands on the themes of his chapter, and Stallibrass's work on the seaside accommodation industry, building on a case-study of Scarborough, is also a useful introduction to the transitional years of the post-war generation.[46] Laura Chase's work on the holiday industry and 'modernity' on the coast of inter-war Essex, Gary Cross's edition of the projected Mass-Observation history and social survey of Blackpool in the late 1930s, and Alastair Durie's introductory forays into seaside tourism in twentieth-century Scotland, are further substantial and thought-provoking contributions.[47] We can also learn from historical studies of seaside tourism in other European countries, from Ireland and France to Denmark, Spain and Greece, and from interpretations based on experiences more distant geographically from this British standpoint.[48] Evidence from the post-war Mediterranean, especially but not exclusively, is relevant to assessing the competitive environment in which British resorts have been struggling during the last third of the twentieth century.[49] The time is ripe, in more ways than one, for a reinterpretation of the twentieth-century British seaside.

It is now impossible, or at least unwise, to grapple with these themes without paying heed to the growing volume of work in sociology, anthropology and cultural geography, sometimes bundled under the capacious umbrella of 'cultural studies', which has offered challenging new perspectives to evaluate and (selectively) appropriate and develop. Links must also be made with the emergent discipline of tourism studies, which has its own journals and university departments. It is unduly present-minded, dominated by economics while beginning to reach out towards (especially) the new cultural geography, but still generates data and ideas which can be useful to an understanding of historical change and continuity.

Some of the key insights and approaches have already been signposted, in the discussion of liminality and the carnivalesque earlier in this chapter.[50] In specifically seaside contexts the work of Rob Shields, developing the idea of Brighton as a liminal space, a 'place on the margin' where the usual rules of conduct are suspended or even inverted, has been particularly stimulating. Relatedly, Erving Goffmann's ideas about public, polite, regulated 'front stage' and disreputable, exciting, taboo 'backstage' aspects of peopled spaces are highly relevant to seaside resorts, especially when we consider that stretches of beach, for example, might be carefully regulated and sanitised during the day but be opened out to 'backstage' activities involving illicit sexuality after dark.[51] Also stimulating is Tony Bennett's working out of the carnivalesque as a theme at Blackpool, where inhibitions can be cast aside, hidden and taboo acts, identities and bodily parts and functions can be brought out and celebrated, and misrule can come forth to display the temporary triumph of leisure and frivolity over the mundane and the workaday. These are not purely seaside-related concepts, of course, whether we look at sixteenth-century Romans as a prototypical site of carnival or at Bowman's portrayal of tourism and sexual relations in contemporary Jerusalem: the very fact of being a tourist, away from the inquisitorial gaze of family, locality and workplace and capable of enjoying a measure of anonymity in a setting where pleasure-seeking is supposed to be paramount and service industries seize the opportunities, has potential consequences in any labelled tourist space, always provided that the tourist is not surrounded by workmates and neighbours who have chosen the same destination. But the seaside, the debatable meeting-point between land and water and imagined source of reinvigoration and stimulation, is a particularly prominent venue for these purposes.[52] Bennett's attempt to situate Blackpool at an alternative, northern, populist pole of popular culture, set in opposition to the metropolis and its pretentions to cultural dominance, also poses interesting questions. His assertion, following Barthes, that Blackpool Tower is a phallic symbol to which other aspects of the resort's identity attach themselves, is perhaps less fruitful, although Lisa Jolly finds support for it in the caressing and enhancing eye of the movie camera.[53] Both Shields and Bennett have been more convincing in transferring theories and suggesting applications than in grounding them in dialogue with substantial bodies of evidence; but they have influenced, and will influence, the agenda of subsequent work.[54]

The beach itself, at the core of seaside resort identity (and liminality), has yet to be explored by seaside historians in the twentieth-century British setting. It falls to Jean-Didier Urbain, in a primarily French and Belgian setting, and John Fiske in a mainly Australian one, to offer provocative approaches to unfolding its meanings, with help from the chatty American descriptions of Lencek and Bosker.[55] Urbain provides the most interesting, though tendentious and demanding, insights: 'The beach is a spectacle. It is a theatre where society unveils and strips itself bare . . . The beach is nobody's native soil. It is a tablet unwritten on, an abstraction, an empty and rootless place'. He points to the early development of social distinctions between different groups of visitors as well as between visitors and locals, and their expression in the zoning and use of the beach. He emphasises the complete distinction between the beach life of the holidaymaker and the routines and surroundings of working life, and the transgression, reinforcement and dissolution of boundaries between classes, sexes and lifestyles which forms much of the modern history of this debatable territory. And he conjures up Foucault's *Discipline and punish*, with its emphasis on technologies for controlling dangerous passions, in relation to bathing regimes of the nineteenth century: 'These disciplinary principles can be perfectly identified in the nineteenth-century medical theory of sea-bathing'. What happened when, in the new century, those technologies were abandoned, as pleasure was licensed to return to the experience of beach and sea, was (as he says) another story.[56]

Another potentially fertile influence on the historian's agenda has been John Urry's *The tourist gaze* and his subsequent developments of this theme, which have drawn attention to the importance of the holiday destination as spectacle, and the ways in which the intersecting gazes of observer and observed leave neither unchanged. Urbain also makes this point: 'To the eye of these strollers, . . . the port, a space of fisherfolk separate from that of the bathers, is henceforth another world. Isolated, distanced or marginalised, that world over there, beyond the wall, outside the leisured universe of the holidaymaker, . . . is an exotic world.' The two gaze upon each other as on strange creatures in a zoo; but it is the tourists who will oust the fisherfolk, or force or encourage them to transform themselves into an acceptable, safe guise, often as the celebrants of 'traditional' rituals, adapted or invented, for the delectation of the new cash crop.[57] But conflicts on this score were to persist through the twentieth century at the British seaside. Urry's distinction between the romantic gaze, which values silent, solitary communing with the desired landscape or site, and the collective gaze, which is more concerned with shared, gregarious, often cheerfully noisy enjoyment of an accessible environment, is also a useful starting-point for arguments which will recur throughout this text. The additional sub-divisions he posits into the spectatorial, environmental and anthropological gazes also offer a purchase for analysis.[58]

The seaside resort is also haunted by the spectre of Karl Marx. This is, after all, an industrial town, dedicated to exploiting natural resources through the business of pleasure and the commodification of dreams. Class conflict is a valuable approach to analysing the social relations of consumption as well as production in this pre-eminently capitalist setting, as the struggles over access to and enjoyment of admired objects of the 'gaze' bears witness: the equation romantic gaze/middle class and collective gaze/working class provides at least a plausible starting-point for analysis. The decline of the British seaside resort has coincided with the decline of the discourses and institutions of a class society (though not the realities of economic exploitation); but class, interacting and coexisting with other methods of analysis, remains essential to the approximation of retrospective understanding. Malcolm Muggeridge, in 1934, commented wrily that Bournemouth, being 'more or less undiluted bourgeoisie . . . ought to suit a Marxist, since it provides unlimited opportunities for the summoning up of class emotions'. He recommended a few days' residence there 'to tune up . . . class-consciousness to a good fighting pitch'.[59] An entertaining paradox is that during the 1870s and early 1880s holidays on the Isle of Wight had revived the physically flagging Karl Marx himself, as he lived the life of a bourgeois semi-invalid at Ryde and Ventnor, and enjoyed the right to be 'comfortably dull' which Muggeridge advanced as one of the virtues of Bournemouth's capitalist civilisation.[60]

The case for the importance of the British seaside that should command the widest assent, however, is the demographic one: the sheer scale of the phenomenon in terms of numbers of residents, toing and froing of residents and seasonal workers as well as holidaymakers, and numbers of people influenced by the seaside and its shifting images. It became, by mid-century, and is still an almost universal experience, and it has affected people's lives. Population figures are dealt with in the next chapter, and migration flows in Chapter 6: suffice here to say that as the seaside approached its peak in England and Wales in 1951, well over a hundred resorts in England and Wales contained nearly 2.5 million residents at an April census, or 5.7 per cent of the population. This makes an unanswerable case for the seaside's importance, even if we leave aside the issues of culture, class and conflict which it raises.[61]

Calculations of this sort are bedevilled by problems of definition: how important does the holiday industry have to be in a town before it can be classed as a resort? This is increasingly pertinent in the late twentieth century, as old resorts transmute into commuter and retirement centres and lose their generic cultural distinctiveness. John Urry has argued that at the core of British seaside resorts' problems at the end of the twentieth century has been the loss of a distinctive, attractive, fashionable identity: a loss of the kind of 'placeness' or place-identity which previously rendered them desirable destinations.[62] The sea itself has become less attractive in its British setting as awareness of pollution has spread and expectations about climate have risen, raising the spectre that on these coastlines the eighteenth-century revolution in tastes which made shorelines attractive may prove to be reversible.[63]

This brings us to that staple tool of tourism studies, the resort product cycle, which is only now coming under serious question for its economic reductionism and neglect of the actual processes that make up the lives of resorts.

Broadly, it could be argued that most British resorts have come to the end of their useful existence: they have passed from discovery, local exploitation, the attraction of national (but not international) capital, the broadening of markets, and the dominance of the artificial over the natural, to saturation, pollution, stagnation and decline.[64] On this basis some resorts may escape, by reinventing themselves, as Blackpool has repeatedly done; but the future for most is bleak.[65] This is certainly too simple: especially as some of the most successful British resorts have stayed comfortably at one of the earlier stages of the cycle, generating a living for their inhabitants without compromising their environment; and the trajectories of resort development (and stagnation) are far too complex to be reduced to a schema of this sort. The resort cycle is a starting point, perhaps, but as a tool of description and explanation the model is too impoverished. We need to generalise, but taking account of the rich and enduring diversity of the British seaside. We are dealing with a recognisable and distinctive kind of town, but with as many variations as a hawkweed or a burnet-moth.[66]

The notion that the British seaside resort retains a robust identity, which in turn reinforces its importance as a subject for investigation and analysis, is shared by Paul Theroux, who expressed it memorably in 1983:[67]

> Every British bulge [of coastline] is different and every mile has its own mood . . . The character [of seaside resorts] was fixed, and though few coastal places matched their reputation every one was unique . . . And yet there *was* such a thing as typical on the coast . . . There was always an Esplanade, and always a Bandstand on it; always a War Memorial and a Rose Garden . . . a Lifeboat Station and a Lighthouse, and a Pier; a Putting Green, a Bowling Green, a Cricket Pitch, and a church the guidebook said was Perpendicular. The pier had been condemned. It was threatened with demolition. A society had just been formed to save it, but it would be blown up next year just the same . . . The railway had been closed down in 1964, and the fishing industry folded five years ago. The art-deco cinema was now a bingo hall . . . The new bus shelter had been vandalized. It was famous for its whelks. It was raining.

These were not universals, but they were recurrent, like the more prosaic resort characteristics discussed above. But for Theroux the charm of travelling round the British coast was the unpredictable variations on and deviations from these themes; and in the chapters that follow we shall pay due heed to them. We begin, indeed, by charting the mixed fortunes of British seaside resorts over this turbulent century.

Notes

1 Bill Bryson, *Notes from a small island* (London, 1995), pp. 124–5. The holidays referred to were presumably taken around 1980.

2 N. Morgan, 'Perceptions, patterns, policies of tourism: the development of the Devon seaside resorts during the twentieth century, with special reference to Torquay and Ilfracombe', Ph.D. thesis, University of Exeter, 1992.

3 R. Shields, *Places on the margin: alternative geographies of modernity* (London, 1991), Chapter 2; Tony Bennett, 'Hegemony, ideology, pleasure, Blackpool', in T. Bennett, C. Mercer and J. Woollacott (eds), *Popular culture and social relations* (Milton Keynes, 1986), pp. 135–54; Helle B. Bertramsen Nye, 'Liminality at turn-of-the-century Brighton', unpublished paper, Lancaster University, 1997; Gary Cross (ed.), *Worktowners at Blackpool* (London, 1990).

4 Peter Bailey, *Popular culture and performance in the Victorian city* (Cambridge, 1998), pp. 71–2, 129.

5 P. Joyce, *Visions of the people* (Cambridge, 1991).

6 Anthony Burgess, *Little Wilson and Big God* (London, 1988), pp. 129, 131–6; Cross, *Worktowners at Blackpool*; P. Gurney, ' "Intersex" and "Dirty Girls": Mass-Observation and working-class sexuality in England in the 1930s', *Journal of the History of Sexuality*, 8 (1997), pp. 256–90; and see also Jeff Nuttall, *King Twist* (London, 1978); J.K. Walton, *The Blackpool landlady: a social history* (Manchester, 1978), Chapter 1.

7 R.S. Neale, *Bath 1680–1850: a valley of pleasure or a sink of iniquity?* (London, 1981).

8 Arnold Bennett, *The Card* (1911: Harmondsworth, 1975), Chapters 4–5; and see above, notes 2 and 5.

9 Graham Greene, *Brighton rock* (London, 1938).

10 Robert Tressell, *The ragged-trousered philanthropists* (1914; London, 1965).

11 George Meek, *George Meek, Bath chair-man, by himself* (London, 1910).

12 Arthur Laycock, *Warren of Manchester* (London, 1906); and see Walton, *The Blackpool landlady*, p. 9.

13 Walter Greenwood, *Love on the dole* (1933: Harmondsworth, 1969), pp. 118–25; C. Musgrave, *Life in Brighton* (London, 1970), pp. 365–6.

14 Philip Norman, *The skaters' waltz* (London, 1979).

15 Matt Thorne, *Tourist* (London, 1998). See also Nicola Barker, *Wide open* (London, 1998), a disturbing evocation of the openness and (in this case) attractive and threatening liminality of a cluster of chalets on the Sheppey shoreline, with the epigraph, 'I dreamed I saw you dead in a place by the water./ A ravaged place./ All flat and empty and wide open.' Here, perhaps, the seaside reverts in earnest to its pre-Corbin state.

16 Jeffrey Richards, *The age of the dream palace* (London, 1984), pp. 181–3, 213–14, 247–8. Many thanks to my colleague Mike Paris for his help with the film references.

17 Thanks to Lisa Jolly for the Blackpool filmography.

18 Stanley Houghton, *Hindle Wakes*; Lisa Jolly, 'Blackpool: seaside sex capital? A critical analysis of cinematic representations of the resort', BA dissertation,

University of Central Lancashire, 1999, pp. 39–43; Richards, *The age of the dream palace*, pp. 318–19.

19 Richards, *The age of the dream palace*, p. 306.

20 Yvonne Cloud (ed.), *Beside the seaside* (1934; London, 1938).

21 Leslie Halliwell, *Halliwell's film guide* (7th edn, London, 1990), p. 76; Jeffrey Richards, 'Cul-de-sac England', in Jeffrey Richards and Anthony Aldgate (eds), *Best of British* (London, 1998). pp. 150–51; Jolly, 'Blackpool', pp. 26–7.

22 Quotations from *Halliwell's Film Guide*, pp. 473, 986. Halliwell's encapsulation of the plot of *The Punch and Judy Man* (p. 823) is disturbingly misleading.

23 Ibid., p. 1123.

24 For Blackpool, J.K. Walton, *Blackpool* (Edinburgh, 1998), Chapters 6 and 7.

25 *The Observer, Life* supplement, 6 July 1997.

26 Martin Parr, 'Modern Times', BBC2, first shown 27 April 1999; *The Observer*, Review section, 2 May 1999, p. 16.

27 Walton, *Blackpool*, pp. 168–9; Beppe Severgnini, *Inglesi* (Milan, 1992), pp. 142–3.

28 Paul Theroux, *The kingdom by the sea* (1983; Harmondsworth, 1984).

29 Bryson, *Notes from a small island*.

30 *Guardian, Saturday Review*, 10 July 1999, p. 2; *Observer, News*, 11 July 1999, p. 17.

31 A. Corbin, *The lure of the sea* (Cambridge, 1992).

32 A. Hemingway, *Landscape imagery and urban culture in early nineteenth-century Britain* (Cambridge, 1992), Chapter 8; Thomas Richards, *The commodity culture of Victorian England* (London, 1991).

33 L.F. Pearson, *The people's palaces: the story of the seaside pleasure buildings of 1870–1914* (Buckingham, 1991).

34 J.K. Walton. 'The demand for working-class seaside holidays in Victorian England', *Economic History Review*, second series, 34 (1981), pp. 249–65; J.K. Walton, 'The world's first working-class seaside resort? Blackpool revisited, 1840–1974', *Transactions of the Lancashire and Cheshire Antiquarian Society*, 88 (1992), pp. 1–30; M. Huggins, 'Social tone and resort development in north-east England', *Northern History* 20 (1984), pp. 187–206; A. Davies (ed.), *Leisure, gender and poverty* (Manchester, 1992); P. Wild, 'Recreation in Rochdale 1900–1940', in J. Clark, C. Critcher and R. Johnson (eds), *Working class culture* (London, 1979).

35 J.K. Walton, 'Railways and resort development in Victorian England: the case of Silloth', *Northern History*, 15 (1979), pp. 191–209; J. Simmons, *The railway in town and country, 1830–1914* (Newton Abbot, 1986), Chapter 8.

36 J.K. Walton, *The English seaside resort: a social history 1750–1914* (Leicester, 1983), Chapter 8; J. Travis, *The rise of the Devon seaside resorts, 1750–1900* (Exeter, 1993).

37 H.J. Perkin, 'The "social tone" of Victorian seaside resorts in the north-west', *Northern History*, 11 (1976), pp. 180–94.

38 D. Cannadine, *Lords and landlords: the aristocracy and the towns 1774–1967* (Leicester, 1980), Chapter 16; Walton, *The English seaside resort*, Chapter 5; J. Liddle, 'Estate management and land reform politics', in D. Cannadine (ed.), *Patricians, power and politics in nineteenth-century towns* (Leicester, 1982).

39 Walton, *The English seaside resort*, Chapter 6; F.B. May, 'Victorian and Edwardian Ilfracombe', pp. 187–206; R. Roberts, 'The Corporation as impresario: the municipal provision of entertainment in Victorian and Edwardian Bournemouth', pp. 137–58; J.K. Walton, 'Municipal government and the holiday industry in Blackpool, 1876–1914', pp. 159–86 in J.K. Walton and J. Walvin (eds), *Leisure in Britain 1780–1939* (Manchester, 1983).

40 J.A.R. Pimlott, *The Englishman's holiday: a social history* (1947; Sussex, 1976); E. Brunner, *Holiday making and the holiday trades* (Oxford, 1945).

41 J. Walvin, *Beside the seaside* (Harmondsworth, 1978).

42 D. Hardy and C. Ward, *Arcadia for all: the legacy of a makeshift landscape* (London, 1984); C. Ward and D. Hardy, *Goodnight campers! The history of the British holiday camp* (London, 1986).

43 Morgan, 'Perceptions, patterns and policies of tourism'.

44 Walton, *Blackpool*, Chapter 6.

45 G. Shaw and A. Williams (eds), *The rise and fall of British coastal resorts* (London, 1997), Chapters 2 and 3.

46 J. Demetriadi, 'English and Welsh seaside resorts 1950–74 with special reference to Blackpool and Margate 1950–74', Ph.D. thesis, University of Lancaster, 1995; H.C. Stallibrass, 'The holiday accommodation industry: with special reference to of Scarborough, England', Ph.D. thesis, University of London, 1978.

47 Cross, *Worktowners at Blackpool*; Themed section on seaside resorts including L. Chase, 'Modern images and social tone in Clacton and Frinton in the inter-war years', pp. 149–69; A. Durie, 'The Scottish seaside resort in peace and war, *c.* 1880–1960', pp. 171–86: *International Journal of Maritime History*, 9 (1997).

48 J.K. Walton, 'The seaside resorts of Western Europe 1750–1939', in S. Fisher (ed.), *Recreation and the sea* (Exeter, 1997), pp. 36–56, and references cited there; J.V.N. Soane, *Fashionable resort regions: their evolution and transformation* (Wallingford, 1993); J.K. Walton and J. Smith, 'The first century of beach tourism in Spain: San Sebastian and the *playas del norte* from the 1830s to the 1930s', in M. Barke *et al.* (eds), *Tourism in Spain: critical perspectives* (Wallingford, 1996), pp. 35–61; P. Battilani, *Vacanze di pochi, vacanze di tutti: breve storia del turismo* (Bologna, 1998); P. Holm, *Kystfolk: kontakter og sammenhaenge over Kattegat og Skagerak ca. 1500–1914* (Esbjerg, 1991); M. Dritsas, 'The advent of the tourist industry in Greece during the twentieth century', paper presented at the EBHA Conference on Business History, Terni, Italy, September 1998.

49 See especially Barke *et al.*, *Tourism in Spain*, Chapters 3–5, 10–12.

50 See above, notes 2 and 3.

51 Bertramsen, 'Liminality at turn-of-the-century Brighton'.

52 E. Le Roy Ladurie, *Carnival at Romans* (New York, 1979); G. Bowman, 'Fucking tourists: sexual relations and tourism in Jerusalem's Old City', *Critique of Anthropology*, 9 (1992), pp. 77–93.

53 Bennett, 'Hegemony, ideology, pleasure: Blackpool' in Bennett, Mercer and Woollacott (eds), *Popular culture and social relations* (Milton Keynes, 1986), pp. 135–54; Bennett, 'A thousand and one troubles: Blackpool Pleasure Beach', in Bennett *et al.*, *Formations of pleasure* (London, 1983).

54 Cross, *Worktowners at Blackpool*; J.K. Walton, 'Popular entertainment and public order: the Blackpool Carnivals of 1923–4', *Northern History*, 34 (1998), pp. 170–88.

55 J.-D. Urbain, *Sur la plage* (Paris, 1994); J. Fiske, *Reading the popular* (London, 1989), Chapter 3; L. Lencek and G. Bosker, *The beach: the history of paradise on earth* (London, 1998).

56 Urbain, *Sur la plage*, pp. 19, 38, 66, 118.

57 J. Urry, *The tourist gaze* (London, 1990); Urry, *Consuming places* (London, 1995); Urbain, *Sur la plage*, p. 70.

58 Urry, *Consuming places*, p. 191.

59. Malcolm Muggeridge, 'Bournemouth', in Cloud, *Beside the seaside*, pp. 113–14.

60 A.E. Laurence with A.N. Insole, *Prometheus bound: Karl Marx on the Isle of Wight* (Newport, I.O.W., n.d.: Isle of Wight County Council). My thanks to Bill Lancaster for this reference.

61 Walton, 'The seaside resorts of England and Wales 1900–1950', in G. Shaw and A. Williams (eds), *The rise and fall of British coastal resorts* (London, 1997), pp. 21–48.

62 J. Urry, *Holiday-making, cultural change and the seaside* (Lancaster, 1987).

63 Corbin, *The lure of the sea*.

64 *Built Environment*, special issue, 18 (1992).

65 Walton, *Blackpool*, Chapter 7.

66 Hawkweeds: 'An exceptionally variable and difficult group, with some hundreds of microspecies', in R. Fitter *et al.*, *The wild flowers of Britain and Northern Europe* (London, 1974), p. 256. Seaside resorts are less resistant to classification, but the broad analogy stands.

67 Theroux, *The Kingdom by the sea*, pp. 349–51.

1

The seaside resort system

A the beginning of the twentieth century Britain, and England in particular, had a system of coastal resorts whose scale and complexity was unmatched anywhere else in the world. This was fitting, as the sea-bathing fashion had begun here in the eighteenth century; and rising wealth, an expanding middle class, an upper working class with more disposable time and income than its counterparts elsewhere, concentrations of urban dwellers in uncomfortably polluted conditions, a long and accessible coastline, the early development of a fully articulated mass transport system in the form of the railways, and the enterprise of entrepreneurs and local government in recognising and responding to opportunities, all conspired to promote a unique proliferation of seaside leisure destinations. In size they ranged from the city with over fifty thousand off-season inhabitants to the fishing hamlet or coastal agricultural settlement which catered for a handful of summer visitors as a supplement to the main business of its inhabitants. They included examples of the fastest-growing urban settlements of the nineteenth century, and continued this tradition into the twentieth. There were, even on the most demanding definition, nearer a hundred and fifty than a hundred of them in England and Wales alone; and within these boundaries they counted more than one and a half million inhabitants at the spring census of 1911.[1] They satisfied a wide range of aesthetic preferences, both in terms of 'natural' landscape and seascape and in those of architecture and planning; and they catered for almost a complete cross-section of society in terms of class, age, gender and religion. Only the poorest of the working class, those most disadvantaged by low and irregular wages, rural isolation or the poverty cycle, and without access to the kind of charity that sometimes sponsored excursions, were denied access of some sort, if only the occasional day-trip. The social mix varied resort by resort, although not in any obviously deterministic way, and changed according to time of the year and day of the week; and the larger resorts were capable of attracting, and keeping, the patronage of various visiting publics, segregating them informally by space and time or regulating their interaction so as to minimise tensions. They had become places which both brought the classes together and threatened to emphasise their differences; but, after a good deal of cultural conflict in (especially) the 1870s and 1880s, the former set of attributes was beginning to prevail over the latter.[2] The seaside had become a microcosm of British society, brought together though it was in towns which were distinctive for their social structure, demography, age and gender profiles, economic organisation and, above all, their central purpose: that of pleasing visitors and making them feel secure and comfortable in their enjoyment of that characteristic institution of the developed world, the beach holiday.[3] The Edwardian seaside was already a major social and cultural fact. This chapter follows its fortunes through the twentieth century, examining the impact of war, the rapid development and changing priorities of the inter-war years, the post-war boom which found room for almost everyone in the capacious bosom of the coast, and the decline which set in during the final third of the century and is still generating analysis, explanation and prescriptions for revival. We begin by putting more flesh on the bones of the Edwardian system.

England and Wales in 1911 had just over a hundred substantial seaside resorts, with resident populations of 2,000 or more at an April census. Imprecision arises from problems of how to categorise towns with mixed economies, and resort areas which were satellites of larger towns, such as Southsea (Portsmouth) and Roker (Sunderland), or small resorts within larger local government districts, such as Silloth on the Solway Firth, tend to slip through this kind of net; but the sheer scale, range and variety of development had no parallels elsewhere. At the top were eight large towns with off-season populations of over 50,000, ranging from Brighton's 131,237 and Bournemouth's 78,764 to Eastbourne's 52,542 by way of Southport and Birkdale, Southend, Hastings, Blackpool and Great Yarmouth. Brighton and Blackpool, in particular, were at the core of seaside conurbations. Hove, with 42,173 inhabitants, was distinguishable from its raffish neighbour only by an aspiring superiority of social tone and claims to respectability, while only a short stretch of sandhills separated Blackpool from its southern neighbour Lytham St Anne's (19,300), and it was reaching out along the northern coastal tramway towards Thornton-Cleveleys (4,669) and Fleetwood (15,875, but with a considerable deep-sea trawling industry). Torquay (38,771), in less dominant or assertive style, overshadowed a string of south Devon resorts, from Seaton to Paignton and

Dartmouth. There were other densely sown strips of coastline in North Wales (from Prestatyn and Rhyl to Penmaenmawr and Llanfairfechan via Colwyn Bay and Llandudno), and Kent (Margate, Broadstairs and Ramsgate). A further close-knit group of resorts followed the Severn estuary on the south bank of the Bristol Channel, from Portishead to Burnham-on-sea and Minehead, with Weston-super-Mare (23,235) having the flagship role.[4] With the exception of south Devon, parts of which had a national and (more so than other English coastlines) an international middle- and even upper-class market with merely a leavening of Exeter trippers and commuters, these resorts were fed by London and the great industrial conurbations, especially the northern textile districts and the manufacturing towns of the West Midlands. They were resort systems, satisfying a variety of needs and preferences, as popular resorts clung on to and developed more select districts and satellites into which self-consciously respectable families and quiet-seeking residents could retreat, and neighbouring landowners and local authorities interpreted their diverse potential markets in different ways and produced contrasting development strategies. There was no simple gravity model whereby the resorts closest to the cities adopted the most down-market postures and social tone increased with distance. The railway system was efficient enough to be a great leveller here, and where resorts were within an hour or so of population centres what differentiated them were internal characteristics of topography, landownership, local government and entrepreneurial preference.[5]

Away from these most densely populated recreational coastlines, resorts were more thinly spread; but there were few parts of England and Wales with a gap of more than ten miles between holiday settlements of some kind. The east coast saw resorts spaced out at regular intervals, from Redcar and Saltburn in the north through Scarborough (37,201) and its north Yorkshire neighbours to the unprepossessing Humberside outlets of Hornsea and sea-beleaguered Withernsea, the working-class playground of Cleethorpes and eventually the Earl of Scarbrough's planned settlement at Skegness. The East Anglian coastline was similarly punctuated, from another planned estate resort at Hunstanton, past the recently 'discovered' (but hardly-developed) north Norfolk coast around Cromer, through the big fishing ports of Great Yarmouth (55,905) and Lowestoft (33,777) (where the autumn herring fleets succeeded the holidaymakers), and on past Felixstowe and the little Suffolk resorts to the contrasting Essex watering-places of Walton, Clacton, snooty, exclusive Frinton and cheerful cockney Southend. Kent, Sussex, Hampshire and Dorset similarly had a sizeable resort every few miles, as did the Isle of Wight. Even the barest and briskest recital of names, enriched with the occasional word of commentary, conjures up something of the variety of what was on offer, and contemporaries were made aware of it by a multiplicity of guide-books, not only to individual resorts and coastlines served by the assiduous publicity machines of the railway companies, but also more general gazetteers which claimed to sum up the essential qualities of each and every resort for the discerning and calculating consumer. For some, the annual holiday was a comfortable routine; for others, it was the result of an informed search through the mountain of available literature for the perfect combination of characteristics.[6]

There were other partially developed English and Welsh coastlines, with smaller and less pretentious resorts at longer intervals. Wales between Pwllheli and Aberystwyth (8,411), served by a sedate but usable rail route from the West Midlands, fell into this category, as did the contrasting sequence of small centres in south Wales, between long-established Tenby (4,368) and the Cardiff maritime suburb of Penarth (15,448 from recent beginnings), taking in more popular Porthcawl and plebeian Barry Island on the way. Most of Devon and Cornwall, apart from the south Devon cluster around Torquay, was in similar case, despite recent attempts at promotion by its main-line railway companies. And there were also a few stretches of coastline which were almost untouched by the resort developer's speculative hand. Some had been pre-empted by another way of exploiting natural resources: the coastline between Tees and Tyne, and for some distance beyond, was largely given over to the coal industry and its offshoots, with Whitley Bay (14,407) breaking the pattern as Newcastle's resort and dormitory; and north beyond Amble Northumberland's fishing villages were hardly disturbed by tourists. An industrial survey of this coast in 1931, from Middlesbrough to the Scottish border at Berwick, did not mention seaside tourism at all, although among the 'minor industries' it noted that hotel, boarding-house and related service occupations accounted for ten per cent of all female insured workers in the area surveyed. But this bias towards masculine manufacturing industry was common. West Cumbria also had extractive industries at key points, as here too the coal measures went under the sea, in close proximity to iron ore workings; and beyond Grange-over-Sands (2,232) only the even smaller resorts of Seascale, St Bees, Silloth and tiny Allonby took advantage of breathing-spaces in the busy, smoke-ridden industrial landscape.[7] The Welsh coastline between Aberystwyth and Tenby was isolated and saw very limited holiday development, despite the development of Fishguard as an Irish passenger port with express rail services from London and Cardiff, and this was perhaps the least-frequented Edwardian coastline in the southern half of Britain, despite its romantic scenery.

Scotland had much longer stretches of deserted shoreline: its holiday centres were concentrated along the shores of the Firth of Clyde, the Firth of Forth and Fifeshire. The Highlands remained the preserve of the few: affluent climbers, deerstalkers, shooting parties, sporting fishermen, lovers of romantic scenery and enthusiasts for the invented traditions of the region. Landowners actively discouraged any hint of resort development: as Ivor Brown said of Jura, 'Despite the mist-collecting habit of the Paps, it has its bays and beaches and might have been a paradisal place of holiday for hundreds . . . but . . . where there are deer in Scotland men, except in Arran, are unwanted. So Jura has but one small hotel and a population of less than nine for each mile of its length.'[8] The Clyde estuary, with its well-developed Victorian steamer services and rail links, propagated a string of small resorts on both banks, while Glasgow and west of Scotland demand also supplemented popular Lancastrian interest to stimulate the growth of the Isle of Man's holiday economy. In the eastern half of Scotland Edinburgh demand promoted a chain of resorts from Dunbar and North Berwick in East Lothian to the more popular Aberdour on the north shore of the Firth of Forth (which also attracted Glasgwegians in numbers) and on to Crail and other little places in Fifeshire, continuing up to St Andrews. On this east coast especially the golf course had become a necessary attraction by Edwardian times, and nineteenth-century Scottish seaside resort development has been characterised as 'from Gulf Stream to golf stream', a dichotomy which takes into account the significantly colder bathing waters of the North Sea. None of the specialised resorts were very large, and there was very little Highland development, although Oban became a significant outpost of the sea-bathing holiday in the north-west. Apart from Ayr, which had its own well-frequented golf courses but also had other fish to fry, the biggest resort populations would have been outside the top forty in England and Wales, with resident populations of no more than 10,000, although Rothesay might play host to as many as 40,000 visitors during Glasgow Fair.[9]

It is tempting to regard the late Victorian and Edwardian years as the heyday of British seaside resort growth, and that is probably true for Scotland; but the resort systems of England and Wales exhibited sustained buoyancy and dynamism throughout the first half of the twentieth century, although growth was increasingly channelled into new kinds of places and styles of holidaymaking. Between 1881 and 1911 the aggregate census population of 145 English and Welsh seaside resorts grew by more than 600,000 to just over 1.6 million, which was nearly 4.5 per cent of the total population: an impressive statistic which reinforces the importance of the themes of this book, especially when we take into account the timing of the censuses, before the season had begun, the immense numbers who passed through the resorts annually as holidaymakers and seasonal migrants, and the large number of relatively short-term residents who experienced resort life as a stage in the life-cycle, especially in retirement. Over the next forty years the total increased by nearly another million, to 2.5 million, in measured steps: the 1931 census found 5 per cent of the population living in seaside resorts, and by 1951 the figure was 5.7 per cent. When we consider the disruption wrought by ten years of world war during this period, this growth actually outpaces that of 1881–1911; and much of it was also expressed in innovative ways.[10] Moreover, the most dynamic of the seaside resorts featured strongly among the fastest-growing towns of all kinds, on a par with London's outer suburbia and the new manufacturing centres of (mainly) the south Midlands. Ten resorts trebled their spring populations between 1911 and 1951, and a few of them grew much faster than this, while a further twenty-two increased between two- and threefold, including Southend, Blackpool and substantial second-rank centres like Worthing and Whitley Bay. By 1951 four leading resorts (Brighton, Southend, Blackpool and Bournemouth) hovered around 150,000 inhabitants. Brighton's lead had been whittled down by this pursuing pack, but Hove, with nearly 70,000, was in sixth place, and its neighbouring if contrasting presence sustained the predominance of the mid-Sussex conurbation. Six further resorts contained more than 50,000 residents (in descending order: Southport, Worthing, Hastings, Eastbourne, Torquay and Great Yarmouth), and a dozen more had between 30,000 and 50,000. Thirteen more were substantial towns of over 20,000. This represented a considerable increase in the number of major resorts in population terms over the forty years: in 1911 twenty resorts had more than 20,000 off-season inhabitants, but by 1951 the figure had grown to thirty-six, with some very large population increments at the top end of the scale. We need now to look more closely at patterns and themes in growth and change, remembering that a statistical treatment is complicated by the loss of the 1941 census to the Second World War and by the problems of adjusting for the postponement of the 1921 census from its usual early spring date to late June, at a time when resort populations were already swollen by visitors and seasonal migrants.[11]

In the first place, the most impressive growth in terms of sheer numbers was concentrated into large towns on well-established resort coastlines. Southend and Blackpool, each of which added more than 85,000 to its resident population, stand out particularly here, followed by Bournemouth's 60,000 extra bodies. Brighton, which had little room for expansion within its municipal boundaries, added fewer than 30,000, but Hove's similar growth and the nearly

40,000 added by nearby Worthing, along with rapid growth from smaller beginnings elsewhere along this coastline, brought this part of Sussex firmly into the pattern. The resorts of the whole county grew by just 43.6 per cent over the forty years, to an imposing total of well over half a million residents, concentrated to the west of Brighton where rail connections with London were best. Moreover, Blackpool's neighbours among the established resorts of the Lancashire coast included Morecambe, which more than trebled its population to 37,006, and Thornton-Cleveleys which displayed similar dynamism on a smaller scale closer to home, although Southport and Lytham St Anne's grew more slowly. The Lancashire resorts forged ahead in percentage growth terms, increasing by 86.6 per cent to nearly 350,000 by 1951. Bournemouth's neighbour Christchurch also tripled in size to top 20,000, while Southend's successful (and sharply contrasting) neighbours at Clacton, Walton, Frinton and Canvey Island made the Essex coast the most expansive resort district of all, growing by more than 150 per cent to nearly 200,000 over the period.[12]

These were the most popular coastlines, readily accessible from the biggest conurbations which were also the best-sited for generating holiday demand across a broad social spectrum; and in each case they catered for the complete range of classes and age-groups, from those who could just afford a day-trip, to the occupiers of inter-war semi-detacheds for comfortable commuters and bungalows for the retired. Away from these privileged coasts with their specialised resort systems and ample room for expansion over long stretches of accessible and inexpensive agricultural land, some of the larger Edwardian resorts failed to prosper in similar manner. Kent and east Sussex signally failed to emulate Brighton and district, as Dover contrived to lose nearly one in five of its resident population, Hastings stagnated, and the chain of resorts round the corner of south-eastern England from Eastbourne to Margate performed at or around the national average, gaining between 30 and 60 per cent on the 1911 population. Closer to London, Herne Bay and Whitstable bucked this trend, more than doubling their populations, and the position further south was probably complicated by a slow recovery from the Second World War as well as poor transport links and lack of innovation. The percentage growth-rate for all the Kentish resorts together was only 38.5.[13] This was in sharp contrast with the dynamism of north Wales, whose resorts grew even faster than Lancashire's, by 88.4 per cent, though from much smaller beginnings. Growth here was concentrated at the eastern end, closest to the industrial centres of Lancashire and the West Midlands, with Rhyl, Prestatyn (especially) and little Abergele showing strongly. But the resort systems of south Devon and the Bristol Channel grew only at the average rate of about 50 per cent, although here too some locations significantly out-performed their neighbours: thus Paignton stood out in south Devon while most of its neighbours grew more slowly than the national norm; and Minehead similarly attracted a disproportionate share of Bristol Channel growth. What we see here is a realignment of demand, and indeed investment, within the existing leading sectors of coastal development, in a situation where growth was the prevailing pattern but some places (including most of the leading Edwardian centres) were able to take more than their fair share of it.

The remoter coastlines were not yet catching up, despite their growing attractiveness to middle-class visitors seeking seclusion and exclusivity. Apart from Paignton, only the north Cornwall resorts of Bude and Newquay in the two south-western counties featured among the thirty fastest-growing British resorts, and by 1951 the former had just over 5,000 and the latter just under 10,000 residents. Torquay and some of its south Devon neighbours aside, resorts in this far south-west were growing more slowly than the national average, and from small beginnings. But this is an area where the bald census population figures are misleading. Post-war holiday statistics credited south-west England with 14 per cent of 'main British holidays' in 1951, when its resorts had only 10 per cent of the total seaside resort population of England and Wales. This clear indication of competitive success is actually understated, because most substantial south-western resorts were towns with mixed economies (fishing, commercial port activities, naval training, china clay) and the proportion of their populations active in the holiday industry was lower than on other coastlines. In turn, these non-resort elements in complex seasonal economies watered down the population growth stimulated by the holiday industry, especially when its growth was counterbalancing decline in other activities. At Brixham, for example, the number of boarding-houses doubled during the 1930s while the fishing industry declined, and the census population increased by just 10 per cent in forty years. On the other hand, the rise of motorised holidaymaking stimulated pockets of growth which are easily missed by census-based surveys, especially when the isolated hotels, or estates of holiday homes and isolated groups of bungalows, or campsites and holiday camps, are practically unoccupied out of season. This was a common theme in Cornwall and north Devon, where resorts beyond railways such as Combe Martin and Woolacombe were attracting large numbers of visitors in relation to small resident populations by the 1930s. Numerically, this kind of growth was still outweighed by the older population concentrations around the railway stations; but it was significant for the future.[14] The south-west was already outpacing the other quiet coastlines of the turn of the century: Norfolk's awakening at that time proved a false dawn, although here again holiday camp and chalet developments were more important than the census figures suggest, while growth in Wales was very slow away from the north coast.

Scotland also failed to sustain the expansion of the turn of the century. Ivor Brown remarked in 1952 that, 'It is a discreditable failure of Scotland not to have done better with its sea-side resorts.' Dunoon he thought cramped and rainy; Rothesay 'shabby at the centre, though its line of shore-villas is trim enough'; and only Largs, 'neater and airier' and with views of the Arran mountains, received a good word among the Clyde resorts. On Arran itself the growth of the resort nucleus of Brodick was responsible for that unusual phenomenon in the western islands, population growth between 1931 and 1951, although it counterbalanced depopulation on the farms. As for the east coast, North Berwick stagnated comfortably while in Fife demand came from within the county, as 'the mining and industrial towns of the east and south of the county send their hundreds by motor-coach to strip and sport on the great sandy crescent beyond the St Andrews links', defying the formidable chill of the water in even the most comfortable summer months. Seaside towns like Montrose, which was presenting itself as a 'Garden City by the Sea' (a title with previous claimants ranging from Southport to the down-market Sussex 'bungalow town' of Peacehaven) in 1939, and even the old Scottish capital of Dunfermline were promoting themselves as resorts in the inter-war years, with apparently limited success. What demand there was for seaside holidays was, as in Fife, overwhelmingly regional and local: the affluent outsiders and (increasingly in post-war years) the coach tours from England headed for the Highlands rather than the seaside. Transport played its part in limiting growth, as the Clyde steamer services declined after the First World War without adequate substitutes, although Clyde estuary resorts continued to advertise steamer excursions to beauty spots alongside the more prosaic motor-coach tours right up to the Second World War, while on the east coast the lack of road bridges over the Forth and Tay confined the horizons of motorists and helped to push the coach tours inland. Population stagnation or very limited growth was the order of the day north of the border, as much popular holiday demand from industrial Scotland was diverted to the fleshpots of Blackpool, Morecambe, Whitley Bay (especially: the majority of holidaymakers there in the late 1960s came from Scotland) and Scarborough.[15]

Among the fastest-growing resorts of England and Wales certain themes stand out as the widespread hallmarks of success in this period. Rapid population growth from small beginnings was associated very strongly with the new informal modes of holidaymaking, as younger holidaymakers (especially) sought to escape from the formality of the now-traditional bandstand and esplanade and the defensive regulations of the seaside landlady, and preferred the more liberal, open-air regime of the chalet or bungalow development and the holiday camp. The most dynamic of the larger resorts were also hospitable to these new growths, or at least unable to prevent them in their immediate vicinity; and they were also making the most of the fashions for sunbathing and outdoor activities by investing in promenades, parks and open-air swimming pools.

The most controversial aspects of these new growths were the so-called 'bungalow towns' or 'plotland settlements' which were proliferating at many points on the English coastline, but especially in the south and east, from the turn of the century, and with accelerating impetus after the First World War. These were unplanned, self-built knots and straggles of seasonally-occupied dwellings, featuring creative adaptations of old tramcars, railway carriages and later bus bodies, which sprang up on the shoreline wherever cheap land and welcoming farmers or astute speculators offered a foothold to bohemian seekers after the simple seaside life or, increasingly, working-class families whose only hope of affording a seaside (or country) holiday was via this makeshift but independent route. Unorthodox or specialised occupational communities also colonised such spaces, such as the psychotherapists who congregated at Walberswick in Suffolk. Those areas of south-east England, in easy reach of London, which had been worst hit by the late Victorian agricultural depression and where old estates were being broken up in the early 1920s, were the most fecund in such developments. They occupied the interstices between more conventional resorts all along the Sussex coast from Selsey to Camber, extending less prolifically into Kent and reaching their apotheosis in Canvey Island on the Thames estuary in Essex. Further to the north there was also Jaywick Sands, a popular but (to local government) embarrassing addition to the holiday portfolio of Clacton, and further developments punctuated the east coast in Norfolk, around Mablethorpe in Lincolnshire, on the Humberstone Fitties near Cleethorpes, and in Yorkshire between Withernsea and Scarborough. Similar settlements developed on a smaller scale in the south-west, outcropping along the coast from Severn Beach through north Devon and Cornwall and around to Beer and Exmouth. There were even examples in west Cumberland, around Braystones; and by the 1930s these informal seaside settlements were accumulating outraged comment from national planners as well as local authorities.[16]

These shanty-town resorts were generally small as well as informal, and came in various guises. The geographer J.A. Steers, reporting on the state of the coastline for the Ministry of Works and Planning during the Second World War, identified three types: the 'isolated hut, or huts in small groups', often in prominent positions in cherished landscapes; 'the unplanned or haphazard holiday camp', a group of fields 'set aside for the reception of caravans, huts, old buses, and shacks of every description', devoid of order, privacy or sanitation; and on the largest scale the 'shack towns', of which the most infamous, in the eyes of both of planners and of opinion-forming custodians of the landscape, was Peacehaven, where the South Downs met the sea a few miles east of Brighton. These larger settlements tended to be more formally laid out, by developers with some financial resources. Peacehaven, the brainchild of the internationally experienced land speculator Charles Neville at the outbreak of the First World War, was a case in point; and, paradoxically, it lacked the randomness of layout which so annoyed the planners elsewhere. It was conceived on an enormous grid pattern, and promoted enterprisingly through press and other advertising (including saturation coverage of the backs of London tram tickets). Plots were sold cheaply for people (especially returning soldiers eager for their 'homes for heroes') to build their own bungalows, and between 1921 and 1926 the population grew from twenty-four to 3,000. Much slower growth ensued, as problems of sewering and other services became increasingly pressing by the 1930s, but Peacehaven attracted people of limited means who liked the fresh air, independence and self-sufficiency which were highlighted in Neville's propaganda. It was the most conspicuous of the 'bungalow towns', and the most reviled, for its conspicuous 'desecration' of the sacred landscape of Downland, which had been written up as an emblem of patriotic southern Englishness; but it was not the largest such development in the inter-war years. That distinction fell to Canvey Island, a low-lying area of reclaimed land in the Thames estuary whose development was initiated by a Southend land agent who laid out cheap plots for impecunious self-builders, and whose brainchild continued to gather its own momentum after his bankruptcy, as it acquired its reputation in London's East End as 'the cheapest possible place for a seaside holiday', with the possibility of a day-trip to the fleshpots of nearby Southend if funds permitted. From 563 inhabitants at the 1911 census Canvey reached about 5,000 at the end of the 1930s, as growing numbers of holidaymakers became permanent residents, and a post-war influx at the peak of the housing shortage brought the 1951 figure to nearly 11,000, making Canvey Britain's fastest-growing seaside resort in population terms over the forty years. On the other side of the Thames Estuary a similar initiative at Minster-in-Sheppey, usually accounted a failure because of the vast areas of empty plots, still boosted the population from about 250 at the turn of the century to 5,500 after the Second World War. A more complex case is that of Lancing, in Sussex, which began as a 'bungalow town' but acquired industries (including a railway carriage works in 1912) and more conventional bungalow estates in the inter-war years, growing from 2,000 to nearly 10,000 people between 1911 and 1951. There were many lesser developments, such as Jaywick Sands near Clacton which had several thousand summer visitors at a time in the mid-1930s and perhaps a thousand permanent residents by 1950, or the 700 dwellings which had grown up on Shoreham Beach's long shingle spit by the outbreak of war.[17]

The smaller settlements were hard hit by the Second World War, as many were in potential front-line locations and were dismantled by the armed forces, provoking post-war controversy over the extent and nature of rebuilding; while the 1947 Town and Country Planning Act prevented further developments of this kind in the post-war years. But at least half the thirty fastest-growing resorts in percentage terms during 1911–51 contained 'bungalow towns' of one sort or another; and at least seventeen also offered hospitality to holiday camps, the other distinctive new growth sector in seaside settlements during these years. The holiday camp acquired a higher profile in the late twentieth century than the 'bungalow town', partly due to the publicity generated by the colourful entrepreneurs who promoted the chains of big commercial camps and partly to a successful television series, 'Hi-De-Hi', which offered an affectionate nostalgic pastiche of their heyday. Even so, and despite the impact a camp might make on an individual resort like Bognor Regis or Minehead, the camps never accounted for more than one-twentieth of the holidaymakers in any given year, although a much larger proportion of the population will have passed through them at some point in the life-cycle. But in the first half of the century the camps catered for a very small minority of holidaymakers, and most of them were what contemporaries called 'pioneer' as opposed to full-blown 'commercial' camps. The former, which began at the turn of the century with tented ventures in Norfolk and on the Isle of Man, and expanded considerably in the inter-war years, were cheap, basic enterprises, often with a political or religious slant, which embraced the simple life and glorified fresh air, self-improvement and a willingness to 'rough it'. As co-operative societies and trade unions moved in during the 1930s, and the government itself began to take an interest on the eve of the war, there was more concern for providing attractive communal holiday centres to meet the growing demand that the paid holidays legislation, which eventually arrived in 1938, was expected to unleash, and the new 'pioneer' camps became less spartan and more entertainment-oriented. It was, however, the unashamedly commercial ventures that emerged in the mid-1930s, the 'luxury' holiday camp chains of Warner and Butlin, which went in for comfortable chalets, full board and in-house entertainment programmes. At this stage most of the camps, excepting trade union ventures like the Derbyshire Miners' Skegness camp, catered mainly for the white-collar clientele which had been the main recruiting ground for early socialists and advocates of 'back-to-the-land' movements; and in contrast with existing resorts their populations were purely seasonal. Census-based studies would therefore miss them. Established resort interests viewed them with suspicion as competitors for established markets rather than openers-out of new ones, and Butlin had to be very persuasive when seeking local government approval for his early camps at Clacton and Filey; but they remained interesting fringe phenomena at this stage. A national map of holiday camps in 1939 showed that those with permanent buildings overlapped with the 'bungalow towns' in Kent and Norfolk, and on the north Wales coast, while the less elaborate tented settlements were concentrated in Lincolnshire between Skegness and Cleethorpes, and in south Wales. In both these cases the visitors were more likely to be working-class families from the mining districts of the Midlands and south Yorkshire and the Welsh Valleys. Holiday camps of a relatively formal kind were an Isle of Wight speciality, but they were almost absent from the 'bungalow town' strongholds of the Sussex coast, and from the generally undeveloped coasts of Cornwall, mid-Wales, Cumbria and the north-east. There seem to be two patterns at work: a search for quiet, rural retreats for the lower-middle class who could not afford to range beyond Norfolk or the Isle of Wight, and cheaper working-class provision on coastlines which lacked conventional scenic beauty but were easily accessible from London and industrial population centres. What is clear is that they were not simply associated with rustic escapism: most of the fastest-growing resorts had holiday camps within or adjoining their boundaries, as befitted their ability to keep up with the changing tastes and preferences of a broad spectrum of visiting publics, including emergent ones.[18]

Resorts were also growing as commuter and retirement centres in these years. The fastest-growing resorts on established coastlines all developed substantial commuter populations, building from established bases at the turn of the century, and new growths like Canvey Island and Lancing were also fuelled in this way. The Sussex coast around Brighton was boosted by rail electrification from London in the early 1930s, but Blackpool and Morecambe benefited from improved steam services as the railway companies woke up to the opportunities, and resorts close to big middle-class population centres were becoming primarily residential, as in the cases of Southport, Hoylake and Whitley Bay. The attraction of retired residents was also positively correlated with rapid growth at this stage, most obviously in Worthing, Hove and Brighton on Sussex's emergent Costa Geriatrica, although to the east Bexhill and Hastings were equally attractive as retirement destinations without sustaining the same levels of expansion. South Devon was also becoming a retirement haven in ways which visibly affected resort demography, as were a range of smaller centres across the country, from Grange-over-Sands to Southwold. Firm foundations were being laid for the much stronger trends of the 1960s and 1970s, when the residential interest really began to make an impact on resort politics and local government policies on a broad front.[19]

It will be clear from this survey that some coastlines developed much more strongly than others during the first half of the century, with Essex and West Sussex being especially stimulated by London demand while Lancashire (above all) and north Wales took the lion's share of the growing popular holiday markets of the industrial north and Midlands. Interesting and novel though the 'bungalow towns' and holiday camps were, demand was still being chan-nelled overwhelmingly into the conventional seaside holiday at established resorts clustered around railheads. Within this pattern, however, some resorts grew much more strongly than others on all coastlines, so that the average percent-ages hid widely fluctuating individual experiences; and we need to consider what the most dynamic resorts had in common. Above all, rapid growth cor-relates with informality and openness to the expanding popular market, as the frequent presence of holiday camps and 'bungalow towns' suggests. Resorts which had been dominated by large landed estates with policies of up-market exclusiveness (a stance which had been highly successful in the mid-Victorian market-place), found difficulty in welcoming the more down-market growth sectors of the inter-war years, and they were increasingly losing their old staple visiting public to foreign competition. Indeed, by the early twentieth century the role of large landowners in resort promotion was coming to an end, and the inter-war years saw the abdication of many landed families from active intervention in resort economies as they disinvested from their families' creations.[20] Other things being more or less equal (especially in terms of ease of access from population centres), what mattered most was to provide a secure but deregulated environment which celebrated the new freedoms for families to bathe together without the constraint (and expense) of the segregated Victorian bathing-machine regime, and to sunbathe as part of enjoying long days in the open air. Extensive sandy beaches were increasingly valuable assets, as was a high sunshine count, and it is interesting to note the large number of rapidly expanding resorts in the sunny south and east which met these criteria. A 'garden city' atmosphere with plenty of investment in parks, promenades, swimming pools and solaria was central to success, although up-to-date, streamlined, attractive fairgrounds and lively evening and wet-weather entertainments also helped. If all this could be combined with the civic amenities coupled with low municipal taxation levels which attracted commuters and the retired, without this coming into conflict with the holiday season, then resorts could advance on several fronts at once. Blackpool and Southend squared all these circles among the largest resorts, followed by Worthing, Whitley Bay, Hoylake, Morecambe, Deal, Paignton and Redcar, all of which doubled or trebled their populations from a 1911 base figure of between ten and thirty thousand. Only Deal and Paignton lacked a conspicuous commuter and retirement element in their populations (Deal had the Royal Marines instead), while local heavy industry contributed to Redcar's growth; but what is also striking is the broad geographical spread of this prosperity, from Devon to Northumberland. Smaller resorts which doubled or trebled in size from a 1911 population of between 5,000 and 10,000 were Clacton, Rhyl, Bognor Regis, Whitstable, Herne Bay, Christchurch and Shoreham. Here there was more concentration in the south-east, with two contenders each from West Sussex and north Kent, and these were the places where commuters made a noticeable contribution. The resorts in the lowest population band, starting at under 5,000 inhabitants, which at least doubled their populations were Thornton/Cleveleys, Felixstowe, Newquay, Skegness, Walton and Frinton, Minehead, Porthcawl, Withernsea, Abergele, Towyn, Bude, Prestatyn (which grew more than fourfold), Lancing (nearly sixfold), Mablethorpe (fourfold) and Canvey Island (twentyfold, but from the very small beginnings described above). The first two of these were affected by industry, but again the sheer geographical range is arresting, confirming that although the fortunes of entire coastlines varied significantly, what really mattered was the nature and 'personality' of individual resorts and their ability to meet the changing desires of their customers.[21] As Nigel Morgan suggested with regard to Devon, resorts were increasingly diversifying to cater for different markets: what we see here is the ones which catered most convincingly for the most expansive ones.[22]

Two further points should be made here. First, the focus on population change tells only part of the story. Visitor numbers would give an alternative perspective, but the kinds of social surveys which might provide plausible statistics were things of the future. The oft-quoted statistic that in the mid-1930s Blackpool had 7 million visitors per year, Southend 5.5 million, Hastings 3 million, Rhyl 2.5 million, Bournemouth, Southport and Redcar two million each, and Eastbourne and Morecambe one million, is a mere compilation of unsourced guesstimates from an article in the *Town Planning Review* in 1935, which offers some notion of rough orders of magnitude but nothing else. Its failure to cat-egorise the holidaymakers (what proportion were day-trippers, for example?) is damning in itself.[23] Moreover, it is too easy simply to equate growth with success. Some of the most prosperous resorts of this period were those which, like Salcombe in south Devon, Lynton in north Devon or Grange-over-Sands on Morecambe Bay, settled down to catering for a small, sedate, prosperous visiting public which generated comfortable retired residents. These were the places which kept their natural attractions by remaining fixed in an early stage of the 'resort cycle' (thereby undermining its viability as a concept) and, with their strong identities and reputations, remained less vulnerable to changing fashions than their more dynamic but unstable rivals. Higher up the scale Eastbourne, for example, grew slowly in population terms, but remained attractive to its mainstream visiting public and in 1950 it had the fifth highest figure among 157 large towns for retail expenditure per head (Bournemouth was second).[24] This does not look like stagnation. Occupying an enduring niche market might be preferable to flourishing by the whims of fashion and then languishing when they moved on. This brings us to the second point. On the basis of league tables based on population growth rates, the most successful British seaside resorts of the period 1911–51 were Morecambe, Bognor Regis, Redcar, Christchurch and Clacton. Redcar, a Teesside commuter and day-tripper resort with developing industries of its own, is a special case; but the others pulled together most or all of the characteristics which made resorts attractive and popular in these years.[25] Increasingly, however, the second half of the century saw them becoming identified with declining visitor numbers, shabby retirement, decaying urban fabric and a desperately unfashionable image among the young. They had ceased to move with the times and had been beached by the changing tides of popular holiday demand in post-war Britain. They had captivated a rising inter-war generation and failed to speak to succeeding ones. They were not alone in this, however; and we move on now to discuss the changing fortunes of the British seaside resort system from the 1950s.

Paul Addison remarked that, 'The 1940s marked the peak of the Victorian resorts', with the continuing dominance of the railways helping to mark out a series of well-beaten paths to traditional accommodation, and much of the entertainment provision and beach furniture remaining recognisably Victorian.[26] Stagnation and decline, in many cases, were soon to follow; but not immediately, and not everywhere. A few resorts just carried on growing. At the head of the list were some of the old 'bungalow towns', which were brought under urban local government regimes and opened out to mainstream demand for (increasingly) affordable seaside residence rather than holidaymaking. Canvey Island, after its remarkably quick recovery from the floods of early 1953 when 58 residents were killed, grew mainly as a dormitory for industrial Essex, with overspill projects bringing 'several hundred families from Dagenham and Walthamstow', and relatively cheap private housing helping to treble the population to around 33,000 in 1980. Peacehaven's population similarly soared, as it acquired its own Town Map for development under County Council auspices, its centre of gravity was shifted away from the shoreline and it was transformed into just another residential suburb with a half-hidden eccentric past. In the 'bungalow town' areas of easternmost Sussex post-war development was concentrated into Camber, but as a planned settlement with carefully zoned holiday bungalows and an off-season population of up to 5,000. These were places whose expansion came with assimilation to wider norms of planning orthodoxy as a condition of development, and with consequent loss of distinctive resort identity.[27]

Relatedly, static holiday caravans were a great growth sector on many British coastlines in the post-war generation. They provided cheap accommodation and very limited scope for the development of year-round settlements or urban amenities, catering as they did for footloose car-based holidaymakers who did not need the relatively labour-intensive services provided by the older boarding-houses which huddled around the declining railway stations; and they increased and multiplied especially on the coasts of Yorkshire, Lincolnshire, parts of East Anglia, both sides of the Severn estuary, north Wales and, most controversially, Devon and Cornwall. On one estimate two million people took caravan holidays in 1955 and 4.5 million at the end of the 1960s. The coastline of Lindsey (Lincolnshire) saw caravan numbers increasing at 1,000 per year throughout the 1950s and 1960s from the 3,000 already present in 1950.[28] Between 1951 and 1965 caravan numbers on the Somerset coast grew from 2,400 to over 5,300, concentrated into new development sites at Brean and Berrow, Blue Anchor Bay and Sand Bay rather than older-established railhead resorts like Weston-super-Mare. By the mid-1960s caravan accommodation catered for similar numbers to the hotel and guest-house sector, which had hardly expanded since the war.[29] This was symptomatic of wider changes in visitor preference, which were encapsulated in the case of Cornwall, where by 1959 the County Council was already declaring some stretches of coastline to be 'saturation zones where further development was to be discouraged'. Chalets rather than caravans were the main growth sector here, showing a 310 per cent increase during the decade after 1954; and here hotels and guest-houses were still being built in significant numbers, with a ten per cent increment between 1951 and 1961 (and a 13.6 per cent increase in Newquay between 1954 and 1964). In 1966 the County Council identified four kinds of 'new centres of the holiday industry', originating under the undeveloped planning regimes of the inter-war years: knots of hotels and associated services (as at Carbis Bay), estates of holiday homes, 'loose groups of holiday homes', and 'chalet, caravan and camping sites in outlying places'; and these all exhibited pressure for further growth. The trend towards more scattered, informal, cheaper accommodation, taking up more space and generating less employment, was as dominant here as anywhere else, provoking worried commentaries and growing intervention and restriction from county authorities.[30]

By 1967, on one calculation, just over 15 per cent of ' "bednights" away from home for non-business reasons' were spent in licensed hotels, compared with just over 20 per cent in 'unlicensed hotels' and guest-houses, 12.7 per cent in caravans, and just over 8 per cent on campsites and in holiday camps combined. These figures are for domestic tourists only (the statistics for overseas visitors were overwhelmingly dominated by guests staying in friends' houses), and they include London and other cities where hotels might be expected to predominate: they will certainly underestimate the share of caravans and holiday camps in the seaside holiday market. Already it is clear that older certainties were being challenged, however, as the freedom of self-catering accommodation lured visitors away from the ambivalent embrace of the seaside landlady, with her old-fashioned accommodation, vexatious rules and timetabled day. Where preferences were also tilting away from older-established but unexciting coastlines, the future was already looking threatening.[31]

Best-guess estimates suggest that Cornwall's visitor numbers (mostly seaside tourists, but with other interests which blurred simplistic classifications) grew from 1.4 to 2.1 million between 1954 and 1964, rising to 3 million by the early 1980s and then stagnating. A survey of visitor origins in 1991 suggested that nearly one-third came from south-eastern England, where many resorts were falling on hard times (as in Thanet) or becoming predominantly retirement centres (much of Sussex). Between 8 and 10 per cent of visitors came from each of the Midlands, the north-west and Yorkshire, suggesting that

Cornwall was also siphoning customers away from older resorts in and catering for these industrial regions.[32] Similar patterns could be identified in Devon.[33] An English Tourist Board survey of 1971 found that over 26 per cent of tourist bednights in England were spent in the West Country (amounting to 28 per head of resident population). Only the Lake District, with 5.5 per cent, had a higher ratio (47). The south-east (excluding London) accounted for one-sixth of bednights, while East Anglia had just over 10 per cent, Yorkshire nearly 8 per cent and the north-west (including the Isle of Man) 7 per cent. The seaside accounted for a higher proportion of tourist activity in some of these regions than in others, of course, and the north-west was close behind the Lake District and the West Country in expenditure per head per night (while the south-east was a long way behind); but what these figures illustrate, with all their problems and limitations, is the continuing shift within England away from older tourist areas towards a new pole of growth in the south-west, which was associated with small urban centres, scattered tourist accommodation and the enjoyment of countryside and sightseeing rather than the by-now traditional seaside menu of entertainments: indeed, the south-western resorts which followed the older pattern, most obviously Ilfracombe, were the least dynamic in the region.[34]

As growth was generally being channelled into more informal, scattered settlements, accessed by road rather than rail, the older resorts over most of the country began to stagnate in population terms. Their entertainments and other services were used by people from the caravan sites when it suited them, although the bigger sites, like the holiday camps, sought to maximise the income from visitors by providing bars and entertainment on-site. The only resorts which featured among the fastest-growing towns of the 1950s, 1960s and 1970s were indeed in the south-west, where climate, scenery and surfing helped to challenge the competition from the Mediterranean and other newer forms of holidaymaking, while transport developments improved accessibility. Overall, Chloe Stallibrass calculated that between 1951 and 1971 the 39 largest English seaside resorts were still growing, but more slowly than the nation at large: an increase of 10.4 per cent in their census populations, as opposed to 11.8 per cent. She also noted the changing nature of resort populations, as retirement took over from the holiday industry the driving force for growth: 'In absolute figures the total population of non-pensionable age at the thirty-nine . . . resorts in . . . 1951–71 increased by 4,000. The increase in people of pensionable age . . . was 207,000.' Five of these resorts had increases of between 85 and 144 per cent in this 'elderly' population band (men over 65, women over 60):

Clacton, Bexhill, Margate, Exmouth and, remarkably, Newquay, despite its position as a popular and rapidly growing resort in the only part of the country where significant numbers of new seaside hotels were still being opened. Elsewhere, the census evidence suggested sharp declines in hotel accommodation at many established resorts between 1961 and 1971, especially in northern England, in the more down-market resorts of Essex and Kent, and at Skegness and Great Yarmouth. Problems of definition plague this material, however, and only six substantial resorts actually showed overall population decline between 1951 and 1971. Meanwhile Exmouth, Newquay and Clacton grew by more than 50 per cent during the two decades (despite the latter's disastrous-looking loss of hotel beds), and a string of south coast centres, together with Lytham St Annes, recorded growth figures of between 25 and 50 per cent. In many if not most of these cases, however, the new populations were of commuters and retirers. The 1960s, especially, saw a new wave of seaside retirement, reaching down to the lower-middle and upper-working classes, as bungalows proliferated around established resort cores in places like Bexhill, Clacton, Herne Bay and (less dramatically but still significantly) across a wide range of resorts and coastlines, most obviously in south-east England and on the Lancashire coast. It was in this decade that my grandfather, a retired Derbyshire coal miner, made his move from North Wingfield to Blackpool, where he and his wife joined my great-uncle, a chiropodist, and my great-aunt. As a result of such trends, the resort elements in local economies were shrinking even as the towns themselves continued to grow. At the end of their product cycle as resorts, they were transmuting into other kinds of place, dormitories and retirement centres which happened to have seaside locations: a trend which is symbolised by the disappearance of Brighton from the 'resort' category in at least two analytical listings. If Brighton was no longer a seaside resort, where did this leave the English seaside? To compound the problem, six other major resorts (Southend, Hove, Worthing, Ramsgate, Hastings and Southport) had fewer than 3 hotels per thousand population and less than 4 per cent of working employees in the holiday trades in 1971. This was dilution of the old identities on a grand scale.[35]

As population growth continued to slow down during the 1980s, there were still a handful of seaside resort-dominated economies among the fifty fastest-growing local government districts of 1981–91. East Dorset was eighth in England, with 13.5 per cent; and Teignbridge, North Cornwall, Suffolk Coastal and East Yorkshire were all in the top twenty, as the post-war bias towards the south and south-west, and to places that lacked the cultural baggage of the older large resorts, remained evident. Brighton, meanwhile, lost 5 per cent of its population, although this development coexisted with the revival of an up-market resort economy and was partly due to saturation point having been passed within the existing civic boundaries. But the days of the seaside resort as urban pace-setter, in any sense, were now long gone.[36]

At the end of the twentieth century, defying rumours of its demise, the British seaside resort system was still in place, challenged though it was by a prolifer-ating array of competitors for free time and leisure spending, and despite the growing importance of residential (commuting and retirement) rather than holidaymaking functions to many old resort economies, as such towns became more like suburbs which happened to be at the seaside. Redevelopment from the 1960s onwards, here as elsewhere, tended to reduce visual and archi-tectural distinctiveness, and expanding leisure provision in the home and in the inland towns also reduced the novelty of a seaside resort visit. As the new millennium approached the lessons of a quarter of a century of decline were still being learned. A central government report, published by Minister for Culture, Chris Smith in February 1999, blamed 'a mix of poor hotels, dowdy town centres and lack of initiative from civic and business leaders' for 'the failure to adapt to the decline of the traditional summer holiday', while offering grants in support of efforts to attract (for example) conferences, English language schools and day-trippers. This was in a context where the *Which?* hotel guide was unable to find a single hotel to recommend in such large resorts as Clacton, Colwyn Bay, Southport, Hastings and even Eastbourne. As we have seen, this was the outcome of a set of trends which were already identifiable thirty years earlier.[37]

There were exceptions. Torquay and Rhyl invested busily in new attractions from the mid-1980s, the former investing in (among other things) a 460-berth marina and new conference and exhibition centres. Torquay and Morecambe benefited from belated English Tourist Board encouragement through Tourist Development Action Programmes, starting in 1986, while from the early 1990s several Local Area Initiatives built on this in other resort districts, and the Tourist Board encouraged diversification of attractions. European loans and then grants became more accessible. Smith's report singled out Redcar, on Teesside, as a town on a depressed coastline which had successfully reinvented itself, and Morecambe was striving busily to pull itself out of the deep trough of the early 1990s, with a reconstructed sea-front featuring sea-bird sculptures and a concentration on niche markets involving (for example) alternative music.[38] Even Margate, which had struggled through the post-war decades in a down-market and increasingly shabby style, with some successful initiatives in the 1950s followed by growing unemployment, drink and drug problems,

was pushing in 1999 to attract a new art gallery to celebrate the town's connection with William Turner, drawing the *Guardian* critic Jonathan Glancey
to rediscover the 'Dutch-gabled abundance of characterful Georgian and
Regency houses' which coexisted with the postcards, amusement arcades and
joke shops. Despite the depressing initial view from the station, here was
architectural heritage and art history to be rescued and celebrated; and this
rediscovery of the marketable aspects of the seaside's past was gathering
momentum in places like this as well as more obvious venues like St Ives, with
its more conventional picturesque qualities and its own local Tate Gallery.[39]
Similar mixtures of cheerful bad taste, joyful tat, engaging architecture,
seaside scenery and an appeal to cultural tourism offered hope across a wide
range of coastal settings, as the tide appeared to be turning once again.
And smaller resorts with distinctive identities and established appeals to niche
markets, such as Whitby, were building on these qualities with visible success,
celebrating whatever literary and historical associations they could call upon
(Captain Cook and Bram Stoker, in Whitby's case, though for some reason
not Mrs Gaskell, who was also available). Southwold celebrated living in a
time-warp, marooned in the 1950s and keeping end-of-the-century innovations like themed swimming-pools and shoreline restaurants at arm's length,
preferring to trade on nostalgia and exclusivity.[40] Here were alternatives to
Blackpool's vigorous pursuit of cheapness, kitsch and the pink pound; and many
of them were flourishing.

But the fear of utter collapse was still pervasive. The fate of New Brighton,
which lost practically all of its resort trappings as even the day-trippers disappeared during the 1970s, showed that the resort 'product cycle' could work
its way through into redundancy and oblivion.[41] Dramatic portents could be
found in the United States, where the fate of Asbury Park, on the New Jersey
coast, seemed to prefigure the worst possibilities for similar British resorts.
This 'blue-collar holiday Mecca' of the 1960s fell victim to competition from
Florida for cut-price vacations, and Atlantic City for casino gambling. Even
the patronage of rock superstar Bruce Springsteen, who gave its name to his
first album and his support to clubs and concerts, failed to save it from becoming 'Ghost-Town-sur-Mer' by the late 1990s, after an attempt at remaking
through a new condominium development had collapsed in half-built ruins
in 1992. By the end of the decade one in five of the population was receiving
welfare and 18 per cent were unemployed. As Ed Vulliamy commented, 'It is
the same story told all over small-town industrial America': a useful comment
because it reminds us that resorts are indeed industrial towns, and that they

need to sustain the demand for their product in a fiercely competitive world economy.[42] Over much of coastal Britain, as on much of the New Jersey seaboard with its similarly chilly and polluted waters, that has been an increasingly difficult task over the last quarter of a century. We now move on to look at the changing composition of the market for seaside resorts and their services in twentieth-century Britain: who have the holidaymakers been, and how has their composition changed over time?

Notes

1 Walton, *The English seaside resort*, Chapter 2.

2 Ibid., Chapter 8.

3 J.K. Walton, 'Seaside resorts and maritime history', *International Journal of Maritime History*, 9 (1997), pp. 125–47.

4 For a full statistical treatment see J.K. Walton, 'The seaside resorts of England and Wales, 1900–1950', in Shaw and Williams (eds), *The rise and fall of British coastal resorts*, pp. 26–9.

5 Perkin, 'The "Social tone"'.

6 Walton, 'The seaside resorts of western Europe 1750–1939'.

7 Board of Trade, *An industrial survey of the North East Coast Area* (London, 1932), pp. 349–51; J.D. Marshall and J.K. Walton, *The Lake counties from 1830 to the mid-twentieth century* (Manchester, 1981), Chapter 8; J.D. Marshall, *Old Lakeland* (Newton Abbot, 1971).

8 Ivor Brown, *Summer in Scotland* (London, 1952), p. 284.

9 A. Durie, 'The development of the Scottish coastal resorts in the Central Lowlands, *c.* 1770–1880: from Gulf Stream to golf stream', *Local Historian*, 24 (1994), pp. 206–16.

10 Walton, 'Seaside resorts of England and Wales', pp. 21–2, 29.

11 J.K. Walton and C. O'Neill, 'Numbering the holidaymakers: the problems and possibilities of the June census of 1921 for historians of resorts', *Local Historian*, 23 (1993), pp. 205–16.

12 For this paragraph and what follows, see Walton, 'Seaside resorts of England and Wales', especially Table 2.1, pp. 27–9, which is the basis for the calculations.

13 E. Brunner, *Holiday making and the holiday trades*, pp. 52–3, for the impact of the Second World War on Margate.

14 Morgan, 'Perceptions, patterns and policies of tourism'; R. Perry, 'Cornwall *circa* 1950', in P. Payton (ed.), *Cornwall since the war* (Redruth, 1993), pp. 39–40; G. Shaw and A. Williams, 'From bathing-hut to theme park: tourism development in south-west England', *Journal of Regional and Local Studies*, 11 (1991), pp. 16–32.

15 Brown, *Summer in Scotland*, pp. 211, 276–7, 283; Durie, 'The Scottish seaside resort in peace and war'; *United Kingdom Holiday Guide*, 1939 (16th Annual edn, London, 1939); Anthony Smith, *Beside the seaside* (London, 1972), pp. 109–10.

16 Hardy and Ward, *Arcadia for all*, pp. 2–7.

17 Ibid., pp. 50–51 and Chapters 3–4; B.E. Cracknell, *Canvey Island: the history of a marshland community* (Leicester, 1959); R.E. Pahl, *Divisions of labour* (Oxford, 1984), for Minster-in-Sheppey; A.D. King, *The bungalow: the production of a global culture* (London, 1984), for Lancing.

18 Ward and Hardy, *Goodnight campers!*, Chapters 1–3 and p. 119.

19 C.A. Moser and W. Scott, *British towns* (London, 1961), especially p. 31; V. Karn, *Retirement to the seaside* (London, 1977), pp. 14–15 and Appendix 1.

20 Cannadine (ed.), *Patricians, power and politics in nineteenth-century towns*, pp. 163–6; Cannadine, *Lords and landlords*, p. 422.

21 Calculations from Walton, 'The seaside resorts of England and Wales', pp. 26–9, Figure 2.1 and Table 2.1.

22 Morgan, 'Perceptions, patterns and policies of tourism'.

23 W. Dougill, 'The British coast and its holiday resorts', *Town Planning Review*, 16 (1935), p. 265n.

24 Moser and Scott, *British towns*, p. 31, Table 13.

25 Walton, 'The seaside resorts of England and Wales', pp. 36–7.

26 Paul Addison, *Now the war is over: a social history of Britain 1945–51* (2nd edn, London, 1995), p. 115.

27 Hardy and Ward, *Arcadia for all*, pp. 66–7, 89–90, 127–8.

28 J. Demetriadi, 'The golden years: English seaside resorts 1950–74', in Shaw and Williams, *The rise and fall of British coastal resorts*, pp. 61–2.

29 Somerset County Council County Planning Department, *Coastal preservation and development in Somerset* (typescript, 1966, B.L. X.80578), p. 21.

30 A. Williams and G. Shaw, 'The age of mass tourism', in Payton (ed), *Cornwall since the war*, pp. 86–8.

31 Glen Bramley, 'Tourism in Britain and some local economic effects' (University of Sussex, n.d., Lancaster University Library TYIeaB), Table 5.

32 Willliams and Shaw, 'The age of mass tourism', pp. 87, 91–2.

33 Morgan, 'Perceptions, patterns and policies of tourism'.

34 Bramley, *Tourism in Britain and some local economic effects,* Table 7.

35 H.C. Stallibrass, 'The holiday accommodation industry', pp. 117–75; Karn, *Retiring to the seaside*, pp. 250–3.

36 R. Forrest and D. Gordon, *People and places: a 1991 census atlas of England* (Bristol, 1993), p. 39.

37 *Guardian*, 27 February 1999.

38 S. Agarwal, 'The public sector', in Shaw and Williams (eds), *The rise and fall of British coastal resorts*, pp. 151–5.

39 J. Glancey, 'Greetings from Margate', *Guardian*, *G2*, 21 June 1999, pp. 12–13.

40 Lynne Wallis, 'Lovely place . . . but you wouldn't want to live there', *Guardian*, *G2*, 28 June 1999: a remarkably single-minded hatchet-job which assumes that it is perverse not to want shopping precincts or multi-storey car-parks.

41 Samuels, 'Research to help plan the future of a seaside resort', in S. Riley, ed., *Proceedings of the 12th marketing theory seminar* (Lancaster, 1974).

42 *The Observer*, Review section, 16 May 1999, p. 3.

2

The holidaymakers

By the beginning of the twentieth century the capacious diversity of the British seaside had room for visitors of all social classes and strata, although working-class access to resorts varied in different parts of the country according to family incomes and holiday traditions. The poorest (including those most encumbered with young children, who were least able to cope with the multiplication of costs and inconveniences) were lucky to manage an occasional day-trip under charitable auspices, although they might have fun at the coast in brief respites from seasonal jobs as waiters, hotel or boarding-house servants, laundrymaids or even itinerant entertainers. But better-off working-class families, with growing children contributing to the budget and a local culture which had come to regard the seaside holiday as a natural part of the rhythm of the seasons, might already be spreading their wings at the turn of the century. In 1913 the suffrage campaigner Ada Nield Chew described such a Lancashire cotton town family's angry encounter with an ignorant and supercilious party of their 'betters', who resented their presence and those of a large number of fellow-Lancastrians who had arrived to spend the Wakes at an unnamed resort in Devon. She claimed from her Rochdale vantage point that her account was 'founded on fact'. Contrary to the expectations of the 'superior' ones, her Lancashire folk had 'a keen sense of beauty, [which] was gratified to the full by the ever-changing panorama of sea, sky, rocks and tree-clad hills'.[1] Blackpool might be a more usual destination, and Chew's family were quite capable of enjoying it just as much in its own way; but it is useful to begin with a warning against easy stereotyping and putting into boxes, especially as middle-class holidaymakers were no strangers to the big popular resorts in their turn.

What is clear is that the Lancashire cotton towns were well ahead of all other urban areas in generating working-class holiday demand on a large scale. Relatively high family incomes and regular employment, coupled with a tradition of seaside visits and the readiness of regional resorts (especially, and spectacularly, Blackpool) to cater for popular preferences, had enabled the traditional Wakes holidays (and some invented new ones) to be given over to extended seaside visits in the late nineteenth century, as cotton workers and their neighbours saved through 'going-off clubs' for fifty-one weeks to enjoy the fifty-second week at the coast. This was a common pattern here by the 1890s among those who were not excluded by low wages or the poverty cycle, and it accounted for a large proportion of Blackpool's estimated four million visitors in 1913.[2] The textile districts of Yorkshire's West Riding followed about a generation behind, as did the Staffordshire potteries and some of the industrial towns of the Birmingham area, where traditional summer festivals continued to be celebrated locally for longer, while Sheffield and the surrounding mining districts tended to take short breaks organised on the 'St Monday' principle (the practice of extending the weekend into Monday and making up the last time by working extra hours later in the week) which offered less scope to the seaside entrepreneur. Other northern industrial areas were slower to acquire the seaside holiday habit. This even applied to the coal and chemical belt of south-west Lancashire, despite the proximity of a string of resorts in Lancashire and north Wales, not to mention the Isle of Man; and Liverpool itself tended to send half-day trippers to New Brighton and north Wales rather than the working-class visitors staying for a week or more who had become the mainstay of central Blackpool. In the north-east of England and West Cumberland the day-trip was likewise the working-class norm, although much industry here was already in coastal locations.[3] South Wales miners and tinplate workers were increasingly in evidence at Porthcawl and Barry Island, and making forays across the Bristol Channel on steamboat excursions; and trips down the Clyde to Rothesay or Dunoon had long been attracting bibulous working-class Glaswegians when in funds, creating amazing scenes when the mad rush for the last boat brought seething masses of swaying humanity to the departure piers.[4] But over most of provincial England south of the Trent low and uncertain wages, coupled with the absence of a pattern of surviving traditional holidays which could be adapted to seaside use and a weak trade union and friendly society system to form a basis for the popular organisations on which working-class holidays needed to be based, meant that the seaside holiday was still in its infancy among wage-earners. Rural workers, in particular, were conspicuous by their absence at the seaside. London, as so often, was a law unto itself, but much of its popular holiday demand at the beginning of the century came from the armies of white-collar workers and shop assistants who were the butts of *Punch*'s condescending derision. Manual workers and their families were largely limited to day trips on 'St Monday' or at August Bank Holiday, the annual break on the first Monday in August which had been instituted by Act of Parliament in 1871 and whose influence was strong in the capital but negligible over much of the industrial north, where the Wakes and similar traditional holidays rendered it redundant. August Bank Holiday had considerable symbolic importance as a popular saturnalia in London, and this has led lazy historians of a metropolitan cast of mind to extrapolate this misleadingly to the rest of the country.[5]

The mainstay of the Edwardian seaside resort was a broad band of middle-class demand, ranging from the plutocratic (bankers, industrialists) through the opulent professionals and substantial employers to the still-growing army of administrators, subordinate professionals, tradespeople and 'black-coated workers'. This even applied to most of the resorts which catered for the industrial north. Blackpool itself successfully protected its North Shore against fairground incursions at the turn of the century, sustaining an enclave of the 'better classes' which reached out along the shoreline to embrace Bispham (brought under the borough's protective umbrella in 1918) and Cleveleys, while the development of the Pleasure Beach at South Shore did not prevent most of this area from retaining an unpretentious middle-class visiting public as well as a growing number of commuters from a stratum dominated by agents on the Manchester exchange, superior clerks and commercial travellers, shading over into the more secluded respectability of St Annes and Lytham.[6] By this time, in fact, the most socially unpretentious seaside resort in northern England was probably Cleethorpes, which doubled as a rather down-market suburb of adjoining Grimsby.[7] Morecambe catered for a mainstream market of black-coated workers, foremen and their families while also welcoming West Yorkshire industrialists, and Southport and Scarborough were dominated by the middle classes. In the latter case the South Cliff provided a decidedly exclusive environment for the northern *haute bourgeoisie*, while the social tone of the North Bay around the cricket ground was lower middle-class and the area around the old fishing quarter was reserved for the genuine proletarians. As V.S. Pritchett remarked in 1934, in words which would carry equal weight a generation earlier:[8]

> Scarborough is so cunningly devised by nature to perpetuate the amenities of the caste system . . . that the 'improper classes' can have the run of the magnificent modern North Bay, or – if they are very improper – of the foreshore and the harbour without being bored by the South Cliff and the Spa. The hills so divide Scarborough, in fact, that it has been able to tout for the masses without losing caste.

The other great generator of popular demand for seaside holidays, London, sent enough day-trippers and short-stay working-class visitors to lend a proletarian image to the central sea-front areas of Southend and Margate, but the condescending attitude which prevailed towards these resorts among the literary middle classes was based more on the presence of the Cockney petty bourgeoisie than on the trippers who frequented the fairgrounds and winkle stalls, and their adjuncts of Westcliff and Cliftonville were the holiday haunts of solid middle-class respectability, as their (brief) endorsements in the *The Queen* newspaper guide for 1907 indicated.[9]

The Queen, which catered emphatically for the servant-keeping classes who were potential purchasers of public school educations and round-the-world cruises, reserved its most extensive coverage for small 'quaint', 'primitive' rustic resorts like Clovelly in north Devon or Selsey ('Selsea') in Sussex; or slightly larger, more conventionally fashionable places with hotels and golf courses like North Berwick in south-east Scotland ('the Biarritz of the north') and Cromer in Norfolk; or (with the fullest coverage) sophisticated places with expensive hotels and pretensions to being climatic stations, such as Bournemouth and Eastbourne, although its coverage also extended to Bridlington and Colwyn Bay. It was these latter places, within the field of vision of affluent or pretentious families while also appealing to the broadest possible middle-class market, that marked out the mainstream visitor experience of the early twentieth century. The description of what Folkestone had to offer sums up how such holidaymakers were expected to spend their time:[10]

> The attractions consist of bracing air, dry soil, good water supply, bathing (shingle beach), winter garden, theatre, museum and free library, pier and other concerts, pretty inland and coast excursions, steamer trips to Boulogne, cricket, polo (at Shorncliffe), golf, tennis, sea fishing, and boating.

As befits the nature of the source, polo is an unusually rarefied attraction, and France as a steamer destination was an artefact of geography; but otherwise the ostensible, respectable priorities of the turn-of-the-century middle-class family are faithfully conveyed by this list, reflecting as it does the growing importance of sport and outdoor pursuits on this kind of holiday menu over the previous generation. The really wealthy, who defined the tone of *The Queen*, were fleeing from their social inferiors and deserting British resorts for the watering-places of Europe and beyond, as the emphasis of its coverage suggests; but the ample layers of comfortable middle-class families below this elevated level were the commercial life-blood of the English seaside in Edwardian times and on into the inter-war years.

There were gradations and deviations, of course. The hitherto-unconsidered coastlines of the plotland settlements, with their self-built houses in rustic settings, attracted the bohemian middle class as well as Cockneys and others who could afford nothing more elaborate. From the turn of the century places like Shoreham Beach, Pagham, Camber and Canvey Island exerted a truly liminal appeal, perched right on the shoreline, where property rights were uncertain (which became a problem at times) and everything conventional was despatched to the margins. H.G. Wells thought of Shoreham's Bungalow Town as 'a queer village of careless sensuality'.[11] Hardy and Ward depicted the sort of people he had in mind:[12]

> Actors and actresses, artists and writers, stars of music hall and early films enjoyed and, in turn, contributed to the libertarian atmosphere of such places. In some cases, too, the simple life and ethnic architecture won the hearts of businessmen and their families who could well have afforded a more conventional bungalow or villa.

As more conventional bungalows, often mutually indistinguishable, multiplied prolifically at the seaside during the inter-war years, they formed permanent and holiday homes for more conventional people, especially in north Wales and above all in Sussex. Here were formally laid out estates for commuters and retirers, which set a premium on idyllic but eminently respectable domesticity. But increasingly a working-class presence gathered momentum in more informal bungaloid settings: by 1929 a ' "simple, weekend bungalow", with a living room, two 12 by 12 bedrooms and kitchen could, exclusive of water, site or sanitation, be built by one man, unaided, for less than £90.' This was a real democratisation of the holiday home, and 'chalet towns' developed at various locations, from Whitesands Bay near Plymouth to Withernsea near Hull. As Anthony King comments, 'All round the coast, within reach of major towns, a proletarian colonisation of seaside land was taking place'; and part of the fun of the seaside here lay in extending and embellishing the holiday home, as well as enjoying the fresh air and freedom of the coastal setting.[13]

These self-build settlements were to be much criticised by architectural aesthetes and town planners, and legislated against in 1947; but meanwhile they made an alternative version of the seaside holiday accessible to people who neither wanted nor needed the existing urban resort culture, preferring their unobtrusive version of the simple life, and defying quantification in the process. The escapist, back-to-nature side of working-class holidaymaking, repudiating Blackpool or Southend as tawdry, artificial and exhausting, is illustrated by Walter

Greenwood in *Love on the dole*, as Harry and Helen lose themselves in the 'springy turf and . . . wrinkled shimmering sea' of a fishing village where the only artificial attraction seems to be a rowing boat. We should be a little wary of this: it comes from the Clarion cycling club school of romantic socialism, and indeed the socialist Larry Meath is presented as the source for the idea of the holiday destination (getting over the hurdle of having to write a letter to the landlady). These were the preferences of a committed minority; but we should not overlook or despise them for this.[14]

Up to the Second World War, at least, the working-class presence at the seaside was most marginal in the small, picturesque resorts, remote from population centres, where artists might congregate and the families of prosperous professionals and unconventional industrialists spend long relaxed summers in beach games and long walks: the Harlech of Robert and Charles Graves, for example. These were, increasingly, the preferred retreats of the more aloof and better-connected middle-class families, helped by the flexibility of travel which the car increasingly provided.[15] But the most efficacious way for those who preferred a measure of exclusivity to avoid their social inferiors as sharers of their holiday environment was to go abroad; and the continuing expansion of the British holiday market during the inter-war years was founded on the increasing purchasing power and holiday entitlements of the lower middle and urban working classes, wherever employment remained reasonably constant. Higher up the scale the retreat to France and further afield, which had begun in Victorian times, was spreading at an accelerated rate. Not that foreign resorts remained entirely exclusive, as complaints about Lancashire accents and unseemly merriment at Ostend indicated as early as the 1920s, and there was always the problem of coexisting with the Germans, which was rearing its head before the First World War, as stereotypes about personal appearance, food, drink and assertive claims to the best bits of beach emerged in the travel literature; but at least the British working class and (in some ways worse still) the aspiring and aspirate-dropping lower middle class could be kept at a safe distance most of the time. There was, however, remarkably little traffic in the opposite direction, except to a few particularly favoured fashionable resorts like Brighton and Torquay, and to those parts of the Kent coast which were closest to France. Harold Clunn, writing in 1929, blamed licensing restrictions, oppressive Sabbatarianism, antiquated hotel facilities and (above all) unimaginative publicity, rather than the weather, for the fact that 'English seaside resorts are so little visited and remain almost *terra incognita* to the average American and foreign (*sic*) visitor to this country'.[16] This was to be an enduring theme.

Inter-war growth in the demand for seaside holidays in Britain was concentrated into well-established resorts within comfortable travelling distance of the great industrial districts, as the population growth indicators in Chapter 1 (in their broad-brush way) suggest; and it was most expansive among the lower middle and mainstream working classes, especially those favoured groups who were in regular employment and able to benefit from the falling prices of basic commodities and the expanded range and availability of consumer goods which characterised most of the inter-war period. There was still scope for debate over just how general the seaside holiday habit had become before the Second World War even in the Lancashire cotton towns, the birthplace of the working-class seaside holiday as of so much else in popular consumerism. On the one hand, Mass-Observation estimated in 1938 that 65 per cent of Bolton's inhabitants would go away for the whole of the town holiday week, and as many as 90 per cent would take at least a day-trip. Sixty-nine per cent of the holidaymakers went to 'popular seaside resorts', and although some of the tables accompanying this statement in the text would produce somewhat different figures, they would not alter the order of magnitude; nor would they dent the overwhelming primacy of Blackpool.[17] Holidays with pay did not come to the cotton industry until after the Second World War, and most Boltoners had to save through a well-established variety of savings clubs, as elsewhere in the region. The town weathered the depressions of the inter-war years better than its neighbours, aided by its specialism in spinning high-grade yarn, and participation rates in the weaving centres around Blackburn to the north may well have been restricted by unemployment. The reminiscences of William Woodruff, whose father was a relatively well-paid overlooker in Blackburn's weaving sheds (but had four children and liked a drink), suggest that Blackpool might glimmer tantalisingly on the horizon for many children who were able to visit it only under exceptional circumstances in the 1920s; but to set against this are the stories of unemployed weavers for whom the 'Blackpool habit' was so ingrained that they would return halfway through their holiday to draw the dole, although such tales have a whiff of the kind of urban mythology that denigrates the unemployed.[18] The work of Paul Wild on Rochdale and Andy Davies on Salford also delineates limits to the accessibility of working-class holidaymaking. Wild argues that the seaside holiday was a minority experience for Rochdale people at the start of the century, if anything declining with Edwardian trade depression, but growing in the inter-war years, although his conclusions are tentative and impressionistic: 'the trend, though fluctuating, was toward a definite increase in the availability of the day trip or holiday for the majority of the population'.[19] Davies is much more pessimistic about the poorer areas of inter-war Salford, and his oral interviews bear out Walter Greenwood's picture of the seaside as being accessible only under very special circumstances; but this was more an inner-city economy with a high level of casual labour than a classic 'cotton town' labour market, and as such it represented a different kind of experience.[20]

By the same token, Liverpool (for example) did not have a seaside tradition (apart from day-trips across the Mersey to New Brighton). Although a social survey in the early 1930s found that four-fifths of a sample of the city's 'ordin-ary clerks, shopkeepers and shop assistants' took holidays outside Liverpool (and most had two or three weeks available), walking and camping holidays in the countryside were preferred to the seaside; and much the same applied to the three-fifths of manual workers who went away during their one or two weeks of holiday, although at this level 'many of the women preferred the seaside'. This was a small sample, and probably a skewed one, but it matches other evidence. Growth in demand for seaside holidays was more apparent in the expanding industrial districts of the English Midlands and the London area, which were catching up with the Lancashire cotton district by the 1930s, as holiday savings clubs on a similar model to those in Lancashire proliferated in the Birmingham area.[21] In 1934 the *New survey of London life and labour* estimated that about half of working-class Londoners holidayed away from home (although this would presumably include the East Enders who took working holidays in the Kentish hop-gardens); and its less-precise comment that, 'An annual summer holiday is today taken for granted by a very large and increasing number of Londoners' at least conveys a notion of critical mass and growth.[22]

Hard figures, however, are impossible to obtain. The estimate in 1937 that 15 million people, around one-third of the population, went away for a week or more is plausible, although the proportion would vary widely by industry and social status, and there is no earlier figure to provide a yardstick for growth. The estimates of visitor numbers in individual resorts which were produced in the late 1930s, adding up to well over 20 million for seven of the largest centres (including 7 million for Blackpool and 5.5 million for Southend), must have included day-trippers in their assumptions; but however untrustworthy they may be in detail, they do convey the sheer magnitude of the seaside holiday market as it had grown over the first third of the century.[23]

Inter-war expansion was fuelled by the growing availability of holidays with pay at working-class level, although many families still found it difficult to budget and the big, accessible, cheap resorts benefited from the inability of many people to afford the holidays of their dreams. Paid holidays of between a fortnight and a month were already the norm in professional and white-collar jobs with large organisations by the late nineteenth century, but they had been provided by only a few industrial employers before the First World War. They became much more widely available among wage-earners during the inter-war years, although for the most part they had to be incorporated into general wage agreements, and it is significant that union negotiators, following the leads given by the Trades Union Congress from 1911 onwards, were prepared to push for them. But it was an irregular process until the late 1930s. The immediate post-war gains, which resumed a trend already apparent in the last years before the war, boosted paid holiday agreements to cover two million workers by 1920. Between 1919 and 1922 more advances were made than in the previous forty years. But the total fell back in the ensuing depression to 1.5 million in 1925, although a further half million were covered by less formal arrangements. This added up to about one in six of all wage-earners, and it was through the unofficial channels that the main advances came: by 1937 formal paid holidays were granted to between 1.5 and 1.75 million manual workers, but informal arrangements more than doubled this figure. As holidays with pay reappeared as a parliamentary concern in the later 1930s, after a series of proposals in the previous decade was interrupted by the depression, and as Lord Amulree's Departmental Committee considered the issue during 1937–38, propelling the Holidays with Pay Act into the statute book in the latter year, so paid holiday entitlements began to snowball in a period of economic recovery. By March 1938 three million waged workers were 'entitled to paid holidays under the terms of district and general agreements', and by September the figure was four million, out of 18.5 million people earning £250 per year or less (and thereby coming under the terms of reference of the Amulree Committee). But when informal arrangements were taken into account the March total was 7,750,000, or 42 per cent of all workpeople. The breakdown included 3 million manual workers covered by collective agreements and 250,000 otherwise provided for; 1,250,000 clerks, draughtsmen and typists; a million shop assistants; a million workers in 'public administration and defence'; and, interestingly, 750,000 'domestic service and miscellaneous'. By November 1938 the number of those earning up to £250 per year with paid holiday entitlements reached 9 million, half of them covered by collective agreements; and by June 1939 the total reached 11 million. The Holidays with Pay Act encouraged the practice rather than imposing it, although orders imposing paid holidays could be introduced in industries covered by

Wages Councils and Wages Boards. In any case, the principle was important, and proved to be contagious. To the relief of planners, and indeed of transport and resort interests, this expansion was not matched by a rush to the coast. It took time for people to acquire the grammar of holidaymaking when they were unaccustomed to it. Here, the British experience paralleled that of the French in 1936, although there were fewer and less vociferous fears of holiday invasion by the 'great unwashed', perhaps because working-class visitors were already a common feature of the British seaside. But the citizen's right to paid holidays, consciously blurring the distinction between white-collar and manual workers, was at last being recognised in both countries.[24] The remarkable thing is that this breakthrough came when the inter-war struggle between a nascent consumer society, and one which set more store by maximising free time than by maximising working hours and income to purchase goods and commercial pleasures, was all but won and lost. But for most people, apart from a dedicated minority of hikers and apostles of 'roughing it', holidays were primarily focused on concentrated consumption anyway.[25]

This is not to say that all holidaymakers found the way to the holiday of their dreams. Practical and financial considerations still intervened. In 1939 a survey published in the *News Chronicle* fixed the watershed at a wage of £4 per week: above this threshold 90 per cent of workers could afford a week's holiday, below it the figure was one-third. This was an arbitrary cut-off point (a little above the average wage for adult male manual workers), and family earnings would be a better basis for calculation, but it clarifies an obvious general point. The highly-seasonal nature of the holiday industry pushed prices up, at least on the south coast, so that (according to the investigators) a week's holiday for a family of four (a couple and two children) might cost £10 in the mid-1930s: more than twice the average weekly wage. In the back streets of Blackpool, however, it would probably cost half that amount (as Mass-Observation evidence suggests), and the contemporary calculations did not allow for the capacity of working-class holidaymakers to crowd into cheap accommodation and make a little go a long way in (for example) the fishing quarter of Hastings's Old Town. The surveys seem to have been based on rather genteel assumptions, overstating the financial burden of the basic seaside holiday at the lower end of the market.[26]

When Mass-Observation organised a competition through a Bolton newspaper on 'How I would like to spend my holidays' in the late 1930s, some of the replies revealed a gulf between aspirations and practicalities, and nearly half mentioned the problems of budgeting for the unpaid holidays which still prevailed in the cotton industry. Eloquent letters imagined the rustic, restful and picturesque charms of the Cornish Riviera, the Welsh countryside, or the Lake District. They might have been written with an eye to what the organisers of such a competition might be expected to favour, of course, but at least three contributors in this vein actually went to Blackpool. Women were particularly keen on a week free from household chores or responsibilities, which the growing Blackpool boarding-house sector could provide as well as anywhere else, as it joined other resorts in shifting away from the apartments system which had required women to plan and shop for meals which the landlady cooked. And the Mass-Observers emphasised that when Bolton people were simply asked what they preferred, the seaside was the predominant choice, with Blackpool far ahead of Douglas (Isle of Man) and Southport. Douglas was a slightly more up-market destination than Blackpool, 'the difference between the vault and the lounge in the pub . . . There is a "class distinction", but the people in each case are of the same origin and live in identical houses; it is an economic class that may well change from year to year with wage fluctuation'. So the choice of holiday was based on a complex mix of cultural preference, convenience, resources and status of destination, and the underlying motives might not be admitted to social investigators nor, indeed, overtly acknowledged by the holidaymakers themselves. Nevertheless, it is clear, and unsurprising, that for some the predominant mode of holidaymaking in the flourishing large resorts was the product of compromise, born of limited resources and knowledge, rather than preference: a conclusion which had implications for the future.[27]

The Second World War interrupted the process of democratisation of the seaside, but also encouraged a frame of mind which encouraged its continuation after 1945. Post-war social surveys show the extent to which holidaymaking had spread through the population, although they do not differentiate between the seaside and other destinations. The Hulton Press readership survey of 1947 found that 56.4 per cent of its sample took holidays away from home in that year, ranging from three-quarters of the managerial, professional and administrative groups, through two-thirds of the mainstream working class, to half of the 'unskilled' workers and state pensioners. This was already a significant advance on the late 1930s. At the top of the scale, 80 per cent of men in the highest class (professional and managerial) and the twenty-five to thirty-four age-group took holidays away from home, while among women of this status the peak of 83–85 per cent carried through from sixteen to forty-four years of age. Interestingly, this figure was nearly matched by young women (aged between sixteen and twenty-four, and mainly unmarried) in routine clerical and skilled manual jobs, where the figure was 81 per cent (compared with 58 for men of the same age and status). Across the working class, however, women's holiday participation rates declined from this early peak, confirming that the poverty cycle still bit deeply into holiday opportunities for working-class people with dependant children. Those least likely to go on holiday were state pensioners, but even here 40 per cent managed to lay claim to a holiday of some kind, although more pessimistic estimates in the mid-1950s pulled this down to one-third. It is noteworthy that a quarter of those (presumably) best able to afford a holiday chose (or were forced by other circumstances) not to take the opportunity; but what is impressive is the breadth and depth of the holiday habit, and its growth in the immediate post-war years. The same survey also found that 'housewives' were less likely to take holidays than unattached women or those working outside the home (51 per cent as against 60.7 per cent) and that only 3.3 per cent of the sample took holidays abroad, at a time when restrictions on the export of currency were still stringent.[28]

The continuing growth of holidays with pay during and after the war helped to boost the spread of the holiday habit, and made a continuing contribution to the expansion and extension of working-class holidays during the period of rising living standards which followed during the 1950s and 1960s. Wartime extensions of paid holidays were encouraged by 'the general spirit of cooperation during the emergency', the setting up of new organisations which fostered collective agreements and generalised them within industries, and a new concern for promoting efficiency through health, safety and welfare.[29] At the end of 1946 'between eleven and twelve million people had entitlement to paid holidays under collective agreements or statutory orders', supplemented by many others who had different arrangements, although for most manual workers this only amounted to a week. A renewed burst of change during 1951–52 boosted the switch to a fortnight: 'Early in 1951 the majority of workers still had a basic holiday entitlement of one week, while a minority could expect a fortnight; the following year the proportions had been reversed'. By 1952 two-thirds of manual workers received twelve days' or a fortnight's paid holiday per year. These changes were achieved largely through collective bargaining, at a time when full employment was combined with a limited development of the consumer sector, with shortages and continued rationing; so additional holidays would look particularly attractive. But extended paid holidays continued to be popular during the ensuing consumer boom, and between 1964 and 1969 the percentage of workers enjoying basic paid holiday of between two and three weeks increased from 7 to 35. The figure fell away to 7 per cent in 1970, but this reflected the growth in entitlements of three weeks or more, from 6 per cent in 1967 to 15 in 1969 and, remarkably, to 52 per cent in 1970. These working-class gains had knock-on effects higher up the occupational structure, and overall the post-war generation saw a very substantial increase in access to paid holidays across the board.[30]

Changes in holiday patterns by the mid-1960s, after a generation of rising real wages, full employment and expanding holiday entitlements, were considerable. A survey by Keele University found that in 1965 just over 60 per cent of adults had two or three weeks paid holiday per year; and although one in four still had no paid holidays at all, this was still a clear advance on the early 1950s. If we remove those aged sixty-five over, only 20 per cent of whom had paid holidays, the change becomes more striking: among workers between sixteen and forty-four years old, 80 per cent were entitled to two or three weeks. Holiday entitlements increased in step with income and educational status, but there were clear working-class gains. The lure of abroad was increasing, though still mainly for the middle classes: a *Reader's Digest* survey in 1963 found that over one-third of administrators, senior executives and top professionals had made overseas visits over the past three years, compared with one-fifth of 'the broad middle class and self-employed artisans' and one-tenth of 'foremen and skilled workers'. The youngest adult age-group, twenty-one to twenty-nine years old, was the most adventurous, and a Mass-Observation survey in 1949 had indicated dissatisfaction with existing holiday arrangements and a pent-up demand for the imagined delights of 'abroad'. Meanwhile, the number of new passports issued annually doubled to just under a million between 1951 and 1966, with most of the increase concentrated into the early 1960s, as external competition for the domestic holiday market stepped up.[31]

At this stage, however, the number of holidays taken within Britain was also increasing. The British Travel Association (BTA) statistics (which are highly suspect, but all we have at national level) suggested a suspiciously rounded rise from 25 million domestic holidays in 1951 and 1955 to around 30 million per year throughout the 1960s (double the estimate for 1937), while holidays abroad went up from 1.5 million in 1951 to hover at or just above 5 million during the 1960s. According to this source the peak figure for domestic holidays came as late as 1973–74, at just over 40 million, while foreign holidays reached 8.5 million in 1972 and then dipped for several years as the oil crisis of the mid-1970s hit fuel supplies and costs, and then recession and deflationary policies hit the British job market between 1979 and 1982. There are complications, however. The BTA defined holidays as constituting four nights or more away from home, so that domestic holidays may have been shortening on average while holidays abroad were likely to be longer. This was in keeping with the plausible assumption that as middle-class and younger holidaymakers increasingly took their money abroad, the British holiday scene was depending more on an older and increasingly working-class market with limited staying and spending power, and on shorter second holidays or long weekends for the more affluent, flexible and mobile groups.[32] This is borne out by the balance between main and additional domestic holidays: the former stagnated at around 25 or 26 million throughout the 1960s, while the latter grew from 1.75 million in 1951 to an interim peak of 5.5 million in 1960, fluctuatiing between 4 and 5 million during the rest of the decade, and rising sharply from 4.8 to 9 million between 1969 and 1971. The BTA's estimates of expenditure levels at 1970 prices are also compatible with these assumptions: annual expenditure on holidays in Britain was estimated at £640 million (at 1970 prices) for 1951, declining steadily to £566 million in 1965, although it then rose vigorously to £630 million in 1969 and remarkably to £782 million in 1970. Estimated expenditure on holidays abroad, meanwhile, rose steadily (again at 1970 prices) from £120 million in 1951 to £465 million in 1970. Expenditure per head on domestic holidays worked out at £25.60 in 1951, £18.90 in 1965 and £22.70 in 1970, while that on holidays abroad was £80 in 1951 and £81 in 1970. This did suggest a considerable gulf, widening between the early 1950s and mid-1960s and then narrowing a little, between the trajectories of domestic and foreign holidays, although it also demonstrates the power of domestic resorts to claim a share in the rising affluence of the late 1960s and to grow in absolute terms over the post-war generation. These are fragile statistics, but their overall message is clear.[33]

A BTA survey of 1968 also suggests the resilience of the seaside as the dominant domestic holiday destination. Seventy-five per cent of British *main* holidays in 1968 involved the seaside, ranging from 93 per cent of those spent in Cornwall and 90 per cent of those in the north-west (Lancashire, Cheshire and the Isle of Man), to 47 per cent of those in the Midlands (where Lincolnshire was the only coastal county) and 14 per cent in the Lake District. The seaside held up well in Scotland and Northern Ireland, forming part of around 60 per cent of holiday experiences (although individual holidays here tended to embrace more diverse environments than in England and Wales). It was clearly too early to speak of sustained overall decline: it was a matter of the seaside taking a limited and down-market share of rapidly-increasing holiday demand, without suffering a net loss of visitors or their spending power.[34]

Within this national picture, however, visitors were already favouring some resorts and coastlines at the expense of others, as we saw in Chapter 1. A survey of visitor attitudes to New Brighton in the early 1970s provided strong support for the local lobby which favoured residential investment rather than resort revival. The Merseyside resort's post-war decline had been catastrophic, accelerating sharply in the late 1960s as changes in the tidal flow of the Mersey ripped out the beach, awareness of pollution increased and the main entertainment complex was destroyed by fire and not replaced. Surveys in 1972 showed that although two-thirds of Merseyside families had recently visited the resort as day-trippers, the proportion from a broader north-western catchment area was only 18 per cent, compared with figures of 46 per cent for Rhyl and 65 per cent for Southport. Much grimmer were the findings that more than half of the sample would not consider visiting New Brighton again for a day-trip, and over 70 per cent would automatically reject it as a holiday destination. A profile of the resort's image among Merseysiders showed it scoring highly only on accessibility and cheapness, with approval ratings between 0 and 15 per cent for beach quality, accommodation, scenery, cleanliness and as a 'good place for a holiday'. The survey report remarked that, 'In the researcher's experience it is rare to find . . . so black and unrelieved an image – perhaps because in the world of fast moving consumers' goods such a "brand" would have "died" or been "re-launched" before getting to such a stage'. This was not just a brand: it was a town, with a sense of collective identity that encouraged it to cling to life in its existing form. Even so, its condition as a resort was clearly terminal.[35]

This was less a matter of tastes changing than of a resort ceasing to give visitors what they wanted and expected, and losing out even to local competitors. Elsewhere in the north matters were problematic but not yet apocalyptic, and even the smaller resorts achieved modest prosperity in the affluent 1960s. Whitby, to take a distinctive but awkwardly sited and deeply provincial resort, recovered from a difficult period in the 1950s. It stemmed the earlier decline in average length of stay, which was 9 days in 1967 as in 1956, and attracted a growing contingent from the Midlands to dilute its dependence on the increasingly depressed economies of the north-east. More than one-third of the visitors sampled in 1967 were under sixteen years old, and only 28 per cent were over forty-five, as families continued to acculturate new generations to the seaside holiday. Just over one-third of the staying visitors here were skilled workers or foremen, and another 20 per cent were white-collar workers, but more than one-sixth were professional and managerial. This was a similar profile to that of Scarborough, which as befitted its easier accessibility and cheap amusements had a larger minority of semi-skilled and unskilled workers; and it was significantly healthier than Blackpool, where in 1972 half the visitors were over forty-five and one-third of them were unskilled manual workers and state pensioners. It was also healthier than Ramsgate, at the other end of the country, where W.D. Peppiatt's survey in 1969 concluded that the resort's current appeal was to 'older visitors "with lower than average incomes", many of whom had been coming to Ramsgate for years', and who were likely to induce a false sense of security by being 'tolerant of any decline in standards', tending to 'shrug off loss of amenities and not to demand any change'. The problem of recruiting the necessary new generation under these circumstances was widespread. Even the younger visitors to Whitby and Scarborough spent slightly less in real terms in 1967 than in 1956, as unemployment levels began to rise, but here as over most of northern coastal England, the holiday industry continued to flourish modestly through the post-war generation, continuing to rely on established markets. Some of the expanding spending power of these decades was increasingly being enticed elsewhere, but in 1970 the crisis of visitor demand was yet to come.[36]

It arrived in many resorts during the 1970s, which were difficult years economically in Britain as well as internationally, and especially the 1980s: it was the latter decade that saw the real explosion of the overseas package tour market, while motorways and enhanced personal mobility extended day-tripper access to resorts and reduced the demand for overnight accommodation which had been so important to the holiday economy. Where the seaside remained a destination, it was increasingly for short trips which were adjuncts to the main holiday menu, except for those who could afford nothing more. It was, however, not until 1979 that the number of foreign holidays taken by British customers passed the 10 million mark, as compared with the 8.5 million of 1972, just before the international oil crisis which put a brake on developments. By 1987 that figure had more than doubled, drawing in growing numbers of working-class visitors as the real cost of package holidays plummeted: between 1969 and the early 1990s the cost of a fortnight's full board in Torremolinos, an identically specified holiday, halved in real terms. It was during the last two decades of the twentieth century that the real challenges came to the popular end of the seaside holiday market, which had hardly been dented by package tour competition even in the late 1960s.[37]

As we negotiate the minefield of contradictory figures generated by the guess-timates of tourism statisticians, it becomes clear that there was a sharp decline in main domestic holidays in Britain between 1975 and 1985, driven by recession and competition, in which the seaside took more than its fair share. On one reading the fall was from 27 to 20 million, while by 1981 more main holidays were allegedly taken abroad than at home. This was counterbalanced by growth in the number of shorter holidays, even in the difficult years between 1974 and 1982, when they increased from 28 to 37 million per year. But a Welsh Tourist Board study calculated that between 1978 and 1988 '39 million nights were lost at seaside destinations, representing half of their staying market for some of the smaller resorts', around 70 of which might attract fewer than 2,000 staying visitors per week by the early 1990s, in contrast with the six major centres which drew more than a million a year. Spending per holiday increased faster than inflation, however, suggesting that even within Britain holiday-taking was being concentrated into more affluent groups in a society where divisions between rich and poor were widening. In 1979 the poorest 40 per cent of Britain's households disposed of 24 per cent of total expenditure, but by 1995 the equivalent figure was only 12 per cent.[38] This meant even more trouble for the more down-market and less distinctive resorts, especially as even the south-west experienced stagnation and decline. Cornwall's tourist numbers remained static at around three million from the early 1980s, and a strong shift towards self-catering made life difficult for the more formal accommo-dation sector. In 1991 46 per cent of a sample of visitors were professional or managerial, but as many as 20 per cent were categorised as unskilled manual workers: a precarious market, all the more so because only one in six of the sample were first-time visitors, suggesting a dangerous (in the long run) reliance on established loyalties. Customer loyalty was valuable, but it needed to be replenished by new blood.[39] Devon, which had increased its share of the domestic holiday market dramatically between 1945 and 1973, peaked at 3.5 million visitors in 1978 according to the official statistics, and fell back to 3 million by 1982, with the seaside suffering disproportionately and the same switch to self-catering, which benefited the smaller north Devon resorts during the 1980s at the expense of their more established competitors.[40] If even the south-west was experiencing problems, the loss of established visitors and the failure to recruit – and hold – new ones in an increasingly volatile and competitive market-place was bound to be much more marked elsewhere. Moreover, the traditional concentration of holidays into July and August remained particularly strong at the bottom end of the market, where people had less autonomy and fewer choices, and this aspect of demand compounded the difficulty of sustaining the holiday economy.

While tourist departures from Britain to foreign beaches continued to expand rapidly, recovering from the interruptions of the mid-1970s and the early Thatcher years, traffic in the reverse direction was very limited. Brighton and Torquay were among the very few British seaside resorts with a tradition of attracting comfortably off overseas visitors, and tourist board advertising after 1969 was consistently directed towards London and 'historic towns' rather than to the seaside. This was foreshadowed by the activities of the Travel and Industrial Development Association, founded in 1929 to promote tourism as a foreign currency earner, which took little interest in the seaside, and by Sir Stephen Tallents's *The projection of England*, published in 1932 (London: Faber and Faber), which listed the boy scouts, foxhunting and the Lord Mayor of London as international tourist attractions but did not mention the seaside. A subsequent propagandist for British tourism, R.G. Pinney, urging government intervention in support of tourism in 1944, did mention seaside resorts, but as an afterthought: horse shows and visits to factories were given priority. Literature aimed at Americans by Americans was sometimes more forthcoming: the 1969 edition of *England on $5 and $10 a day* recommended Dover (but not explicitly as a seaside resort), Brighton, Bournemouth, Hastings, Torquay, north Devon and various Cornish fishing villages, although it had no truck with the rest of the British coastline, concentrating on London and otherwise preferring Shakespeare, the cathedrals, Oxbridge and the Cotswolds. Post-war British resorts lacked the advertising resources and travel agency links provided by the package tour firms. Not that they always used what they had to the full: Peppiatt's report on Ramsgate complained that only £16,000 had been spent on advertising in 1969, only three-quarters of the amount the law allowed, and despite its location the town had failed to attract visitors from Europe.[41] Blackpool, which did use all its resources, was more successful in attracting Irish visitors than in its efforts to pull in Germans or Russians, although it did attract a small number of high-spending gamblers from Saudi Arabia, and at the end of the century its growing attractiveness to gay tourists was beginning to pull in Americans and northern Europeans, as was Brighton.[42] This point is developed in Chapter 6. Meanwhile, Dover had been trying to take advantage of its convenient location by producing French and German supplements to its guide-books as early as the 1930s, but success seems to have been limited, as was the case elsewhere on the promisingly sited Kent coast.[43] The most lucrative and successful way of tapping foreign demand came to be through language schools, which brought large numbers of young Europeans to south coast resorts from Hastings to Bournemouth (especially) by the 1980s and 1990s, creating a major source of income and employment at the cost of occasional demonstrations of xenophobia among the locals.

Despite some evidence of recovery in the 1990s, however, the problems of the more down-market resorts at the century's end were underscored by a European Union survey which reported that 35 per cent of British households could not afford a week's holiday away from home. This reflected the widening gulf in living standards between the better-off and the poor which had marked the social polarisation of the Thatcher years and continued through the 1990s. The British figure compared with 12 per cent in Germany and 14 per cent in the Netherlands, and was on a par with Ireland and France, which were also significantly worse than the average for Western Europe. If the respondents included in their definition of 'holiday' the bleak caravan sites of the Yorkshire, Lincolnshire and north Wales coasts, and found even these cheap possibilities to be out of reach, and if we assume that a similar proportion of the remainder as in the 1950s and 1960s chose not to take holidays, the evidence suggests stagnation or even decline in the proportion of the population going on holiday, even as the average number of holidays taken by the more fortunate continued to increase.[44] The conference trade, in which resorts with resources were busily investing (especially to fill accommodation in the difficult weeks just before and after the main summer season), tended to draw upon the same relatively well-off groups, reinforcing the general picture of 'to them that have shall be given', for resorts and visitors alike.[45] But this was not the whole story, as John Ezard has pointed out. The moral he drew from a short visit to the revamped Skegness Butlin's camp of 1999 was that, despite new 'weather-protected baby domes' to insulate holidaymakers from sea and weather, and the company's own obvious distrust of old holiday styles, 'the bucket-and-spade holiday is by no means totally dead'. He noted the resilience of Skegness, an undistinguished resort for (mainly) the East Midlands working class, which should have been particularly vulnerable to the trends of the 1970s onwards. It lost 3,200 of its 8,100 'serviced bedspaces' between 1950 and 1998, but gained more than 15,000 caravans over the same period; and the town benefited from the boom at the turn of the 1980s and 1990s, which spawned second holidays in self-catering accommodation alongside the additional wave of foreign holidays and the new destinations. The town strove to keep its established, loyal visitors (in 1998 57 per cent had been coming for five years or longer) while moving with the times sufficiently to build for the future. People still wanted donkey-rides. And the discourse of decline, which dominates commentaries on holidaymakers and their preferences in the context of British resorts, is given aid and comfort by the enduring lack of reliable statistics. As Ezard says, 'Without resort-by-resort figures to serve as a baseline, you might wonder how national tourist organisations can state . . . that we took 26.5 million seaside holidays in 1997 and spent £4.7 billion. Those figures could be about as reliable as an off-form palmist's reading on Wigan pier.' This problem has bedevilled all attempts to get a firm purchase on the changes in the seaside visiting public throughout the century; and at its end it probably makes the decline of the British seaside holiday look worse than it is.[46]

A review of the English Tourist Board's statistics for 1997 confirms this prognosis. They are arranged by Tourist Board region and by county, and it is indeed impossible to disaggregate them for individual resorts. They also give North Yorkshire, Somerset, Kent, Devon and Cornwall more tourist trips and bednights than Lancashire, which the presence of Blackpool in the latter county renders utterly implausible, especially as the whole county is accorded only 4 million overnight visits, only 46 per cent of which are regarded as being for holiday purposes. Blackpool's own surveys show far higher figures than this. The notion that the average length of stay in Cornwall (nearly 6 nights) and Devon (just over 5) is longer than in Kent (2.7) or East Sussex (3.5) does fit in with other evidence, but it is based on the same problematic data. All that can be salvaged are the league-tables of visitors to attractions, whose evidence of the overwhelming popular appeal of the big north-western amusement parks further undermines the staying visitor figures. The official statistics have been used sparingly and with reservations, in this chapter as elsewhere, and Ezard is right to point up their deficiencies.[47]

Among the key changes we can identify, especially in the post-war years, has been the transformation of the journey to the coast, which in turn has had its own impact on visitor profiles and the nature of the seaside holiday. Here, the evidence for change has been overwhelming. An examination of the switch from rail to road, and of its consequences for the British seaside, forms the next stage in the argument.

Notes

1 Doris Nield Chew (ed.), *The life and writings of Ada Nield Chew* (London, 1982), pp. 188–94.
2 For this and what follows, see Walton, 'The demand for working-class seaside holidays in Victorian England'.
3 Huggins, 'Social tone and resort development in north-east England'.

4 Durie, 'The development of the Scottish coastal resorts in the Central Lowlands *c.* 1770–1880'.

5 See Walton, 'The demand for working-class seaside holidays in Victorian England'.

6 Walton, *Blackpool*, Chapter 4.

7 Cannadine, *Lords and landlords*, pp. 67, 288, 410–11.

8 R. Bingham, *Lost resort? The flow and ebb of Morecambe* (Carnforth, 1991); J. Grass, 'Morecambe: the people's pleasure', MA dissertation, Lancaster University, 1972; V.S. Pritchett, 'Scarborough', in Yvonne Cloud (ed.), *Beside the seaside*, p. 226; J.K. Walton, 'Scarborough', in P.J. Waller (ed.), *The Oxford illustrated history of the English urban landscape* (Oxford, Oxford University Press, forthcoming, 2000).

9 M. Hornsby, *'The Queen' newspaper book of travel: a guide to home and foreign resorts* (London, 1907), pp. 45, 68.

10 Ibid., p. 25.

11 King, *The bungalow*, illustrations 56–8.

12 Hardy and Ward, *Arcadia for all*, p. 2.

13 King, *The bungalow*, pp. 174–5.

14 Greenwood, *Love on the dole*, pp. 119–22.

15 Robert Graves, *Goodbye to all that* (London, 1957); Charles Graves, *-And the Greeks* (London, 1930); S. O'Connell, *The car in British society: class, gender and motoring 1896–1939* (Manchester, 1998), Chapter 3.

16 Harold Clunn, *Famous south coast pleasure resorts: past and present* (London, 1929), p. xx.

17 Cross, *Worktowners at Blackpool*, pp. 47–8.

18 William Woodruff, *Billy boy: the story of a Lancashire weaver's son* (Halifax, 1993), pp. 41–4, 123–6.

19 Wild, 'Recreation in Rochdale 1900–1940', p. 147.

20 Davies, *Leisure, gender and poverty*; Greenwood, *Love on the dole*.

21 D. Caradog Jones (ed.), *The social survey of Merseyside* (Liverpool, 1934), Vol. 3, pp. 271–3; Walton, *The Blackpool landlady*, pp. 38–9.

22 Pimlott, *The Englishman's holiday*, pp. 215, 232; Walvin, *Beside the seaside*, p. 107.

23 Pimlott, *The Englishman's holiday*, pp. 215, 240.

24 A. Russell, *The growth of occupational welfare in Britain* (Aldershot, 1991), pp. 65–72, 114, 116; Pimlott, *The Englishman's holiday*, Chapter 13; Walvin, *Beside the seaside*, pp. 103–7.

25 G. Cross, *Time and money: the making of consumer culture* (London, 1993).

26 Pimlott, *The Englishman's holiday*, p. 232; Walvin, *Beside the seaside*, pp. 109–10; Walton, *The Blackpool landlady*, pp. 171–8; Cross, *Worktowners*, p. 45.

27 Cross, *Worktowners at Blackpool*, pp. 40–51.

28 A.H. Halsey (ed.), *Trends in British society since 1900* (London, 1972), pp. 540, 548–9; Walvin, *Beside the seaside*, p. 136.

29 Russell, *The growth of occupational welfare in Britain*, pp. 71–2.

30 Ibid., pp. 114–20.

31 Halsey, *Trends in British society since 1900*, pp. 548, 550.

32 Demetriadi, 'The golden years, pp. 52–4.

33 Bramley, 'Tourism in Britain and some local economic effects', Tables 1 and 4.

34 Ibid., Table 9.

35 J.A. Samuels, 'Research to help plan the future of a seaside resort', pp. 63–4, 69–77.

36 P. Lavery, *Patterns of holidaymaking in the Northern Region* (Newcastle, 1971); Walton, *Blackpool*, pp. 145–6; Peppiatt's survey quoted in F. Stafford and N. Yates (eds), *The later Kentish seaside* (Gloucester, 1985), p. 169.

37 'Demetriadi, 'The golden years', pp. 56–9.

38 Welsh Tourist Board study quoted in N. Morgan and A. Pritchard, *Power and politics at the seaside* (Exeter, 1999), pp. 47–8; C.P. Cooper, 'Parameters and indications of the decline of the British seaside resort', in Shaw and Williams (eds), *The rise and fall of British coastal resorts*, pp. 84–5.

39 A. Willliams and G. Shaw, 'The age of mass tourism', in P. Payton (ed.), *Cornwall since the war* (Redruth: Dyllamson Truran, 1993).

40 Morgan, 'Perceptions, patterns and policies of tourism'.

41 Demetriadi, 'English and Welsh seaside resorts'; Stafford and Yates, *The later Kentish seaside*, p. 169; R.G. Pinney, *Britain – destination of tourists?* (London, 1944), pp. 26, 48–50; S.M. Haggart and D. Porter, *England on $5 and $10 a day* (New York, 1969).

42 Walton, *Blackpool*.

43 Dover *Holiday Guide*, (1935 edn Dover: Dover Corporation), pp. 106–11.

44 Stephen Bates, 'Hard-up Brits who cannot afford holidays', *Guardian*, 25 June 1999, p. 6.

45 Morgan, 'Perceptions, patterns and policies of tourism'.

46 John Ezard, 'Give them a break', *Guardian*, *Travel*, 31 July 1999, p. 2.

47 English Tourist Board website, http://www.travelengland.org.uk, 'Tourism professionals', tourism statistics for 1997.

3

Travelling to the coast

The seaside holiday could not have achieved its twentieth-century ubiquity without systems of mass transportation to take the millions of visitors to the resorts; and the journey itself was an important part of the holiday experience, developing its own folklore in families and communities, born of shared anticipation and tribulation and punctuated by the observation and celebration of familiar landmarks. Changes in the prevailing mode of holiday transport, with their implications for the nature of sociability on the journey, the extent of freedom of movement during the holiday itself, and the patterns of traffic flows and problems within the resorts themselves, form a central theme in the social history of the British seaside. This chapter narrates the transition from rail to road as the main mode of holiday transport within Britain, highlighting the contrasting implications of the coach and the private car, and assessing the implications of this transition in the broader context of changing living standards, social expectations, and attitudes to the balance between planning, control and individual self-expression within the resorts themselves.

The beginning of the twentieth century was close to the peak of the railway system's dominance of passenger transport and therefore of journeys to pleasure. All the resorts of any size on the mainland had direct railway access from at least the 1870s and 1880s, although most of the lines were built primarily for other purposes (developing commercial ports, linking up with seaborne passenger and mail services, opening out mineral resources or linking industrial towns by coastal routes), and only a relatively few short branches from the main trunk network were constructed specially for the holiday traffic.[1] A few resorts still relied on steamboats for access, most obviously the Isle of Man and the Isle of Wight, which had their own internal railway systems to ease the dispersion of visitors arriving at Douglas, Ramsey and Ryde to a variety of bathing-places and other attractions, while the Clyde paddle-steamers took

Glasgwegians to resorts in the estuary such as Rothesay, which harboured summer commuters as well as more conventional holidaymakers, as well as to Manx destinations. Steamboats also supplemented railways: a fleet of vessels took Londoners to Southend, the Essex coast and as far as Great Yarmouth, and also to Margate and Ramsgate, following a pattern which had begun with the sailing vessels which had brought grain to London from Thanet in the eighteenth century; and the Bristol Channel had steamer services whose most obvious role was the ferrying of working-class South Walians to Weston-super-Mare and Ilfracombe.[2] The steamers brought their own sense of adventure and opportunity to the holiday journey, especially where alcohol consumption afloat was part of the experience. But, overwhelmingly, what mattered was railway access and the nature and quality of the service, and new developments at the turn of the century applied the finishing touches to remote corners of the system, provided additional routes to places which were already served by existing companies, and expanded the capacity of existing lines to meet expanding demand, usually after a rising crescendo of complaint about delays at the height of the holiday season. The railway companies' advertising campaigns to boost seaside and other forms of tourist traffic were also becoming more assertive and creative at the start of the new century, generating enduring and alluring images for some of the places they promoted.

Most of the new lines which opened at the turn of the century, in the last years of the railway system's expansion, were branches to small resorts in the West Country. In Cornwall Bude acquired its branch in 1898 and Padstow in 1899, while the Looe branch was connected to the main line in 1909, and in 1905 a second route to Newquay opened by way of Chacewater. In south Devon and Dorset branch lines opened to Budleigh Salterton and Lyme Regis in 1897 and 1903, the latter using the newly available and cheaper light railway construction standards, while in north Devon the little resorts of Lynton and Lynmouth acquired a winding narrow-gauge track across difficult country from Barnstaple in 1898. North Norfolk, also a late-developing holiday region, saw a new line to Mundesley in 1897, which was extended to offer an additional route to Cromer in 1907; and new halts serving a proliferation of small holiday camps were a feature of railway developments in this area. Elsewhere there was very little, apart from the rustic light railway from Lampeter to Aberaeron in mid-Wales. A significant straw in the wind was the Great Western Railway's decision not to extend the Helston branch line in Cornwall to serve the Lizard, as management became aware of the potential for using buses for feeder services, which began here as early as 1903. A few resorts were never connected to the railway network, the largest being Beaumaris, the county town of Anglesey, which remained five miles from the Chester and Holyhead Railway; while Southwold's eccentric narrow-gauge branch line offered few of the usual advantages, although in 1911 it contrived to pay a dividend for the first time. But actual additions to the system at the turn of the century were geographically peripheral, and much more significant were improvements to existing heavily trafficked seaside routes.[3]

Most impressive here were developments in northern England, especially on the Lancashire coast, where the sheer scale of the holiday traffic drove companies into installing extra route and terminal capacity which might only be used to the full on a few summer Saturdays each year, and the growth of seaside residence among commuters encouraged investment in new trains and services. The line from Liverpool to Southport was electrified in 1904, and local services between Lancaster and Morecambe received similar treatment in 1908. The terminal stations at Morecambe Euston Road and Morecambe Promenade were rebuilt in 1888 and 1907, and the Midland Railway's special residential express service with club carriages pampered the long-distance commuters to Leeds and Bradford with comfortable, exclusive accommodation. Rival companies to the south had similar ideas, as 'club trains' were introduced from Blackpool, Southport and Llandudno to Manchester; and from 1911 a less exalted group of two hundred commuters into London from the Thanet coast, the Association of Regular Kent Coasters, combined to reserve special coaches with tables for members' card games. Blackpool's terminal stations were also rebuilt at the turn of the century, with vastly extended excursion platforms (giving the town's two termini a total of 29) and sidings, while Llandudno had seen a less-ambitious expansion in 1892, and on the other side of the country Scarborough acquired an additional excursion station and four miles of carriage storage. Middle-class demand fuelled the building of 'spacious new station facilities' on the south coast at Bexhill, Bognor and Worthing in the early twentieth century. Between 1900 and 1912 passenger bookings at Black-pool North station increased by 44 per cent, and receipts by 84 per cent. To the south, a new direct line from Kirkham enabled non-stop trains to by-pass the congestion of the existing routes from 1903, when the track between Preston and Kirkham was quadrupled. A year later the seaside suburban and holiday lines on north Tyneside, from Newcastle to Tynemouth and Whitley Bay, were electrified, and (as elsewhere) services became more frequent as well as being speeded up. The other really outstanding developments linked London with the West Country, as the Great Western Railway by-passed Swindon and provided new named express services, most evocatively the 'Cornishman' of 1895 and especially the 'Cornish Riviera Express' of 1904. This last initiative fuelled a highly successful advertising campaign which appealed to science (climate and health), modernity (special carriage window glass to allow in ultra-violet light on the journey), and the notion of Cornwall as a ' "primitive" land of magic and romance'. The extensions of railway tentacles in the south-west were part of this process of opening out new, distant and potentially lucrative coastlines, and the London and South Western Railway was similarly extend-ing its through services to the West Country.[4] Several other long-distance through services linked the industrial north and midlands with the south and south-west, involving co-operation between companies. These included a through restaurant car train from Liverpool and Manchester to Brighton and Eastbourne in 1905, and a similar service between Manchester and Bournemouth which anti-cipated the long-running future 'Pines Express' in 1910. Services to Ilfracombe in summer 1909 even included a through train from Halifax.[5]

The economics of railway services to the coast are still uncertain, but the railway companies' investment in them extended to lively advertising campaigns. John Hassall's 'Skegness is so bracing' poster for the Great Northern Railway in 1908, featuring a robust fisherman skipping with frisky vigour along an open stretch of sand, acquired iconic status and was endlessly reproduced. No doubt the two-and-a-half-fold increase in the number of tripper arrivals at this small Lincolnshire resort between 1907 and 1913, from an already impressive 321,000, was evidence of its success.[6] Hassall's poster became famous because it was unusu-ally arresting, but many railways followed the example of the Great Western in 1886 and set up specialist publicity departments, and leaflets and excursion programmes became increasingly sophisticated, with links being made between poster campaigns (usually conventional descriptive renderings of scenery) and illustrated promotional booklets. Several companies enlisted travel agencies to help co-ordinate the development of passenger services, and by 1905 the Great Western was producing a 200-page guide to holiday lodgings, with its book on *Holiday haunts* following a year later.[7] Railway hotels were part of the invest-ment and publicity process, and although only a few were in seaside resorts (mostly in Scotland and aimed at golfers) they were developed with a view to creating additional traffic rather than making extra money out of existing traffic flows.[8] And representations of resorts began to invade the journey itself, as carriage interiors were embellished with photographs of seaside and other tourist destinations served by the company in question.

The First World War disrupted this transport system considerably. Worst-affected were the steamer services, as vessels were called up for war service. The Isle of Man was cut off from its visitor markets, leading to bankruptcies in the tourist industry which had political consequences, as boarding-house keepers who were unable to pay local property taxes were threatened with forced sales and the Island's government refused to listen to pleas for relief. The resulting campaign rocked the Island's constitution to its foundations, providing an arresting illustration of the potential political significance of a tourist industry. Elsewhere the consequences were less apocalyptic, although Ilfracombe suffered from the loss of its Bristol Channel steamers; but the railways were also affected by wartime conditions, although some resorts confounded expectations by flourishing even when excursion services were cut and fares were forced up owing to coal and rolling-stock shortages. Blackpool was one such, and Brighton was emphatically another. According to Harold Clunn, Brighton attracted a huge influx of leisured people who were unable to take their usual holidays and winter breaks abroad, together with convalescent soldiers (especially officers) and 'aliens seeking security from the air-raids over London'. The alleged East End provenance of this group suggests an element of myth based on xenophobia or anti-semitism; but all this meant that immense pressure was placed on the wartime train services, as 'the trains to and from London during the business hours became disgracefully overcrowded', with a veto being placed on the purchase of new season tickets, and new hazards for travellers: 'People would queue up for the trains a whole hour before their departure, card sharpers reaped a big harvest, and sometimes hundreds of pounds would change hands during a single journey.'[9]

However exaggerated this retrospective view might be, rail travel became associated with discomfort and delay under wartime conditions, and this must have helped the rapid expansion of motor services using adapted (and boneshaking) army surplus vehicles when peace came, with demand being further boosted by price wars between a multitude of small operators, and by rail fares held at artificially high levels in the post-war transition. A Ministry of Transport traffic census during Whit Week in 1921 (a great Manchester holiday, but widely observed throughout Lancashire) counted 21,676 vehicles travelling on the Blackpool–Preston and Garstang roads, of which only 912 were horse-drawn. There were 3,105 charabancs (which would have carried at least 60,000 people), 6,536 motor-cycles and 9,704 private cars.[10] Ten years later an Easter traffic census found 40,498 vehicles traversing Blackpool's three main approach roads between Good Friday and Easter Monday, a four-day total which included

27,210 cars, 3,123 charabancs and only 181 horse-drawn vehicles. This was at the beginning of April: the late Easter of 1930 had brought out 47,571 vehicles between 18 and 21 April, with 30,259 cars and as many as 3,935 charabancs.[11] This was still a fraction of the rail traffic, but a growing one; and it offered genuine alternatives, helping to keep prices down, as at Rochdale where by the early 1920s six coach firms were competing with the railway for excursions and holiday bookings.[12]

The inter-war rise of car ownership among (especially but not entirely) the middle classes brought the number of registrations past the million mark in 1933. Many vehicles were licensed only for the summer months, and the concentration on pleasure travel which this suggests, at a time when winter motoring was still cold and inconvenient, ensured that the car would make a disproportionate impact on holidaymaking. Clunn advanced a standard argument in 1929 that 'the motoring habit' would favour the smaller and less-fashionable resorts by encouraging touring holidays which would embrace entire coastlines. Car ownership certainly made it easier for seekers after quiet and exclusivity to head for smaller and more remote resorts which were difficult to reach by rail, and the car's flexibility encouraged touring, camping and caravan holidays, as well as making it easy to take picnics on day-trips to the seaside, by-passing local cafe proprietors in the process. Caravanning developed from the 1920s, and although the cheapest new models cost between £50 and £100, accessibility was greatly improved by the growth of hiring firms. On one estimate as many as 150,000 families hired a caravan to visit one or more of the new touring caravan sites in 1935, many no doubt using the Automobile Association's annual guide to such places, first published in 1933. Camping by car was part of a more down-market trend to cut elsewhere the additional costs imposed by motoring, and the established hotel and catering industry complained of a flood of new cheap bed and breakfast outlets which competed with them. Most of the new motorists followed well-beaten paths, however, despite the rhetoric of freedom which was directed at the new consumers of space and scenery; and the roads to the big established resorts were already becoming congested in the summers of the mid-1920s.[13]

By the 1930s the coach (more sophisticated than the charabanc) was at the core of the dominant imagery of the popular seaside day-trip, associated with freedom, camaraderie and endless crates of brown ale, with supplies being replenished at wayside pubs. Charles Graves provided an amused outsider's view, narrating an excursion from London's Victoria Embankment, a kaleidoscopic medley of motor-coaches, to Southend. At the half-way pub stop:

Twenty motor-coaches were drawn up before the only inn in sight. Half the passengers wore coloured paper hats. An old lady played the piccolo. Other old ladies joined in the chorus.

Over a glass of stout, the driver recommended Monday as the best day for observing tripper habits and customs:

> That's the day the laundry girls have off. Yesterday one of my mates took a coach-ful of them down. There were thirty-two of them, and they had twenty-four crates of beer on board. Well, when they got to Southend it was decided that they had perhaps better not get out, so they stopped at Billericay and ended up with whisky and port . . . Last Monday . . . there were 315 motor-coaches from London alone to Southend. One hundred and ten of them were full of laundry hands, from the age of seventeen to eighty. You couldn't move a foot or hear yourself speak in here on Monday night.

Similar stories were told about trips to Blackpool. The second-hand, anecdotal character of this evidence matters less than the strength of the imagery it conveys, whose basis in experience (if not in exact correspondence with statistical fact) was readily verifiable on the ground.[14] And the charabanc excursion, organised by pub, church or neighbourhood, offered the security of travelling among a group of known faces with shared preferences and expectations. Moreover, across the board, competition between road and rail helped to bring down fares for cheap seaside excursions, thereby democratising access to the holiday experience still further.[15]

The increasing use of roads for holiday traffic gave rise to investment in by-passes and realignments on routes to the coast in the inter-war years, as county councils responded to congestion and the threat of accidents. Lancashire, with its particularly well-patronised resorts in easy reach of population centres, was an extreme example which anticipated future developments elsewhere. As John Whiteley comments,[16]

> The roads to the west coast had never been turnpiked, and as a result, even where adopted as main roads, were in no condition to meet traffic demands. The improvement of access to the three main Lancashire resorts – Morecambe, Blackpool and Southport – was therefore a county council priority from the 1920s until work stopped in 1939.

The road from Preston to Blackpool had been bothering the county council since the 1880s, as traffic increased, and in 1909 it was improved for the heavy motor traffic which was expected for Blackpool's Aviation Week, although urgent repairs were needed soon afterwards. The post-war growth in road traffic prompted

investment very quickly, eased by Ministry of Transport funding and special
relief work schemes for the unemployed. A new wide road between Lancaster
and Morecambe was an early priority in 1921–22, as were improvements to
the main access road to Blackpool from the north, where there was no direct
rail link. More than half of this Garstang–Blackpool road was realigned and
widened during the 1920s and early 1930s, while Preston was by-passed on
the southern route from the cotton towns and much of the very busy Preston–
Blackpool road was reconstructed between 1929 and 1936. Preston's town
centre was just as much a problem for road traffic to Blackpool as its railway
layout had been for summer train services, and further west Anthony Burgess
remembers returning from day-trips to Blackpool and seeing 'entire villages
sitting on the green, watching the cars, their sole Sunday entertainment'. Watching
the traffic jams was a Sunday pastime that persisted through the 1930s, from
Preston's Moor Park as well as in the villages. A second new road to Morecambe
was also built in the 1930s, when access to Southport was also improved. This
surge of activity encouraged the further growth of road traffic to the coast, whether
by charabanc, coach or (increasingly) private car, changing the nature of the
holiday journey; and similar developments, more tentatively and on a smaller
scale, were occurring elsewhere. The arterial road from London to Southend
was prominent among them.[17] But even where, as in the south-west, road
improvements were not yet being made, road traffic was growing anyway. There
were particular problems in south-eastern England, where by 1938 nearly
20 per cent of households owned a car as compared with less than 12 per cent
in the north. The Brighton to London road was already prolific in summer evening
traffic jams in 1925, and bottlenecks were common elsewhere, with half-mile
tailbacks at a one-way bridge across the River Stour on the way to Bournemouth. North Wales was experiencing similar problems, but the south-west
had the worst bottlenecks by the 1930s. M.P. Fogarty pointed out in 1945
that 'growing congestion in the resorts themselves and on the railways and roads'
was the second great problem for tourism in Devon, after the shortage of cheap
accommodation; and in August 1938 'the daily volume of traffic recorded . . .
by the Ministry of Transport on the Torquay–Paignton road was greater than
on any other road in the country – not far short of double the traffic on the
London–Brighton road.'[18] Problems were already being stored up for the future.

Parking at seaside resorts also became an inter-war issue, and not only in
the larger centres. The convenience of motorists, whose custom was attractive
to trading interests, had to be weighed against problems of road safety and loss
of amenity.[19] Not only did Blackpool have to deal with tens of thousands of

cars at peak periods, building (by 1939) a multi-storey car park with a thousand places and another parking area for 650 coaches, and having to make hard decisions about whether to charge for or resist parking on the promenade, while Brighton had to cope with up to 25,000 vehicles per day along the sea-front by 1936 (including heavy lorries from Shoreham harbour): the issue reared its head even in small and remote resorts like St Ives in Cornwall.[20] Here car parking tolls were introduced as early as 1925, but the initial charges of sixpence for up to two hours and a shilling beyond were soon felt to be deterring free-spending visitors, and as the carborne trade continued to increase, efforts were made to find a site for 100 vehicles. In 1931 a proposed 'concrete parking raft on pillars' on the sea-front was rejected, and by 1933 the police were only prosecuting in extreme cases, issuing 'hundreds of verbal cautions'. Eventually, in 1936, houses were demolished at Pudding Bag Lane, in the heart of the old fishermen's quarter, and the car park was placed there. Here as elsewhere, the rise of motor traffic precipitated conflict between those who wanted to preserve traditional quaintness and keep motorists at arm's length, and those who preferred to encourage the new visitors and the spending power they represented. In this case the obvious losers were the St Ives artistic colony, who 'lost one of their favourite subjects', and the fishermen who 'lost their lofts and their homes', as the car park marked the first stage of a longer process of demolition and displacement.[21]

This was the golden age of the bicycle as well as the private car, as the craze continued its late Victorian advance into the Edwardian years and perhaps reached a peak of popularity in the 1920s and 1930s, although the organised cycling clubs themselves were losing members by this time.[22] The Cyclists' Touring Club's accommodation listings showed a rich diversity of destinations, tending to confirm that cycling took its votaries to rural and scenic destinations, diluting the influence of the seaside as such, while the cyclist's mobility and independence, like that of the motorist, militated against the kind of settled holiday by the railhead to which seaside accommodation providers had become accustomed. The Wye Valley, north Wales and the Lake District were particularly popular cycling areas, but certain kinds of seaside destination were also attractive. North Devon stood out, with the 1930 handbook listing eleven approved lodgings beyond the railhead at Combe Martin, fourteen at Lynton and Lynmouth and as many as twenty-four at Ilfracombe, which was more than at Blackpool, Bournemouth or Brighton. Certain Cornish destinations were also prominent, including Bude, Tintagel, Boscastle, St Ives and the Lizard, while Lyme Regis had sixteen lodgings, and on the Isle of Wight Ryde was on a par with Bournemouth at twenty-three, and Ventnor had as many as seventeen. The cyclists, like the motorists, were colonising new, picturesque destinations which were beyond railways or poorly served by them, and the CTC's favoured places reflected the inter-war preoccupation with fresh air, exercise and scenery, coupled with liberation from the old, restrictive, formal Victorian watering-place atmosphere.[23]

Not that the railways were actually suffering from this competition as yet: visitors by train continued to grow in numbers in all British resorts during the inter-war years, when road transport took the pressure off a seasonally overloaded system rather than (as yet) challenging it. One estimate claims that holiday traffic on the railways trebled in ten years from the late 1920s, and the system was close to breaking point on some summer Saturdays. A magazine survey in the mid-1930s suggested that just over 60 per cent of holiday-makers still travelled by train, despite recent rapid increases in the use of coaches and private cars.[24] Railway investment in resort traffic continued. Where commuters could be encouraged alongside the trippers, electrification might be on the agenda. The first major scheme to be carried through was the London to Brighton route, which was electrified in 1932 and was famous for its luxury Pullman trains on the Southern (and from 1934 Brighton) Belle.[25] This was an isolated vision of sophisticated modernity, as befitted Brighton's reputation in other respects; but in 1937 electrification was extended from Waterloo to Portsmouth (with emphasis on the Isle of Wight connection) and a year later in mid-Sussex (including the Bognor Regis branch). Elsewhere, much was made of new steam-hauled expresses from London to a variety of coastal destinations. The competition between the Great Western and the Southern Railway for the Devon and Cornwall holiday traffic was particularly fierce and well-publicised, with the Southern's Atlantic Coast Express entailing eight separate departures from Waterloo in 1938. Station expansion continued, with heavy investment on the south-east and south coast at Margate, Ramsgate, Clacton, Hastings and even little Seaton.[26] The 'Big Four' railway companies continued a co-operative advertising scheme with the resorts which was to last for fifty years from 1913, and Alan Jackson tells us that 'The London and North Eastern . . . paid half the advertising costs for Butlin's pioneer holiday camp at Skegness.' The London, Midland and Scottish (LMS) went one better by investing in its own holiday camp at Prestatyn, as well as in a new Art Deco hotel at Morecambe, complete with Eric Gill mural, in a gesture more worthy of Brighton than of this aspiring provincial resort. It also introduced a Fylde Coast Express from London Euston, with a new locomotive named *Blackpool* allocated to it in the beginning, but this was an unusual initiative.[27] Naming locomotives after resorts was at least a token gesture towards the importance of the traffic, and several other LMS locomotives were similarly labelled; but otherwise only the Southern's post-war 'West Country' locomotives carried resort names, and this as part of a wider topographical celebration of the region.[28] Traffic to the coast was usually much more mundane, even workaday, however, as miles of sidings were raided every summer for superannuated rolling stock which trundled to the seaside behind a motley array of wheezy old freight locomotives, releasing crowds of desperate travellers into generously proportioned lavatories from non-corridor trains at journey's end, a problem which persisted from earlier years and was the subject of graphic commentary from a Mass-Observation observer returning from Blackpool in 1937:[29]

> Observer was bursting to pee and would have done it through the window, but for putting fear into the children, so that I had to bend my body . . . and gradually relieve myself into my trousers and hope for the best . . . By the time I arrived at Worktown [Bolton], 12.40 a.m., I was wet through and nearly double . . . After a great relief, I made my way to the barrier, at the same time searching for my ticket and . . . found it in my trousers pocket wet through and in a little ball . . . I handed it to the collector and told him that I was sorry but I had to piss in my pants and he had quite a laugh about it.

This provides, in its way, a good illustration of the railways' limited concern for their working-class passengers on the special holiday services, where (despite the inroads made by coaches), much of the trade was still a captive market.

For many holidaymakers the railway journey continued to be something of an adventure, requiring careful advance packing and planning, especially on the long journeys to the West Country which were increasingly in vogue and for which long distances and poor roads towards journey's end discouraged all but the most enthusiastic motorists. But in the 1930s even the short trip from Preston to Blackpool could take on the trappings of a great annual saga, with queues right down the hill on the station approach, children racing to and fro with news of other families, and 'all the well-worn buckets and spades lashed to the case handles with string.' The politics of the journey at the great Wakes exodus brought problems of their own, as people gravitated to friends, avoided enemies, and forged new alliances which might outlast the week away. Mass-Observation described the slightly longer train journey from Bolton to Blackpool at the town holiday of 1938:[30]

> Lots of children and cases line the train platform; babies, handbags, toddlers, parcels – everyone is loaded down. Nobody moves much and the scene is a parade of all

in 'Sunday Best' in honour of the occasion. Most of the women are wearing coats and hats, although one observer still notes traces of the mill on two young women 'with the mill fluff on their tams'. Men wear freshly pressed, often new suits . . . A group begins to sing and their mood spreads infectiously across (the station) to children and adults alike . . . Accordion played, 'Count thy blessings, one by one'. Everyone singing . . . [On the train] . . . For the first part of the journey there is almost always restraint and silence. Girls read *Woman's Own*, *Passing Show* or *Silver Star*; men smoke; and the train moves on to the stops at Chorley and Preston . . . Beyond Preston the traveller . . . reaches the world of sand-barrens, on which the star grass grows . . . The train follows the line of the dunes and the Tower comes into view, dominating the flat landscape. No longer is the mill chimney the inescapable symbol; the 'other world' has been reached. Inside the train, the mood changes; the travellers are now bound together as 'fellows' by this common rallying point. The restraint clearly visible at the outset has dropped from sight. Cotton and factory chimney are finished with . . . (Sweets and cigarettes are handed around and singing begins) . . . The skyline has changed; the land has changed; the mood has changed. It's all Blackpool – all magic – now. The ordinary, the common, the usual is all far behind, left in the mill town.

This romanticised, composite picture nevertheless gives a sense of community, occasion and rising excitement which is difficult to capture in other sources, however we might feel obliged to stand back from it and remember that its compilers remained outside the culture they sought to lay bare and penetrate. It might also be dangerous to generalise from it to (say) the experience of Midlanders going to Weston-super-Mare; but it is a representation of the working-class holiday journey which cannot be lightly set aside.

Among the comfortable middle classes the longer family holiday was a major operation, requiring special arrangements on the railways' part to deal with piles of unwieldy cabin trunks full of summer clothes for all weathers and occasions, which were sent on in advance on special luggage services to minimise delays on the actual journey. Alan Jackson points out that, 'If the absence was to last more than a fortnight or so, other pre-holiday tasks (apart from the endless packing) included placing dust covers over the furniture and depositing the family silver and other valuables in the vaults of the local bank'. And then there were the excitements of the journey itself, especially for the children who had to be kept amused, with the reassuring rituals of lunch and afternoon tea in the dining car and, for the remoter destinations, a final amble along a rustic branch line.[31] This mode of middle-class holidaymaking survived the Second World War by a decade or so, but its heyday was Edwardian and inter-war.

A lively survival from the earliest days of the seaside holiday journey, suitably adjusted for changing times, was the steamer trip down the Thames to Margate. The irrepressible Charles Graves provided a colourful description of the voyage of the *Crested Eagle* in about 1930:

> It is 9.30 a.m and there are 1,200 of us on board, bank clerks and book-makers, compositors and tobacconists, . . . plump young men and thin old men, old ladies already sipping their bottle of stout, curly-headed children with buckets . . . We go on the top deck, where, before we have reached Greenwich, there are twenty couples dancing to a banjo and two tin megaphones . . . We sing, we clap, and we laugh. We dance without formal introductions. We can have drinks all round the clock from 9.30 a.m. upwards . . . [and] for 5s6d you can eat yourself silly.

At the end of the four-and-a-half hour journey, the variegated delights of Margate awaited; and, for the day-tripper, an evening return,

> more cheerful than ever. More singing, some flirting, more eating and drinking, more banjos and laughter; a distinct touch of sunburn, our lungs full of sea air, ourselves full of lobster, of salmon and cucumber, . . . calf's head and bath-chap.

This was now the journey experience of a small minority of holidaymakers, for the steamer traffic had never regained its pre-war vitality, and the railway and the charabanc dominated proceedings. It is documented here by a chronicler of the high life at elite resorts, happily letting his hair down among the lower orders in a book dominated by Deauville, St Moritz and Monte Carlo, and romanticising a little from the fringes of the culture he describes.[32] But it is an arresting vignette all the same, all the more so because part of a specialised but recognisable genre. Four years earlier Douglas Goldring had also travelled on the *Crested Eagle*, this time on a Sunday excursion to Southend, and recorded his impressions in a book mainly devoted to Sweden and Brittany. He celebrated the vitality of the excited East Enders who were his companions, with their eager consumption of bottled Bass, chocolate, fruit and salacious Sunday paper divorce reports, and defended their morals against the censorious gaze of prurient bishops; and he too presented this as a romantic journey along the river which was London's life-blood and through which the heartbeat of its history pulsed. The paddle-steamer might be in decline, but it still had its celebrants, and not only on the Thames: the traffic revived in the Bristol Channel from the mid-1930s, for example, in response to economic recovery in south Wales and enhanced spending power for miners and tinplate workers.[33]

Where the seaside journey was too mundane, the romantically inclined might seek to complicate it. Jack Common and his friends, in their early teens during the First World War, would work out fantasies of exploration by walking from Heaton, near Newcastle, to the coast, which was only a matter of eight or nine miles away and served by a circuit of fast electric trains. Our families went there regularly through the summer, those with railway associations cheaply by privilege ticket. But that wouldn't do at all. Whoever heard of an expedition taking an electric train up the Amazon? Or travelling with a lot of women and kids?

So they concocted secret plans, assembled provisions and set forth through the grim industrial landscape of the Tyne to their glorious destination:

> from North Shields on, the air was full of the great sea-glow, a salt radiance brightened all the long Tynemouth streets. And at the end of them, the land fell off at the cliff-edge into a great shining nothingness immense all ways over the lazy crimping of seas on their level floor.

There were ruins and rock-pools, caves and limpets, and Whitley Bay's Spanish City amusement park; and at the end of the long summer day the weary walk home. This kind of odyssey, which has its Swansea counterpart in a story by Dylan Thomas, should not be omitted from accounts of the holiday journey.[34]

The Second World War brought similar travel disruption to that of the First, although this time holidaymaking was recognised from the beginning as a necessary and legitimate contribution to efficiency and the war effort. This did not mean either that resorts were readily accessible, or that frivolous travel was encouraged. The south and east coasts of England had front-line status and were effectively closed to tourists from the summer of 1940 onwards, and ordinary trains were slow and subject to all manner of disruption. Passengers were invited to reflect on whether their journey was really necessary, and civilian motor traffic was severely restricted. All this did not prevent Blackpool from enjoying unprecedented prosperity during the war, boosted by military training on the beach, munitions work and the proximity of free-spending Americans at the Warton air base; but holidaymakers still found their way to the north-western resorts from their industrial hinterlands. This was unusual, however, and an important effect of the war was to create a bottled-up longing for seaside pleasures which issued forth in record levels of crowding on holiday train and bus services in the immediate aftermath, as the Wakes traffic to Blackpool on the last Saturday of July in 1945 brought a record-breaking 102,889 passengers into the town, while 1,200 coaches a week began to arrive when this traffic (but not private motoring) was derestricted.[35] But the late 1940s were the last period of railway domination of the holiday traffic, as simply getting to the coast overrode all the delays and discomforts that might be encountered along the way.

After the immediate post-war adjustment period was over, road transport really came into its own. Even in the four years between 1951 and 1955 the proportion of holiday journeys taken by train in Britain fell from 47 per cent (itself a sharp reduction from the pre-war figures) to 37 per cent, marking the shape of things to come. At Whitby, with circuitous rail routes and a pre-dominantly middle-class visiting public within easy day-trip range by road, half the visitors came by train in 1946 but only 30 per cent as early as 1956. Rail passengers into Blackpool between May and November fell from 3.2 million in 1937 to 0.63 million in 1966, even though about 50 per cent of holiday-makers still used public transport, with bus and coach services bringing in up to 76,000 people on a peak day. Traffic surveys in late August found an average of more than 55,000 people coming in by road per day between 10 a.m. and 4 p.m. on the two main access routes. The planners found this to be tolerable, although they had to admit that on the promenade, 'The high volume of vehicular traffic and pedestrians results in conflict and interaction between them. This now seriously detracts from the environment of the sea front and presents hazards and frustrations to both drivers and pedestrians'. Despite Blackpool's traditions of crowding, and its visitors' gregarious pre-ferences, 'The presence of motor vehicles detracts from the enjoyment of the crowded holiday atmosphere'. The town had to ask itself how it was going to cope with what seemed to be the impending 'full motorisation of its visitors' (*sic*). Thus was a common problem writ large in the liveliest and most popular of resorts. Meanwhile, on the national stage, over the generation between 1951 and 1972 the proportion of holidaymakers travelling by car rose from 27 to 70 per cent, and when buses and coaches were included in the road transport figures the rise was from 53 to 85 per cent, while the railways' share declined from 47 to 12 per cent.[36]

All this made for a transformation of the holiday journey, with new land-marks and new problems. As James Walvin remarked in 1978, 'Ring-roads and by-passes, motorways and diversions, all have become part of the scenery on the way to the sea – often as far back as fifty miles from the coast itself'. Towns like Tadcaster and York became infamous obstacles to travellers to the Yorkshire resorts, while in the West Country bottlenecks like Bridgewater began to pass into motoring legend. The towns and their layouts were often seen as the prob-lem, in a familiar transference of blame from motorist to victim; and the lives of their inhabitants were disrupted, polluted and made dangerous at every summer weekend. So were those of the inhabitants of desirable destinations: Lamorna, the best known of the Cornish coves near Land's End, had 'a serious traffic problem, often reaching a complete stalemate on Bank Holidays' by 1964. As Anthony Smith suggested in 1970, however, the larger resorts maintained their hold over most carborne visitors, who had nothing but small-scale road atlases to guide them and kept a preference for 'man-made fun' rather than 'natural wonder, open-space rustic charm, empty beach and the shriek of the oyster-catcher'. Reinforcing this pattern, the rise of the coach had already been evident among the higher-class visitors to the North Devon resort of Ilfracombe by the 1920s, and twenty years later Lancashire cotton workers were an important element in the coach tour market here, which had grown to the extent that some hotels 'were wholly controlled by coach companies'. By the 1960s these trends added up to a clearly marked absolute as well as relative decline in rail use, although on some lines traffic peaked in the 1950s before falling away, and in the West Country as a whole the high water mark came as late as 1957.[37] As early as 1965 only 20 per cent of Minehead's staying visitors, and 18 per cent of those to Weston-super-Mare, came by train; the corresponding figures for day-trippers were as low as 6 per cent and 10 per cent. For Burnham-on-Sea, which had to be reached by bus from Highbridge station, the railway had an even more residual role, with 7 per cent of staying visitors and only 2 per cent of day-trippers making the complicated journey: a good illustration of what happened to transport patterns when branch lines closed. As the Somerset County Council planners noted, too, carborne visitors made much more impact on the landscape, over a wider area, than those who came by train.[38]

The cuts in rail services which followed the Beeching Report of 1963 added momentum to this trend. Casualties were particularly heavy in the south-west, on lines with very little freight or other off-season traffic. The branch lines to most of the small south Devon resorts did not survive beyond mid-decade, while those to Bridport and Swanage staggered on into the 1970s as (just) did those to Ilfracombe and Minehead. Most of the little Isle of Wight lines were closed before Beeching, in the 1950s, and the splendidly archaic branch to Hayling Island disappeared in 1963. East Anglia was another area where old-fashioned leisurely branch lines with ancient rolling-stock were severely culled, in this case mostly before the early arrival of diesel trains and rationalisation in the region around 1960, although the branch to Hunstanton survived until 1969. Further north Mablethorpe, Hornsea, Withernsea and a string of little resorts in North Yorkshire lost their trains between 1964 and 1970, as did most of the fishing villages and seaside resorts of north-east and south-west Scotland. Significantly, traffic levels in north-west England were sufficient to ensure that no resorts were cut off from the railway on this side of the country between

Silloth in north Cumberland, which lost its branch line in 1964, and the remoter seaside destinations of south-west Wales. Porthcawl, much nearer to population centres, was a more surprising Beeching era casualty, along with several small places on the English side of the Bristol Channel. But there was a lot more to this than the pruning of branch lines. Many resorts lost some of their through services from population centres as duplicate routes were axed, such as the direct line from Preston to Southport, the alternative route from London to Eastbourne, the Midland and Great Northern line which linked north Norfolk with Midland population centres, and the Somerset and Dorset route through the Mendips which served Bournemouth from the north and Midlands. And the purge on sidings housing surplus rolling-stock helped to ensure a rapid decline in excursions and summer Saturday 'extras', because the wherewithal to provide them was no longer there. Resorts lost their excursion sidings to car parks and their station buildings to retail developments. And even the largest places saw a considerable scaling down of the railway presence: Blackpool itself lost its Central Station in 1964, as the route via Lytham terminated on the southern edge of the town, and three years later the direct excursion line from Kirkham was abandoned. The old route to Central Station became a sequence of roads and car parks, eventually linking up with the M55 motorway which became the resort's new lifeline in 1975, and the surviving South Station was served only by an all-stations local branch line train, while direct connections to Manchester and beyond were channelled into North Station. This was a characteristic story on an unusually grand scale. Nationally, the downward spiral was almost halted in the 1980s, after threats of rail closures to resorts as important as Skegness. There was very little positive to set against the cuts apart from extensions of electrification in the south-east and south, especially between London and the Kent coast in 1959 and from Waterloo to Bournemouth in 1967 and on to Weymouth in 1988; but these developments were justified by commuter rather than holiday traffic. The outcome reflected the relegation of the railways to a relatively minor role in the holiday journey during the fifty years after the Second World War.[39] The reopening of several seaside lines as preserved steam railways does nothing to offset this pattern, as they count as part of the menu of holiday attractions at Minehead or Kingswear rather than as a serious alternative means of access.

Meanwhile, the bus companies were moving into the market with increasing vigour, boosted by the end of petrol rationing, coupled with increases in permitted vehicle sizes, from 1950. The Royal Blue company, serving the south and south-west, was quick to respond, offering non-stop weekend services from

London to Ilfracombe and Weymouth in that same summer. In the following
year overnight services to the Festival of Britain made many potential holidaymakers realise that this was a tolerable mode of cheap travel, and by 1952
non-stop provision from London was extended to Torquay and Brixham,
Minehead and Lynton, Newquay and Perranporth, and Swanage. Most of these
destinations figured among the early railway branch closures. Service expansion continued almost uninterrupted through the 1950s and 1960s, apart
from a hiatus at the time of the Suez crisis, with its fuel rationing, in 1956–57
which had knock-on effects in the late 1950s. Road improvements and new
bus stations boosted the growth in traffic, although the company's historians
pointed out sourly that, 'The running times on Saturday non-stop journeys
(in 1969) are of academic [*sic*] interest only, in view of the traffic conditions
which had been allowed to develop on the main roads to and from the West
on peak summer Saturdays.'[40] By this time, anyway, the snobbery of the early
1950s which had preferred trains to coaches for holiday travel, despite their
'flying smuts and upholstery that would explode in a storm of dust as you sat
down', had been completely laid to rest.[41]

The changing patterns of holiday travel were presented in a spate of
planning documents from the mid-1960s onwards, when local authorities
strove to come to terms with the new problems, as the rise of the private car
outpaced that of the coach as a contributor to holiday traffic and congested
roads. By 1976 Devon County Council was becoming increasingly concerned
to control car use on the north Devon coast. Already about one-sixth of Devon's
three million visitors found their way here, with nearly 18,000 at a time at the
season's peak; and the Council was acutely aware that the completion of the
M5 motorway in 1977 would boost the number of people within three hours'
travelling time from 2.7 to 4.5 million, increasing visitor pressures; and practically all were carborne by this time. Policies involved discouraging car park
expansion and channelling parking into two approved parks at Woolacombe
and Saunton; discouraging road improvements to ration traffic; encouraging
selective car parking charges; and providing alternatives to the car for coastal
access. This was, since 1966, a designated Coastal Preservation Area, and its
uneasy relationship with the car reflected fears of further loss of amenity, although
the visitors' own main complaints were of traffic congestion and lack of car
parking spaces. Official attitudes to landscape preservation were here in direct
conflict with the expressed desires of holidaymakers, who nevertheless came to
enjoy the peace and scenic beauty that they themselves threatened.[42] It proved
very difficult to square this circle.

The larger resorts also had serious problems in adjusting to the demands of the almost-exponential rise in the number of carborne visitors, especially as the new mode of transport was much more space-hungry than the old, and parking charges, restrictions or inconveniences were likely to put the resorts that introduced them at a competitive disadvantage against more motorist-friendly rivals. The old railway excursion sidings could be pressed into service for motorists, of course, as happened most impressively on the southern approaches to Blackpool, where multi-tracked carriage sidings and engine sheds gave way to capacious car parks. But this was a general theme, transforming plans and townscapes all along the coastline.[43]

Blackpool's was an unusually elegant solution; and there remained plenty of on-street parking and congestion even here, although plans for an inner relief road which would have ripped out distinctive Victorian townscape and led to the demolition of over 370 properties, mainly boarding-houses, were never carried out.[44] Everywhere, however, the car was a damaging and disruptive influence, intruding into landscapes, clogging up central streets and promenades, colonising vacant land, encouraging demolitions, siphoning demand away from established accommodation areas where parking was difficult, and bringing inner-city risks and fumes to holiday areas. Making room for it detracted from the distinctive character and quality of seaside life, especially as demolitions for car parks tended to remove older buildings in prominent positions, and helped to reduce the comparative attractiveness of resorts as compared to other leisure forms and opportunities. This trend was accelerating on a broad front in the last quarter of the twentieth century, and it was also apparent in the sphere of popular entertainment, where the seaside lost many of its 'traditional' attractions, found that visitors' home towns and new inland sites were competing to provide new ones, and began to lose its distinctive identity as a provider of pleasures. The development, heyday and decline of the place-specific images and patterns of seaside entertainment, which had become part of the holiday tradition, will form the central theme of the next chapter.[45]

Notes

1 J. Simmons, *The railway in town and country 1830–1914* (Newton Abbot, 1986), Chapter 8.

2 J. Whyman, 'A Hanoverian watering-place: Margate before the railway', in A. Everitt (ed.), *Perspectives in English urban history* (London: Macmillan, 1973), pp. 138–60; May, 'Victorian and Edwardian Ilfracombe'.

3 M.H.C. Baker, *Railways to the coast* (Wellingborough, 1990); Simmons, *The railway in town and country*, pp. 294–5, 297–8.

4 Baker, *Railways to the coast*; Simmons, *The railway in town and country*, p. 250; David N. Smith, *The railway and its passengers: a social history* (Newton Abbot, 1988), p. 130; A.A. Jackson, *The middle classes 1900–1950* (Nairn, 1992), pp. 242–4, 305; James Vernon, 'Border crossings: Cornwall and the English (imagi)nation', in G. Cubitt (ed.), *Imagining nations* (Manchester, 1998), Chapter 9; Morgan, 'Perceptions, patterns and policies of tourism'; R. Burdett Wilson, *Go Great Western: a history of GWR publicity* (Newton Abbot, 1970).

5 Smith, *The railway and its passengers*, p. 131; Simmons, *The railway in town and country*, pp. 254, 268.

6 Simmons, *The railway in town and country*, p. 266.

7 Smith, *The railway and its passengers*, pp. 156–8; Burdett Wilson, *Go Great Western*.

8 J. Simmons, 'Railways, hotels and tourism in Great Britain 1839–1914', *Journal of Contemporary History*, 19 (1984).

9 S. Norris, *Manx memories and movements* (Douglas: Norris Modern Press, 1941); J.K. Walton, 'Leisure towns in wartime: the impact of the First World War in Blackpool and San Sebastian', *Journal of Contemporary History*, 31 (1996), pp. 603–18; Clunn, *Famous south coast pleasure resorts*, pp. 21–3.

10 A.Crosby (ed.), *Leading the way: a history of Lancashire's roads* (Preston, 1998), p. 217.

11 Lancashire Record Office (LRO), CBBl 105/1, Watch Committee minutes, Chief Constable's traffic census, 24 April 1931.

12 Wild, 'Recreation in Rochdale', p. 147.

13 O'Connell, *The car in British society*, pp. 86–90; Clunn, *Famous south coast pleasure resorts*, pp. xxi–xxii.

14 Graves, *-And the Greeks*, pp. 191–3.

15 Walvin, *Beside the seaside*, pp. 111–12; Wild, 'Recreation in Rochdale', p. 147.

16 J. Whiteley, 'The beginning of the motor age', in Crosby (ed.), *Leading the way*, p. 232.

17 Ibid., pp. 192, 218, 232–6; Burgess, *Little Wilson and Big God*, p. 84.

18 O'Connell, *The car in British society*, p. 85; M.P. Fogarty, *Prospects of the industrial areas of Great Britain* (London, 1945), p. 380.

19 C. O'Neill, 'Windermere in the 1920s', *Local Historian*, 24 (1994), pp. 205–16.

20 O'Connell, *The car in British society*, p. 86; Walton, *Blackpool*. p. 132; E.W. Gilbert, *Brighton, old ocean's bauble* (2nd edn, Hassocks, 1975), p. 234; and for problems in a lakeside resort see O'Neill, 'Windermere in the 1920s'.

21 Eddie Murt, *Downlong days: a St Ives miscellany* (St Ives, 1994), pp. 129–31.

22 Harvey Taylor, *A claim on the countryside: a history of the British outdoor movement* (Keele, 1997).

23 Cyclists' Touring Club, *Handbook and guide 1930* (London, 1930), accommodation listings.

24 Walvin, *Beside the seaside*, pp. 113–14; Brunner, *Holiday making and the holiday trades*, p. 38.

25 James S. Gray, *Brighton between the wars* (London: Batsford, 1976), illustration 90.

26 Smith, *The railway and its passengers*, p. 134; Jackson, *The middle classes*, p. 305; Baker, *Railways to the coast*, pp. 49–50.

27 Baker, *Railways to the coast*, p. 151; Jackson, *The middle classes*, p. 305.

28 F. Burridge, *Nameplates of the big four* (Oxford: Oxford Publishing Co., 1975), pp. 67–71, 91.

29 Cross, *Worktowners at Blackpool*, p. 227.

30 J. Hudson, *Wakes week: memories of mill town holidays* (Gloucester, 1992), pp. 17–19; Cross, *Worktowners at Blackpool*, pp. 59–60.

31 Jackson, *The middle classes*, pp. 306–7.

32 Graves, *-And the Greeks*, pp. 195–9.

33 Douglas Goldring, *Northern lights and southern shade* (Boston and New York, 1926), pp. 192–4; Morgan, 'Perceptions, patterns and policies of tourism', p. 176.

34 Jack Common, *Kiddar's luck* (1951; Newcastle, 1990), pp. 111–13; Dylan Thomas, 'Who do you wish was with us?', in *Miscellany Two* (London, 1966), pp. 78–91.

35 Walton, *Blackpool*, pp. 137–9.

36 G.H.J. Daysh (ed.), *A survey of Whitby* (Windsor, 1958), p. 168; Lancashire Record Office, CBBl 32/4, pp. 3–4, 35; Harold Perkin, *The age of the automobile* (London, 1976), p. 155.

37 Walvin, *Beside the seaside*, p. 145; Anthony Smith, *Beside the seaside* (London: Allen and Unwin, 1972), pp. 110–12; Morgan, 'Perceptions, patterns and policies of tourism', pp. 169, 185, 191; Smith, *The railway and its passengers*, p. 135; S.B. Hough, *Where? An independent report on holiday resorts in Britain and the Continent* (London, 1964), pp. 39–40.

38 Somerset County Council Planning Department, 'Coastal preservation and development in Somerset' (typescript, 1966: copy in BL, X.80578), pp. 27–8.

39 Baker, *Railways to the coast*.

40 R.C. Anderson and G. Frankis, *History of Royal Blue express services* (Newton Abbot, 1970), Chapter 8.

41 Hudson, *Wakes week*, p. 15.

42 County Planning Department, Devon County Council, 'North Devon coast study (Woolacombe, Croyde, Saunton)', typescript, 1976 (BL X.702/5240), pp. 1, 5, 29.

43 Walton, *Blackpool*, p. 151.

44 *West Lancashire Evening Gazette*, 25 June 1973.

45 Urry, *Consuming places*.

4

Seaside pleasures

From its earliest days the English seaside resort has made its living by offering distinctive entertainments and artificial attractions as well as the natural (but culturally mediated) features of shoreline and sea. Indeed, one symptom of the decline of many resorts in the last third of the twentieth century has been the loss of the (by then) traditional resort attractions (as, in most cases, they ceased to attract), and the failure of the seaside to generate new ones as opposed to sustaining the old, where possible, on heritage life-support systems. But at the beginning of the century the peculiar menu of seaside entertainments, a set of invented traditions with varying pedigrees, was well-established and flourishing, supplemented by more mainstream amusements imported from the inland towns to cater for tastes that could be met at home throughout the year but were also required as part of the holiday bill of fare. There was the pleasure pier, as promenading area and place of assignation, with its distinctive architecture of eclectic frivolity and its musical, comic and dramatic entertainments, from the unpretentious band for open-air dancing and the small 'end-of-the-pier show' or 'concert party' comprising comic and sentimental songs and sketches, to the substantial orchestra with real (if intermittent) pretensions to 'high culture'.[1] The pierrots, white-faced performers in clown costumes who provided songs, jokes and sketches on beaches and in parks as well as on the pier, had superseded the Victorian 'nigger minstrels' with their patter, banjos and arch or sentimental 'plantation' songs. Pierrots were a recent seaside institution, supplemented or rivalled by 'concert parties' in mock naval uniforms or a variety of other disguises.[2] On the beach Punch and Judy was a well-established seaside favourite alongside musicians, shooting galleries or vendors of medical recipes, while entertainment of a kind might also be offered (without necessarily being intended as such) by itinerant evangelists or more orthodox outreach services from the Church of England or the

Free Churches, or even by political meetings, especially socialists or suffragettes who found it difficult to get a hearing elsewhere.[3] Stalls selling ice-cream, or the hard sugary confection called 'rock', or oysters and other sea-food, expressed another aspect of the 'otherness' of the seaside, the consumption of unusual food, which in its 'rock' form might be taken home as a souvenir alongside the various other gifts and keepsakes for family (especially mothers) and friends which often took distinctive seaside form (shell ornaments, pottery figures bearing the name and even the municipal crest of the resort, and other items for mantelpiece display). Fairgrounds were springing up on or next to popular parts of the beach in the larger resorts, in permanent form and on a scale which dwarfed the itinerant fairs which visited the inland industrial towns at holiday time. Some were becoming major and heavily capitalised entertainment centres in their own right, as at Blackpool, Southend, Margate and even ostensibly sedate Southport, whose fairground was 're-constructed on much-improved lines' in 1912–13 and emulated Blackpool's better-known Pleasure Beach with its water chute, river caves, helter skelter and Hiram Maxim flying machine.[4] Relatedly, eccentric forms of transport were a seaside speciality: Volk's electric railway or the 'Daddy-long-legs' tram on stilts at Brighton, or the various cliff lifts at resorts from Lynmouth to Scarborough, or even the narrow-gauge railways that provided unreliable access to small resorts like Southwold or Lynton. The horse tramway along the sea-front at Douglas (Isle of Man), and later the Blackpool electric tramway system, were to become unique, and therefore attractive because sufficiently archaic, with the passage of time; and the seaside resort was to become the last outpost of the horse-drawn landau, providing another relishably old-fashioned travel experience alongside the shock of the new on the fairground rides (some of which were themselves to focus nostalgia as they passed from novelty to tradition). The children's bucket and spade holiday was in full swing, enlivened by sandcastle contests promoted by the new cheap national newspapers, and enriched by the scope for investigating rock-pools and collecting shells or seaweed, getting wet and muddy in the process in ways which would not have been sanctioned at home, and thereby confirming the notion that some of the rules of normal conduct were in suspension. Donkey rides, for adults as well as children, were a well-established seaside institution, sometimes supplemented by goat-carts and (for one memorable Blackpool season) camels.[5] And then there was the sea itself, still approached artificially through the commercialised rituals of the bathing-machine in most resorts, although mixed and 'macintosh' bathing were spreading even among the ostensibly 'respectable', and the bathing-machine regime had always been an official bulwark of respectability rather than compulsory or rigorously enforced, even in its mid-Victorian heyday.[6] Boat trips and fishing boosted the earning opportunities of the surviving communities of inshore fishermen, some of whom were already fully converted to a new role as caterers for tourists.[7] All these distinctive pleasures marked the seaside out as somewhere special and desirable, even if some of them were already open to satire and not to be taken too seriously.

The larger resorts also had 'pleasure palaces' behind their promenades and sea defences, offering familiar inland entertainment programmes which nevertheless displayed a seaside flavour. There were aquaria, as at Brighton and Scarborough, which offered music and other entertainments as well as denizens of the deep in elaborately decorated buildings; and there were Winter Gardens, another seaside genre with few inland counterparts, which provided glassed-in promenades with potted plants for decorous sociability, but came to combine these limited attractions with concerts and even music-hall performances, especially where the main clientele was now working-class. These shaded over into an array of Towers, Halls and Alhambras catering unashamedly for a working-class market, usually northern or metropolitan, with popular concerts and music-hall, zoos, circuses, aquaria, roof gardens, exhibitions of exotica and of 'other' cultures (Zulus, native Americans), and fairground rides, all for a single admission fee of (usually) sixpence. The distinctively 'seaside' aspects of these ventures lay in their sheer scale and elaboration, and the exotic exuberance of their architecture and decor, which (in the largest and most popular resorts) went beyond most if not all that was on offer in the big industrial towns or even London, although outside Blackpool few of the investors (whether individual entrepreneurs or more usually shareholders) reaped sustained dividends from the short summer season.[8]

This pattern of provision marked out the seaside resort's status as a liminal environment, neither land nor sea, a 'place on the margin' where the usual constraints on respectability and decorum in public behaviour might be pushed aside in the interests of holiday hedonism, and of carnivalesque escape from the petty restrictions of everyday life in displays of excess, challenging authority and flouting the everyday norms which restrained bodily exposure and recommended civilised moderation in consumption and demeanour.[9] This was not quite as exciting in practice as a bald statement of the principle might appear, for even where (as in the resorts which catered for the 'Wakes Weeks' of the northern factory towns) the potentially censorious gaze of neighbours, workmates and Sunday School teachers was not an ever-present fact of holiday life, visitors brought their own internal controls with them, and resorts which were conscious of the financial power of the 'respectable pound' were at pains to restrain any liminal tendencies in a strict straitjacket of by-laws and frozen disapproval. It is no coincidence that resorts like Frinton and, on a larger scale, Eastbourne took stern measures to prevent their more frivolous visitors from getting carried away by the seaside atmosphere and scandalising the staid. Frinton was prominent among the fastest-growing Edwardian and inter-war resorts, despite its developing status as a music-hall joke, which was based on a reputation for toffee-nosed exclusivity and was given added post-war emphasis when the entertainer Freddie Frinton took its name. Awareness of the seaside's propensity for encouraging unbuttoned behaviour might prompt its own pre-emptive antidotes, which could in turn be taken up and turned around for use by the champions of liminality.[10]

Developments after the First World War changed the balance of the picture in important ways. Most obviously the atmosphere of the beach changed, with the pre-war trend to relaxation and informality in bathing and bodily display becoming sharply accentuated, boosted by the vogue for sun-bathing and more generally for sport and healthy outdoor activity. Relatedly, the initiative in entertainment and amenity provision shifted to the local authority, following patterns which were already apparent in resorts like Bournemouth, Southport and Torquay before the war, as parks, gardens, promenades, swimming-baths and sporting amenities proliferated while the piers and late Victorian pleasure palaces offered an updated but recognisable mixture as before. Scarborough was pushing such policies strongly by 1914, as its Corporation sought to lease its theatres and other places of entertainment out to 'experienced caterers', with clauses safeguarding the quality and content of shows, while running 'games' itself and investing eagerly in new amenities. The Floral Hall, an all-weather glass entertainment pavilion on the North Bay, opened in 1910, while South Cliff gardens were completed in 1912, the Mere on Seamer Road offered boats and a small cafe from 1913, and the South Cliff bathing pool, the jewel in borough engineer Harry Smith's crown, was still being built when the war broke out, with its opportunities for 'swimming galas and carnivals', its terraces, promenades, balconies and cafes. These were typical local authority enterprises in the immediate pre-war years, although Scarborough was unusually prolific. They set the tone for what followed. Private enterprise also built on pre-war initiatives: fairgrounds proliferated, expanded and became more sophisticated, and the seaside was a happy hunting-ground for cinema promoters. A distinguishing feature of the larger seaside resorts, indeed, became an unusually wide choice of cinema and programme. Otherwise, however, new initiatives from private enterprise were modest and sporadic. We begin with the beach and how its place in the seaside experience changed in the inter-war years.[11]

James Kirkup, the poet, son of a South Shields joiner who had 'a hard life in harsh surroundings', remembers enjoying the more prestigious of the town's two beaches in the brief summers of his childhood in the early 1920s. His home town was industrial, at the mouth of the Tyne, but it had boarding-houses, beach furniture, buckets, spades, ice-cream, Punch and Judy, and 'one summer there were nigger minstrels with ukeleles and striped trousers. I rather fancy that Shields folk thought such things were out of place on our sands. Then there was a man who made wonderful sculptures in the damp sand: he could do mermaids and dolphins, and castles and sailing-ships and battle-cruisers, with burnt-out matchsticks for guns'. His poor but respectable family avoided 'the low sands', with their dirty beach, ragged children and 'bus-loads of rowdy trippers in hot, dusty, best-suited clumps drinking jugs of ale, eating saveloys and cream cakes with uproarious enjoyment'. Kirkup's family preferred 'the big sands', with their promenade, hot water for tea, bathing-tents and clean sand, for picnics, play and paddling, and rides on Shetland ponies, 'brought up out of the mines for a breather'. Fat ladies would paddle in comic post-card style, 'with their flowered frocks tucked up into the elastic in the legs of their bloomers', producing shocking utterances about what the waves had done to their knickers. 'Sea-water was supposed to be "good for the corns" . . . and "strengthening for the ankles"', and it might be taken home in bottles for therapeutic use in emergency. Here, in a particularly proletarian setting, was a telling interaction between tradition, liminality and consciousness of social boundaries, which was replicated elsewhere; and Kirkup captures the seduct-ive combination of pleasure, discomfort and unease which accompanied the ambiguous enjoyment of sand and salt water, with their distinctive accompany-ing amenities. This was a very individual viewpoint and a setting which lay outside the usual field of vision of the resort historian, but in many ways it was transferable across a broad range of experience.[12]

Kirkup's description captures a point at which ways of using the beach and sea were changing in important ways. The decline of the bathing-machine, that device for controlling bathing by vesting access to it in licensed proprietors, requiring payment for their services, and segregating the sexes into separate bathing areas, was already incipient before the First World War and acceler-ated in the 1920s, becoming precipitate during the following decade. Central government became increasingly unwilling to allow new restrictions on bathing, and the older ones were allowed to fall into decay in the inter-war years. A

Home Office memorandum in 1922 referred already to 'the old-fashioned plan' of allocating 'particular parts of the beach . . . to a particular sex', and Colonel Day, M.P., was ridiculed in the House of Commons by Home Secretary Joynson-Hicks in 1927 when he asked for 'legislation forbidding undressing on beaches for bathing purposes'. There were already such by-laws at Margate, Folkestone and Southwold, and according to the Home Secretary there was no reason to believe that the existing laws could not cope. When Day asked, 'Is the Home Secretary aware that in many cases large groups of people undress on the beach without any covering at all?', Joynson-Hicks replied, 'I am quite sure that in any case of that kind the Hon. Member . . . would not be present'. The civil servants were equally relaxed: on the previous day D. Veale of the Ministry of Health informed a Home Office colleague that his department did not look favourably on restrictive by-laws on this subject, as being 'likely to interfere with bathing by the poorer classes among the inhabitants as distinct from visitors who can afford to pay'. By the mid-1930s this spirit of democratic tolerance was extending to the two ministries' interpretation of the Town Police Clauses Act of 1847, the basis for bathing regulation. Policy was now to limit by-laws to preventing danger, avoiding all mention of indecent exposure of the person. Sunbathing and undressing on the beach were not covered by the Act, which only referred to bathing in water; and the civil servants were disposed to resist the 'agitation working up among Local Authorities for greater restrictions upon bathing, sun-bathing and walking about in bathing-costumes' away from the beach, the last of which even Canvey Island wanted to prohibit in 1938. It was regarded as an offence against good taste rather than public morality, and legislation was resisted. Where local authorities owned or leased their foreshores, they could take civil action to enforce their rules; but consensus as interpreted by senior civil servants worked in favour of increasing freedom to enjoy the beach without paying for municipal facilities or fearing prosecution for inde-cency. As the bathing-machine and all it stood for withered away (although even Blackpool still had one bathing-van proprietor in 1938), the Ministry of Health's model bathing by-laws could be allowed to pass formally into disuse in 1948.[13]

The growing tolerance of 'mackintosh bathing' (putting a bathing costume on in your lodgings and wearing it under a mackintosh to get to the beach, rather than paying for a bathing-hut or machine) and changing on the beach, along with the increasingly common replacement of machines by huts, cabins and tents in association with the growing acceptability of 'mixed bathing' from the turn of the century, reflected the more systematic use of the sea as something to paddle and play in and around. The rise of the bathing-hut was a mixed blessing, as those who rented them tended to treat their immediate surroundings as private property, deterring casual promenaders and picnickers; and local authorities could adopt exclusive principles in letting huts, discriminating against outsiders and creating select areas for denizens of the 'better side' of town, as at Frinton. But, more positively, all this was part of the sea becoming a focus for shared family enjoyment rather than part of a regulated regime of medicinal bathing for isolated individuals. Municipal provision of deck-chairs, an Edwardian innovation, and encouragement of sun-bathing through 'lidos' and sun-terraces, expressed growing though not uncontroversial acquiescence in the changing patterns of popular demand. Bathing-huts could be rented to provide a territorial base for this relaxed regime of picnics and family parties, while the new salt-water swimming-pools in the larger resorts, with their diving-boards and spectator terraces, were an extension of this pattern. The inter-war development of sun-bathing (whose origins antedated the First World War, long before the French Riviera of the late 1920s where persistent legend places them) and the cult of the outdoors made an immense difference to the enjoyment of the beach. Changing health fashions were at the core, as growing medical attention was paid from the turn of the century to the role of sunlight in treating, and preventing, tuberculosis and rickets. Providing access to sunlight became an important goal of the eugenics movement, as one of its more benign tools for improving the race. These strands were brought together by Dr Saleeby, chair of both the National Birthrate Commission and, from 1924, of the Sunlight League, one of whose goals (taken from a paper by Dr Palm on rickets in 1890) was, 'The systematic use of sunbaths as a preventive and therapeutic measure in rickets and other diseases', together with 'teaching the nation that sunlight is Nature's universal disinfectant, as well as a stimulant and tonic'. For this, said Saleeby, 'The beach is incomparable. It gives the child everything'. All this provided a powerful boost to a fashion for sunbathing which was growing of its own accord and also entailed a revised physical aesthetic, so that tanned, brown bodies became a symbol of health rather than a disfigurement brought on by outdoor labour. This is remarkably reminiscent of the revaluation of the sea and the medical endorsement of salt-water bathing which underlay the original rise of the seaside resort. But Saleeby's strictures on how exposure to the sun should be regulated and controlled were less effective than the earlier prescriptions of Russell or Granville: he knew that his recommendation of early rising, to catch the sun's light without its heat, would fall on stony ground, and his urging of the careful phasing-in of exposure, a very little at a time, was no more successful. The regulated sunbed did not become the new seaside analogue of the bathing-machine: new fashions in health reinforced a broader change in preferences, rather than creating it. Sun-bathing was an individualistic, hedonistic pursuit, although it might be collectively pursued when enjoyed in serried ranks, and it received its measure of medical approval without ever falling under the doctors' spell. It also had to be embraced by resort authorities without shocking the puritanical through indiscriminate over-exposure of hitherto-hidden body parts. The development of briefer and more revealing bathing attire, easier to don and remove as the bather wriggled behind a sheltering towel, was central to process and controversy, although consensus had moved on by the later 1930s to embrace the modest two-piece costumes for women which appeared at that time, and even to cope (from the late 1940s) with what became known as the bikini.[14]

The most convincing embodiment of the new seaside ethos of sunshine and freedom was the lido, which had its inland incarnations but was predominantly a seaside innovation. Drawing on happy experiences at Weston-super-Mare and Saltdean, near Brighton, as well as at Fishponds near Bristol, Julie Burchill has commented on the lido's heady combination of the 'opulent and socialistic, encouraging individuals by the hundred to find true happiness by merging into one big faceless, sun-worshipping mob'. Not only were they 'a blank space on which any fantasy may be projected'; they were also, subversively, 'an open invitation to do nothing'.[15] Their combination of art deco architecture, blue water and lawn expressed a classic inter-war leisure aesthetic, celebrating the relaxed side of modernity in ways which pulled together many of the attractions of inter-war resort development. The bathing-pools with their diving-boards, filtered water supplies and tiers of spectator accommodation, offering frolic, sport, scope for display of physical pride and prowess and (the other side of the coin) acceptable voyeurism, were a more concentrated and energetic variant, safer, more predictable and often more comfortable to the feet than bathing in the unmediated sea. They were prominent among the municipal investment fashions of the inter-war years, as Blackpool's enormous South Shore pool of 1923 claimed kinship with the leisure architecture of ancient Rome and (for example) Margate's Clifton Baths pool of 1927 could accommodate 1,000 bathers and 3,000 spectators, while Folkestone followed suit in 1936 and Ramsgate belatedly acquired the Marina Bathing Pool, 'the grandest of the Kent open air pools'.[16] A press report on a morning at Scarborough's South Bay pool in 1926, with 3,500 spectators paying sixpence (2.5p) each, captures the preferred ambience:[17]

> At the popular periods when the band is playing it is . . . a case of waiting
> one's turn to occupy a cubicle . . . Thousands, also, enjoy the fun which is rarely
> lacking in the stupendous energies of those disporting themselves in the water,
> the music of the band, the amenities of the well appointed cafe, and the picturesque
> setting of it all . . . A weekly aquatic display . . . offers a 'break' in the usual
> programme here . . . organised by Miss Bessie Jones, the swimming instructress
> at the Pool, and Mr H. Boyes . . . Under-water swimming, swimming through
> a hoop, boat-rowing, steam-tug, torpedoes and other novelties were performed
> . . . a noteworthy display of high diving from the 25 ft diving board . . . falling
> statue, Charlie Chaplin, Charley's Aunt, corkscrew and swallow dives . . . some,
> as the titles suggest, being humorous caricatures.

Not that this was mere passive spectatorship: 'As usual, not two minutes had
elapsed after the exhibition before bathers were plunging into the pool to try
some of the stunts they had seen, and to find that these were not easy after
all.' This was the cult of the active, open-air holiday, spiced with its own sense
of humour, at its liveliest.

The vogue for fresh air, exercise and outdoor fun went hand in hand with
a spreading interest in photography, as the pre-war vogue for holiday snaps
became more widely democratised in the inter-war years. Manuals were produced to reinforce the conventions of seeing which guided the photographer's
eye, and Robert Goodsall's order of priorities in 1939 is interesting as both
distillation and propagation of conventional preferences. He began with,
'Children romping with Rover the dog, building sand castles, bathing, sailing
boats and astride the beach donkeys', moving on to beach games, bathing, 'low
tide', children's pranks, and only then the more conventionally picturesque aspects
of boats, fishermen, harbours and local crafts: 'Cumbersome tar-boarded sheds
along the beach where old craftsmen with loving care fashion trim little rowing
boats.'[18] Such picturesque manifestations were under threat from apostles of
tidiness and uncompromising modernity at precisely this time, and this direction
of the photographer's gaze was probably a minority taste among the aspiring
amateur photographers who were Goodsall's target readership. Conventional
representations of the consensually picturesque, carefully composed as holiday
trophies and evidence of authentic presence, were perhaps more important at
holiday venues where scenery had a high profile; but at the seaside, the fresh-air
priorities were family and fun.[19]

Another photogenic outside venue, according to contemporary conventions,
was the public park, which became as necessary a part of the well-equipped
resort's inventory of attractions in the inter-war years as the bathing pool. As
resorts embraced planning schemes, so they sought to offer tidy, controlled

green spaces which offered facilities for healthy exercise as well as promenading, listening to bands and admiring formal gardens. There were plenty of Victorian and Edwardian precursors from which to develop. Landowners had often granted ornamental estates to local authorities as amenities, as in the case of Worthing's Steyne Gardens or Southport's Hesketh Park, donated by the Rev. Charles Hesketh, who attached conditions which encouraged the development of surrounding building estates on his land. This was a common strategy. Southport's Marine Lakes and Victoria Park also predated the First World War, making the best of the sea's retreat and helping the town to lay claim to the title of 'England's seaside garden city' which was perceived to be an inter-war selling-point. Bournemouth acquired the old turbary commons for conversion into public parks between 1894 and 1906, and likewise traded on a reputation for greenery and open spaces.[20] But provision was greatly expanded between the wars, as the park vogue extended even to Blackpool, which had previously shown dismissive resistance to planning schemes while the Corporation regarded the beach as sufficient public open space. Stanley Park, opened in 1926, was described thus in the official guide for 1938:[21]

> One of Blackpool's proudest possessions . . . is Stanley Park – where nearly 300 acres have been transformed into a perfect paradise for lovers of nature and outdoor sport . . . The picturesque Italian Garden, with its classic colonnade, guarded by two de Medici lead lions . . . is the central attraction, while the floral cuckoo clock is always a source of wonder . . . Stanley Park is not merely a show place, however, for it abounds in every kind of sport – bowls, tennis, putting, boating and golf.

This was not exactly the conventional representation of Blackpool, but it was how the resort sought to present itself to broadening markets in the inter-war years. The last sentence was important, for no self-respecting inter-war resort could afford to neglect this kind of sporting provision. Above all, golf was absolutely necessary for any resort which aspired to middle-class patronage. It had been central to the appeal of Scottish resorts since the late nineteenth century, especially the east coast links courses which made St Andrews and environs famous, but also on the Clyde coast at (for example) Ayr. A 'representative selection of the principal Golf Courses' of Scotland in 1930 listed seventy-eight places with at least one seaside links (some had several). Forty-seven were on the east coast, including fifteen between Crail and Dunbar beside the Firth of Forth; but there were also twenty-four along the Clyde estuary.[22] English and Welsh resorts were acquiring courses apace at the turn of the century, with Lytham, St Annes and Southport on the Lancashire coast in the vanguard. These were the challenging courses on which Open Championships might be played, but the game sucked in a wide range of abilities as well as middle-class occupations. P.G. Wodehouse's imaginary resort of Marvis Bay, where in the mid-1920s 'the hotel links were a sort of Sargasso Sea into which had drifted all the pitiful flotsam and jetsam of golf', illustrates the obsessive hold the game acquired in middle-class culture:[23]

> there are many kinds of golf, beginning at the top with the golf of professionals and . . . working down through the golf of ossified men to that of Scottish University professors. Until recently this last was looked upon as the lowest possible depth; but nowadays, with the growing popularity of summer hotels, we are able to add a brand still lower, the golf you find at places like Marvis Bay.

Wodehouse also emphasised the growing popularity of golf among young women, so that it joined lawn tennis (especially) as part of middle-class courting rituals: and much seaside leisure activity was part of this process, at all social levels. The great spectator sports, cricket and football, were more masculine domains; but a good cricket club was an asset to a middle-class resort, as Sidmouth's eagerness to highlight its picturesque ground bore witness; and where festivals could be arranged or county matches laid on, as at Scarborough or Hove, there were added advantages. Professional football was a more peripheral and adventitious development at the seaside: only Blackpool sustained a relatively successful inter-war club, as befitted the importance of a transplanted and socially mobile Lancashire working class to its economy, while Grimsby Town, who had roughly equal status, played in Cleethorpes. Brighton, Torquay and Southend were foredoomed to struggle. This was, socially, at several removes from the golf, tennis or bowls club which was much more characteristic of the seaside, and football was, after all, still a winter game.[24]

Celebrations of outdoor exercise in a seaside setting, placing lithe, bronzed bodies as central symbols of what resorts had to offer, were at the core of the inter-war seaside as its advertisers and promoters preferred to present it. Alongside all this, the 'artificial attractions' of more directly commercialised entertainment continued to flourish. The lower strata of pierrots and concert parties often plied their trade on the sands or in the parks, and continued to flourish through the inter-war years. That potent symbol of the Victorian seaside, the pier, was more than capable of adjusting to inter-war trends. In principle it is the essence of liminality, with more convincing credentials as phallic symbol than the tallest tower, as it points a stiff masculine technological probe into the mysterious feminine world of the sea, linking the elements to generate the special frisson of pleasure and the privileged gaze that go with occupying the bridging-point of two worlds. Some of this magic persisted in the inter-war years, and although the golden age of the pier was already passing, new uses could still give new life. The construction of new piers practically came to an end in the early twentieth century, as all the most plausible places outside Scotland, which never took to them, had acquired at least one, and their finances became increasingly uncertain: only nine were built between 1900 and 1910, including a replacement for Great Yarmouth's popular Britannia Pier and the impressive new Grand Pier at Weston-super-Mare. The last Edwardian pier was at Fleetwood, and subsequently the only further venture was the third pier to be built at Deal, constructed as late as 1954–57 to replace a Victorian structure damaged beyond repair in the war. The accumulated expertise of specialist pier builders had decayed by the inter-war years, although steel and reinforced concrete made some aspects of it irrelevant, at least to engineers. The occasional new proposal, as at Hove, came to nothing, and a long period of conservation and development of existing structures set in.

The new developments were important, however, reflecting expanded markets for entertainment and new customer preferences in what was still an attractive setting. Piers in the larger resorts had acquired entertainment pavilions, dance-floors, cafes and kiosks at the turn of the century. Morecambe's Central Pier, in 1906, offered dancing all day, with two bands daily; a morning promenade concert; two concert and variety entertainments daily ('All the leading stars, no duds'); two sacred concerts every Sunday; steamer services to other resorts; and 'Grand Aquatic Performances and Sensational Diving into the Sea'. Similar fare continued into the inter-war years, although steamers declined on the Lancashire coast after war losses. The ramshackle piers, with their bandy-legged struts, sometimes seemed to stagger under the weight of their indoor attractions, from which the susurration of the waves could still be heard between the performances.[25] The First World War, which (like the French Wars a century earlier) drove wealthy holidaymakers back to their own island coastline, propelled some favoured piers up-market for a time. Thus both the Brighton piers took on high-class orchestras to meet the new demand, as fashionable promenaders reappeared in strength. But this was a temporary reversal of sustained down-market pressures: orchestral music gave way to dancing in the post-war years, and then even to 'wireless concerts', while the Palace Pier's Pavilion moved over from concerts to a new use as (in Harold Clunn's disgusted words) 'a so-called Palace of Fun', with 'stalls, automatic machines and sundry other attractions for the use of the general public'. Games of chance and 'What-the-butler-saw' machines were essential to the profitable future of many piers up and down the country.[26]

Piers had, indeed, ceased to be fashionable (while remaining emphatically popular) in the inter-war years, as Lytton Strachey and his allies began the debunking of all things Victorian. Harold Clunn pronounced in 1929 that Brighton's West Pier 'is probably the most elegant in Great Britain', but retreated immediately into the nervous acknowledgement that 'opinions on the merits of such structures as pleasure piers and railway stations vary enormously' and that his praise was only 'a personal expression of opinion'. He was only too aware of the rising tide of mockery which encouraged Malcolm Muggeridge to describe the characteristic pier as 'a kind of pasteboard Taj Mahal', as the playful orientalism of pier pavilions, like its fountainhead the Brighton Pavilion of George IV, became fair game for the spleen of the modernists and classical revivalists.[27] These were the sentiments of a self-proclaimed elite, and they were not shared by the customers whose preferences prompted and endorsed the new investments and initiatives. The New Palace Pier at St Leonard's is a particularly impressive example. It was effectively rebuilt in 1933, with a deck area more than four times that of the largest Blackpool pier of the 1890s. There was room for more than a thousand dancers on the sprung maple floor of its ballroom, and it had a sun-lounge as well as a cafe. It also had, reputedly, 'the most extensive and modern range of Automatic Machines on the South Coast', as well as dodgems, skittles, darts, shooting ranges, bars, shops and kiosks. It was, in fact, a full-scale fairground suspended above the waves, and in 1936 it attracted a million visitors. The Grand Pier at Weston-super-Mare acquired an even bigger, glass-roofed Pavilion at the seaward end in 1933; and these extravaganzas followed a spate of earlier initiatives at (for example) Eastbourne, Great Yarmouth, Clacton and Penarth. These developments, concentrated into the more popular resorts, identified the pier as a prime site for investment in the new popular pursuits of the inter-war years. It was still a vital focal point for seaside pleasures, and entirely compatible with the visions of modernity with which most of its visitors identified, although Ernest Kingsman's eager expansion of new pleasures on the privately-owned Clacton Pier was less than popular with those strands of local opinion which preferred a planned, tidy, select version of modernity to a streamlined vision of democratic technological pleasures.[28]

There was also extensive inter-war investment, especially by local authorities, in pavilions, theatres and (in some up-market settings) municipal orchestras which continued the traditions of classical music for what was seen as a discerning seaside audience. Brighton's orchestra, which had been a great success during the war, was abolished in 1924; but Bournemouth, Torquay and Folkestone took this path, and in 1936 Bognor Regis joined them, belatedly, as part of a bid to attract the 'better classes', although the winter garden which was supposed to house its musicians fell foul of the policy disputes which bedevilled the local authority. An orchestra provided valuable and well-targeted publicity when its concerts were broadcast on the radio, as happened three times in Bognor's first season, but these were always controversial ventures, and the less demanding (and expensive) programmes of quartets, octets and concert parties were much more widespread and enduring.[29] More usual was the lighter music provided by pier or winter gardens orchestras of up to fifty pieces on a commercial basis during the season, as with M. Jules Riviere and Herr Theodor Sverdloff, whose very names added *gravitas* and prestige, in Edwardian Morecambe.[30]

But the seaside nostalgia of later generations was founded in the smaller pierrot troupes of around ten performers, originally male-dominated but usually more evenly balanced by the inter-war years, who had taken over from the blackface minstrels as burnt cork gave way to zinc oxide at the turn of the century. These entertainments displayed varying degrees of sophistication and financial substance, ranging from the small groups who moved from pitch to pitch with their piano or 'strill' (portable harmonium) and collected what they could by 'bottling' the audience, to regular occupants of dedicated pavilions on piers or foreshores or in municipal parks, charging for seats and paying rents based on auction or tender, and having access to lighting and special effects. Some impresarios, such as Scarborough's Will Catlin, acquired pierrot concessions in several resorts across the country: in the same season Catlin's Royal Pierrots could be found, under local managers, at Scarborough, Colwyn Bay, Bournemouth, Withernsea and Yarmouth, as well as beyond the resort world at Erith. This is a reminder that pierrots went inland outside the holiday season, working small theatres, music-halls and park pavilions, although many troupes returned year after year to the same resorts. But there were elements of seaside liminality about their acts, which featured female impersonators (including some groups whose whole act fell into this category) and exotic garb: beyond the conical hats and pom-poms, there was a pervasive vogue for Japanese floral kimonos worn by male artistes, although blazers and yachting caps also had their votaries. The performers were at pains to stress the inoffensive nature of their acts, which had to appeal to children and their parents; but this was the milieu that nurtured (for example) Larry Grayson, and a lot of the names and slang have since acquired camp connotations which perhaps add spice to the nostalgia in some quarters.[31]

Pierrots, as relatively informal outdoor performers, seem to have flourished most in smaller resorts where there was little competition from a weightier entertainment industry: they struggled to make headway against the competition at Blackpool, for example, except when a company found a niche on one of the piers. The small East Coast resorts of Redcar, Saltburn and Withernsea were particular strongholds, for example. They were, perhaps, already in incipient decline on the eve of the Second World War. The 1938 film *Bank Holiday* is merciless about a show of this kind, which (in a resort full to the gunwales) plays to an audience of one (who is waiting for the pubs to open) until a thunderstorm suddenly fills it. Certainly, many shows of this kind failed to reappear after the war, and those that did soon began to struggle. By the mid-1960s the last survivors were folding and the nostalgic histories were beginning to appear, refusing to accept that the more sophisticated revues which were appearing at the piers and pavilions were the true heirs of what was seen as a distinctive seaside tradition.[32]

The pierrot shows nurtured talent for the music-hall and other media, and some of their owners recognised that the cinema could complement rather than compete with their offerings: Filey's Andie Caine opened the town's first cinema, and Will Catlin even produced his own films.[33] The cinema was a valuable and lucrative wet-day resource, especially for resorts which had limited shelter or indoor entertainment for visitors who were expected to vacate their lodgings when neither eating nor sleeping; and even in Blackpool in the late 1930s the big cinemas put on special morning performances. Here as elsewhere, the seaside had more than its fair share of cinemas, including luxury ones, alongside the other offerings.[34]

In the big popular resorts the Victorian pleasure palaces continued to offer their broad range of attractions at all-in prices. Theatres and music-hall flourished, while Blackpool Tower's zoo, aquarium and circus continued to attract, and to lay claim to educate as well as entertain the customers. But its most popular offering was dancing in the Tower Ballroom, and this was the great seaside craze of the 1920s and 1930s. Special evening dance excursions (the 'Passion Express', as the Bolton one was known) ran from the industrial towns, and even the villages of the Lune Valley, to Blackpool and Morecambe during the latter decade. They ended at the Tower with canoodling couples filling the Palm Lounge, Aquarium and galleries before being assertively moved out by attendants just ahead of closing time at 11.30. Earlier, the dancing was formal and carefully policed, and up to 5,000 people would pack the ballroom balconies during the season to watch the dancers and enjoy the music of the Mighty Wurlitzer, whose broadcasts became symbolic of one version of the Blackpool holiday.[35]

The thrills, spills and scope for exciting encounters which were associated with the fairground also came to have a special relationship with the seaside, even though travelling fairs had long brought their own suspensions of every-day reality and constraints to the popular holidays of inland towns and villages, and even on a smaller scale to weekly markets in the industrial centres. The fairground on a dedicated site, with exciting and technologically sophisticated rides and spectacles, became a feature of the larger seaside resorts from the turn of the century, and during the inter-war years the most popular resorts saw impressive investment in these popular and controversial emblems of carnival, with their challenges to gravity (in all senses), equilibrium, calm and modesty. Margate's Dreamland, which included bars, dining halls and a ballroom as well as a fairground, was completely renovated during 1934–35 to include a new Super Cinema and licensed cafe, while Blackpool's Pleasure Beach provided a sequence of new rides, calling in the architect Joseph Emberton to produce clean-lined, modernistic buildings in keeping with the proprietors' deter-mination to provide a healthy, respectable environment and disarm critics.[36] Some of the travelling showmen who made the smaller resorts part of their summer circuit were equally anxious to proclaim their respectability, and the Corrigan family whose inter-war Yorkshire circuit included Hornsea, Bridlington and Scarborough were also investing in new rides and trying to keep potential critics at arm's length. They eventually settled down after the Second World War to provide permanent fairground amusements of their own in Filey, Scarborough, Bridlington and further afield in Fleetwood and Ramsgate, as well as catering for the caravan holidaymakers at the giant site at Primrose Valley to the south of Filey.[37]

Smaller and more disreputable stalls were also part of the seaside entertain-ment experience, especially on Blackpool's 'Golden Mile'. In the late 1930s Mass-Observation was fascinated by the popularity of the stalls here, which featured (alongside fortune-telling and games of chance) freaks of nature and people presented as enduring extremes of starvation and confinement. There were also 'fakirs, ecstatics and holy men', appealing to an interest in the 'mysteries' of 'the Orient' as an 'other' constructed through journalism and popular literature. Waxworks shows played to these and other fascinations, featuring exhibitions of murderers and the ravages of venereal diseases. Two of the most compelling exhibits were the unfrocked Rector of Stiffkey (who was alleged to have maintained unduly close relations with the prostitutes he was 'saving') and Colonel Barker, a woman who had married in male guise. Interest in what Mass-Observation called 'intersex', and more generally in unortho-dox sexual activity, was a strong theme, perhaps allowing for prurient and vicarious escape from the conventions of everyday life. Luke Gannon, the most high-profile impresario on this front, was married to a fortune-teller but came from Burnley and lived in a semi-detached house on South Shore. His and related activities exercised Blackpool Corporation's inspectors and attracted Home Office interest when a visitor complained about an exhibition of a young woman fasting in a coffin in 1933: 'People are paying 2d each to see the frail young woman in the coffin, and I think it is most injurious to public moral. I expect the fast is a fraud, and I hope it to be so, but the effect is the same on the sightseers if they believe it to be genuine'. The Corporation responded to enquiries by forwarding reports from its Inspectors, who had talked to several exhibits and found them to be in good health, while the model of a 'starving bride' had been amateurishly adapted from a draper's model purchased from a local outfitters. The Corporation sought to regulate such shows more tightly by a clause in its Improvement Act of 1935, but to little avail. Similar dramas were played out on a smaller scale elsewhere, and such spectacles were not unique to the seaside: a fasting lady in a coffin had been exhibited at fairgrounds across the Midlands in 1934, for example. But the sheer concentration of these exhibits in popular seaside settings, and the publicity they often attracted, assimilated them into the collective place-myth of the seaside.[38]

Blackpool's Illuminations also attracted more publicity and bigger crowds than similar ventures elsewhere. This device for extending the season in autumn was pioneered here in 1912, interrupted by the First World War and post-war fuel and power restrictions until 1925, and had become such an institution by the Second World War that revival in 1949 was treated as a sparkling symbol of retreating austerity. This was a municipal initiative, trumpeted as 'the greatest free show on earth', and its tableaux and special effects helped to create a hedonistic atmosphere, although Mass-Observation in 1937 reported little actual discussion of their appearance and content. Its commentary on what visitors actually did on their Blackpool holidays was, in fact, revealingly banal.[39]

An observer from Mass-Observation followed two married couples around for the day. They had no children with them (a broader visual survey found that only 9.5 per cent of a Blackpool visitor sample were children, although what constituted a child was undefined), and they were millworkers. They spent their time walking along the promenade, sitting in deck-chairs by the North Shore pool, reading the *Daily Express*, taking a tram ride to the South Pier to listen to the pierrots, and, in the evening, going to the cinema. They were seen to spend 11s 3d (56p) between them. Expenditure was clearly constrained, and the big commercial attractions were avoided. Jollity and high spending was in evidence all around this quartet, whose experience cannot have been 'typical'; but as a way of experiencing Britain's most popular and highly commercialised resort this way of spending the day needs to be taken into account. It was not all high spending and raucous laughter: there was a quieter side.[40]

In the smaller resorts, this kind of day was all there was, supplemented by excursions to places of interest in the district, and by regular special events such as carnivals and regattas. In settings like Deal this kind of holiday was a lifestyle choice, rather than being imposed by shortage of funds, although the kind of middle-class family that predominated in this setting was usually careful with its money. Deal's attractions in its Charter Year of 1949 were typical of many middle-sized resorts in the pre- and post-war years, although the wartime loss of the pier was lamented. There were four cinemas; the Astor Hall, which hosted 'dances, concerts, exhibitions, whist drives, etc.'; golf, bowls and tennis; concerts by the band of the Royal Marines, whose local barracks was itself an attraction; sea-fishing; riding; and the annual regatta. The town guide had features on the Goodwin Sands lifeboat and 'some interesting local churches', and letters from imaginary visitors emphasised local history and vernacular architecture. The one from 'Mary Guest' foregrounds the pleasures of shopping, the cinema and: 'My favourite pastime during the day is sitting! Just sitting, in a deck chair. At times I read or knit, or just relax and do nothing. After a week of it I am feeling a different woman, really toned up.' The combination of recuperation and relief from household chores echoes the priorities of the women who wrote to Mass-Observation, and emphasises the limited requirements of many holidaymakers of this generation, which the British seaside was readily able to satisfy.[41]

Such visitors were likely to find the restrictions on seaside revelry which set Britain apart from the Continent to be acceptable and even reassuring. Harold Clunn, in 1929, argued that British holidaymakers were being driven to the Continent in search of a more relaxed attitude to Sunday observance and the sale of alcoholic beverages, lamenting the lack of open-air cafe life in England; and his survey of the South Coast resorts includes a series of attacks on vicars and other supporters of 'Mrs Grundy' who opposed Sunday trams, bands and cinemas. In practice, prevailing resort attitudes varied widely, from Blackpool's Edwardian openness to Hove's enduring attachment to restrictions. Clunn endorsed a description of Hove as 'one long yawn' for the holidaymaker: 'a more inhospitable town it would be impossible to find throughout the length and breadth of Great Britain'. But its growth and apparent prosperity in these years suggests that it met the requirements of a significant segment of the market, reinforcing the theme that the success of British seaside resorts as a category of town during the first half of the twentieth century represented the sum of a diversity of entertainment regimes.[42]

Tastes began to change in the post-war generation, especially as a gulf began to open between the tastes and preferences of younger people and their parents. The quieter pleasures of Deal began to lose their appeal, and alternative destinations became more accessible. Changes in tastes between the wars could be accommodated within the overall system of provision, but the new consumer cultures were more demanding. These changes began to work their way through in the 1950s, precipitating (for example) the terminal decline of pierrots and band concerts, and making it increasingly difficult for even the largest resorts to afford top-line entertainers. Many resorts and businesses were clearly slow to react to changes in demand, in contrast to the responsiveness of the 1920s; but New Brighton, for example, was still flourishing on the older model right through the 1950s, and it was only in the following decade that problems began to spread and criticisms to mount.[43]

Even in the mid-1960s, however, observers often found more to praise than to decry about the British seaside. Offering an 'independent report on holiday resorts in Britain and the Continent' in 1964, which (for example) did not mention Mallorca, S.B. Hough extolled the 'seemliness and general high standard of appearance and amenities of these [south-eastern] British resorts . . . They are distinctly better in these respects than those across the Channel from them. The British resorts are bigger and better organised, with better buildings, roads, gardens and sea-fronts.' He had special praise for resorts like Hastings and Bournemouth which offered 'quality' to the substantial middle classes (singling out Hastings' 'elaborate arrangements for bowls' and Bournemouth's symphony orchestra), and picked out Ilfracombe for 'an unusual number of concert parties and theatre attractions for a place of this size', illustrating the persistence and desirability of traditional entertainments. On the other hand, 'Whitby would be entirely charming if there were less of a tendency to a fish-and-chip and cheap-snack-bar and amusement-arcade atmosphere', and if more of its cafes served afternoon rather than high tea, although it did have 'better hotels on the west cliff, and a Chinese restaurant', still a novelty in the provinces. These class-bound perceptions did not shut out Blackpool, however, where 'the social atmosphere, as well as the sea air, is forceful and invigorating', and the fifteen live shows were 'as many as most capital cities'. Barry Island, the playground of the South Wales working class, was recommended to 'the visitor from southern England, looking for something "different", who could immers[e] himself in its atmosphere', take a trip to Cardiff's Tiger Bay, and find the experience 'quite as foreign as many places across the Channel'. South-west Scotland was a little too foreign, however, as resorts like Ayr 'may appear a little hard and grim to English eyes'. This idiosyncratic southern middle-class perspective has the merit of bringing out the flourishing aspect of British seaside attractions and entertainments in the mid-1960s, and the survival of traditional attributes, at the dawn of the great changes which were to follow.[44]

Disinvestment in distinctive seaside entertainment buildings whose architecture and programmes had lost their appeal to a rising generation was a feature of the 1950s onwards in many resorts. Victorian attractions were becoming vulnerable: Blackpool lost the turn-of-the-century Palace, originally the Alhambra, which had been built to rival the Tower, only to be swallowed up by it and then replaced in the early 1960s by a department store whose architecture owed nothing to seaside conceits. The Grand Theatre, a Frank Matcham masterpiece of 1894, also came under threat, only to be saved by its admirers after a fierce and sustained campaign against owners who saw more money in destruction. At least the three piers survived, providing fairgrounds, shows and slot-machines and continuing to complement each other, although there were many casualties elsewhere among these most evocative reminders of Victorian and Edwardian leisure preferences.[45]

Piers proved terribly vulnerable to storm, fire and maritime collision, as well as to the consequences of neglect by proprietors who had come to find their upkeep an expensive liability. Of the eighty-five piers to have been built around the coasts of England and Wales, sixty-five of which existed at the system's peak in 1900, just fifty-three remained in 1976. Nine were Victorian casualties, some of them being replaced after suffering serious damage. Three more went in the Edwardian years from storm and collision damage, and three more between the wars, among which Ramsgate remained unrepaired after a First World War mine exploded against it. But a pattern of closure and demolition really began in the 1950s, when piers were beginning to feel their age, and all things Victorian were still deeply unfashionable. Minehead was a direct wartime casualty in 1940, and others never recovered from being breached during the war to prevent use by invading armies, or from other war damage, or from wartime neglect of already elderly structures. There were nine demolitions between 1950 and 1961, of which only Deal was replaced. They were all at small or marginal resorts, with the exceptions of St Leonards, which had been the object of such extensive investment in the 1930s, and Lytham; but by the mid-1970s decay was spreading into the heart of the system, as Rhyl lost its pier and Hunstanton, Shanklin and Bangor were closed to the public, while Clevedon and the West Pier at Brighton were the storm-centres of conservation controversies which are still running (and worthy of a book in themselves), and several other piers were partly closed or had lost key buildings to fire. Subsequent losses included both the piers at Morecambe, which were not seen to be at risk in the 1976 survey. In some places, on the other hand, there was renewed investment in piers and their amusements, although critics complained that this often detracted from their Victorian character and assimilated them to broader, duller patterns of leisure building. Simon Adamson's survey highlighted the piers at Clacton and Walton-on-the-Naze, where full-scale fairgrounds and aquaria were introduced; Southend, where the local authority made a brave investment decision to restore the structure in the mid-1970s; and Bournemouth, with the more traditional attractions of promenading, angling, a cafe and a summer variety programme. Hastings' Triodome of 1966 perpetuated a frivolous Art Deco seaside spirit very effectively. Cromer even kept its end-of-the-pier concert party, which was playing to very small audiences when it won the grudging respect of Paul Theroux in 1982, but survived to the end of the century after all the other examples of a once-universal seaside *genre* had disappeared during the 1960s and 1970s. Like the archaic transport systems (electric trams at Blackpool, horse trams at Douglas, cliff lifts, steam railways, landaus) which survive and flourish in seaside settings (unless, like the Mumbles Railway, they were closed just before their value as survivors became apparent), the Cromer concert party has acquired cult status, feeding on nostalgia and near-extinction, to pull in block bookings from elderly day-trippers from urban East Anglia. But the standard (and widespread) post-war pier fare involved an obsession with the profit to be made from amusement arcades with slot-machines, along with provision for the bingo craze of the 1960s; and new pier architecture tended to be box-like and utilitarian, in dismaying contrast to the filigree and fantastical of the Victorians, while concrete often replaced or encased the characteristic wrought-iron work. The successful investment stories show that piers were not entirely passé, however. In a few places, 'The old railway-type refreshment rooms and drab paintwork and bare floors gave way to well-equipped restaurants carpeted throughout; night clubs and lounge bars with cabaret replaced the old theatres and music halls and well-equipped shops superseded the kiosks.' In many more there were new arcades, fairground rides, and even bowling alleys. Such adaptability became more controversial, but also more viable, as the piers began to benefit from the nostalgia and heritage boom of the 1980s; but the future of many remains uncertain.[46]

Victorian seaside pleasure buildings more generally fell out of favour from the 1950s and especially the 1960s onwards, even when less vulnerable to age and the elements than the piers. One of the most spectacular, New Brighton's turn-of-the-century Tower, which outstripped Blackpool's by over a hundred feet in the height stakes and dominated the Mersey approaches, succumbed to lack of wartime maintenance and was demolished as early as 1919, although the pleasure gardens which surrounded it were much longer-lived.[47] Some, like Scarborough's Aquarium, were already moribund by the early 1920s. This underground Moorish palace, with its swimming bath, concert hall, circus, shooting galleries and artificial caves, had enjoyed a brief heyday in the late 1880s but struggled thereafter, to be wound up in 1914, bought by the Corporation in 1921 and sustained precariously through the inter-war years, 'leased to the proprietors of every kind of side show'. The planning team who reported on Scarborough in 1938 saw it as an eyesore and a health hazard, and only the war and its austere aftermath delayed its demolition and replacement by a car park.[48] As money became more available for redevelopment in the 1960s, Blackpool's Palace, on its prime site next to the Tower, became one of many live entertainment centres to give way to shopping or (along with the cinemas) to bingo, which itself became an emblem of the popular seaside; and Whitby was unusual in keeping its Pavilion of 1878 and adding a new extension. The overwhelming trend was for the landscapes of leisure to lose their Victorian landmarks as times and tastes changed.

Some Victorian entertainment complexes in the larger resorts, like Blackpool's piers, Tower and Winter Gardens, were capable of adaptation or reinvention to cope with new fashions and preferences. The Tower Ballroom was gutted by fire in 1956, and its decor was restored in all its turn-of-the-century splendour, with lasting success; but this was exceptional on both counts, and had the fire come a few years later a complete transformation in the tastes of the 1960s would probably have resulted. More representative in outline was the saga of the Aquarium at Brighton, like Scarborough's a product of the vogue for such 'rational recreations' in the 1870s. It also had to be rescued by the Corporation early in the new century, with a municipal orchestra in residence from 1908 to 1918; and between 1929 and 1931 it was rebuilt at a cost of £117,000, with a completely new facade on its prominent promenade position, and the old winter garden turned into a concert hall. There was also an impressively large new ballroom. After wartime neglect, lessees allowed the Victorian splendour to decay and tampered with the decor; but, implausibly, new life was brought to the structure by adapting its original use, as dolphins were introduced and placed in new tanks in what had been the ballroom, and the Aquarium became a successful dolphinarium during the 1970s. Emulators elsewhere included Morecambe, and more recent sea-life centres have brought an updated aquarium concept back to the mainstream of distinctive seaside attractions.[49]

The casualties were not only Victorian. The outdoor swimming-pools of the Edwardian and inter-war years, the Art Deco swimming-baths and lidos, the rockeries, walks, shelters and sunny cafe terraces which were so characteristic of the 1920s and 1930s, all came under attack or crumbled into neglect, along with the cinemas, pavilions and Floral Halls. Blackpool's losses included the South Shore open-air swimming-pool of 1923, replaced by the Sandcastle complex whose only distinctively seaside attribute was its name, at a time when every town of any size was acquiring its 'leisure pool', and the indoor Derby Baths of 1938. Julie Burchill, celebrating the renaissance of Saltdean Lido, comments on its lost counterparts elsewhere, in words which might also be applied to conventional open-air pools: 'many seaside towns have a sad, rectangular crater on the seafront, like an open grave where pleasure has been buried'.[50] This was part of a wider story of changes in popular culture, preferences and provision, which is summed up by Tim Gale for the period 1974–88 as 'bringing the seaside inside', but began a decade and more earlier as private enterprise and local authorities alike lost confidence in traditional products and began casting around for alternatives.[51] The problem was to find them, in any recognisably seaside idiom; and most of the zoos, night-clubs, shopping malls, slot-machine parlours and improved fairground rides of the late twentieth century could have been anywhere, and just happened to be on the coast because there were established markets which could be sustained and rebuilt.

By this time many resorts were beginning to renew their popular entertainment facilities to match changing visitor expectations, in an attempt to break out of what had seemed to be an inexorable spiral of decline. Rhyl, which still had 1.7 million staying visitors in 1993 (and 2.5 million day-trippers) according to a County Council survey, was particularly effective at tapping into European regional development grants, beginning with the Sun Centre in 1979. This was a pioneering example of what was to become a common genre, the indoor leisure centre with 'a soft-edged leisure pool in a pseudo-tropical environment'; and after a short hiatus it was followed by the Skytower in 1988, and then in the early 1990s a Sealife Centre, Children's Village and Events Arena, while the New Pavilion Theatre was added to the Sun Centre. Tim Gale comments that, 'this saw Rhyl attempt something that few other resorts have dared to try, that is to reinvent an otherwise static and partially-obsolete product'. But it left the local authority deeply in debt at the turn of the century, and 'several projects were left unfinished as funds dried up, and the private sector has been slow to respond to this pump-priming'. Indeed, First Leisure pulled out of the resort in 1997 after vandalism damaged its Superbowl and Ocean Beach Funfair. The outcome of this brave experiment in 'enterprise planning' remains uncertain.[52]

Elsewhere in the 'post-industrial' north-west there were further stirrings. Southport was re-emerging as a popular resort, with new private investment in its Pleasureland amusement park in 1999 featuring the Traumatizer, 'the "tallest and fastest" suspended looping coaster in Britain', and the Skycoaster, 'horizontal bungee jumping, albeit slightly more restrained . . . not for the faint hearted'. This was a remarkable development in a resort whose dominant image had become staid, up-market and residential.[53] In 1997, the English Tourist Board statistics for the most popular attractions not charging admission put the region's three big seaside amusement parks in first, third and fourth places, with Blackpool's Pleasure Beach drawing in an estimated 7.8 million visitors, Southport's Pleasureland 2.1 million and Morecambe's Frontierland 1.3 million, ahead of Blackpool Tower, which headed the north-west's paying attractions with 1.2 million visitors, while Blackpool's Louis Tussaud's waxworks came sixth with 400,000. This suggested considerable resilience in the popularity of pleasures at the seaside (if not necessarily generic seaside pleasures) in a region of traditional strength. Specifically seaside locations fared less well in other parts of the country, however. The Lynton and Lynmouth Cliff Railway headed the list in the south-west, where it came third in the regional table with 528,198 paying customers, followed closely by Flambards Theme Park at Helston and (in ninth place) by Paignton Zoo. This was a long way behind the big north-western figures, suggesting a more scattered holidaymaking public with diverse tastes. The same applied in the south-east, where Brighton Pavilion's 393,059 customers put it in sixth place, while the Paradise Family Leisure Park at unglamorous Newhaven came ninth with just over 300,000 punters. Southend Pier's 350,000 visitors, which put it in fifth place in the east of England table, was similar; and here Butlin's Funcoast World at Skegness was down in sixteenth place, with only 135,000 admissions. Outside the north-west, commercial seaside entertainment rarely made a strong showing in terms of visitor numbers; and some of the most popular venues were theme parks whose location was only incidentally maritime. The resilient drawing-power of north-western seaside attractions was not being replicated in the rest of the country.[54]

The enormous end-of-the-century success of Blackpool and Brighton in providing exciting and exotic venues for clubbers (including gays: 'as camp as Blackpool Illuminations' was passing into the language in 1999) likewise found little resonance across the British seaside at large; and the fashion for eating out, with the invention of the celebrity chef and the pursuit of innovatory tastes and textures, also failed to strike sparks in most resorts. Fish and chips remained the quintessential seaside meal, as it had been for a century, at the popular end of the market; and a quest for evidence of the 'food revolution' on the coast in 1997 concluded that 'for every adventurous restaurant' (as in isolated examples at Padstow in Cornwall, St Leonard's and Aldeburgh) 'there are a thousand low-budget seaside cafes with menus unchanged since the Fifties', and fierce resistance to anything new or fancy from what restaurateurs regarded as a deeply conservative public. 'Of 117 restaurants with a star rating in [Egon] Ronay's 1997 guide, only a handful are by the sea.' Problems of seasonality, together with limited supply of or demand for local fish in most places, helped to explain this further evidence of the seaside's failure to march with new (if up-market) trends, and the evidence on eating out as entertainment rather than refuelling runs with the grain of the other problems of sustaining or creating seaside distinctiveness.[55]

The current state of seaside pleasures at the end of the millennium is summed up by the late summer Bank Holiday weekend of 1999 at Whitby. Here, the west beach was quite well-populated, with every kind of traditional activity on offer: sandcastles, children buried in the sand to be photographed by adoring parents, donkeys, cricket, chasing with crabs and seaweed, and picnic sandwiches with added sand. Looking across the harbour, an endless pilgrimage up and down the steps to the Abbey was visible, an indicator of the continuing lure of historic buildings and heritage tourism, although the parish church displayed a handwritten sign explaining that Dracula was not actually buried in the graveyard. But the great crush of visitors was in the narrow streets on either side of the harbour, and the preferred recreation, overwhelmingly, was shopping. The seaside resort as shopping mall was perhaps its dominant identity at the end of consumerism's century, and Clacton, with its Clacton

Common themed shopping experience, or Fleetwood with its Freeport, were among the resorts which tried to capitalise on this. For most people, most of the time, the sea was incidental.[56]

Nevertheless, very simple and uncommodified pleasures play an important part in the hold the sea still has on British consciousness. Paul Theroux noticed a strange phenomenon early on his tour of the coastline in 1982:[57]

> wherever a road came near the seaside: cars parked and piled up, and people in them, always very old people . . . They sat in their cars and stared out at the sea. They were on every beach road . . . I saw them everywhere, eating sandwiches, drinking tea out of plastic cups, reading the paper, looking fuddled. They always faced the water. They were old couples mostly, but they never seemed to be holding conversations . . . they did not seem to be looking at anything in particular. Their expressions were a little sad and empty, as if they were expecting to see something beyond the horizon or under the surface of the waves.

He commented that, 'It looked sombre enough to be an English recreation'; but he wondered about the more cosmic significance of going out to gaze into the void from the precarious shelter of a little parked car; or indeed, perhaps, a promenade shelter. The English in their old age like to gaze upon the sea: a new generation has been recruited since Theroux's tour. It is sublime, calm and tempestuous by turns, rhythmic, in tune with a timetable but not subordinate to it, linked with old dreams of Empire, national destiny and naval prowess, and perhaps also of freedom and escape, but also with advancing thoughts of eternity. The sea as solace, if only through the magic of its apparently ignored proximity, is not the least of its attractions; but for most people its enjoyment depends on access and amenity, however basic, provided by human hands. This even applies to the habitues of coastal paths who find more strenuous and direct forms of communing. And it is here, among other places, that the apparently banal role of local government, as provider, facilitator and regulator, becomes central to the story, as we move on to focus on seaside environments.

Notes

1 R. Fischer and J.K. Walton, *British piers* (London, 1987).

2 M. Chapman and B. Chapman, *The pierrots of the Yorkshire coast* (Beverley, 1988), has a good range of illustrations.

3 Reynolds, *A poor man's house* (1908; London, 1980).

4 Seed's *Southport and district directory* (Preston, 1914), p. xv.

5 Chapman and Chapman, *The pierrots of the Yorkshire coast*, p. 13. For camels, Blackpool Public Library, photographic collection, ref. 1207.

6 J. Travis, 'Continuity and change in English sea-bathing, 1730–1900', in Fisher (ed.), *Recreation and the sea*, Chapter 2.

7 Reynolds, *A poor man's house*.

8 Pearson, *People's palaces*; Walton, *The English seaside resort*, Chapter 7.

9 Shields, *Places on the margin*.

10 Walton, *The English seaside resort*, Chapter 8. For Frinton, which had a frivolous younger set who played practical jokes and enjoyed noisy parties in the inter-war years, Laura Chase, 'The creation of place image in inter-war Clacton and Frinton', Ph.D. thesis, University of Essex, 1999.

11 Scarborough Public Library, Scarborough Pamphlets No. 363, Harry W. Smith, *Catering for the wants of the holiday maker* (1915); R. Roberts, 'The corporation as impresario', in Walton and Walvin (eds) *Leisure in Britain*; Morgan, 'Perceptions, patterns and policies of tourism'.

12 James Kirkup, *A child of the Tyne* (Salzburg, 1996), pp. 103–9.

13 Public Record Office (PRO) HO45/22142, HO45/20127.

14 Chase, 'The creation of place image in interwar Clacton and Frinton', pp. 152–7; C.W. Saleeby, *Sunlight and health* (London, 1923), pp. xi, 140; Stafford and Yates, *The later Kentish seaside*, pp. 115–16; cf. Corbin, *The lure of the sea*.

15 Julie Burchill, 'Off at the deep end', *Guardian, Weekend*, 8 May 1999, p. 3.

16 Walton, *Blackpool*; Stafford and Yates, *The later Kentish seaside*, pp. 116–17.

17 Scarborough Public Library, 'Newspaper cuttings, Scarborough and District', Vol. 2, p. 77, undated but labelled 1926.

18 Robert H. Goodsall, *On holiday with a camera: at the seaside, in the country* (London, 1939), pp. 26–9.

19 J. Urry and C. Rojek, *Touring cultures* (London, 1997).

20 Ward Lock and Co., *Worthing* (London, 1912), Worthing section, p. 26; Southport Corporation, *Sunny Southport: official guide 1929–1930* (Southport, 1929), p. 25; Liddle, 'Estate management and land reform politics', p. 156; D.S. Young, *The story of Bournemouth* (London, 1957), pp. 136–8.

21 *Blackpool: Official Guide* (Blackpool, 1938), unpaginated; Walton, *Blackpool*, Chapter 5.

22 *Golfing in Scotland at 100 holiday resorts* (2nd edn, Cheltenham: J. Burrow, n.d., *c.* 1930 (Anon)).

23 P.G. Wodehouse, *The heart of a goof* (London, 1926), p. 20.

24 A. Durie and M. Huggins, 'Sport, social tone and the seaside resorts of Great Britain, 1850–1914', *International Journal of the History of Sport*, 15 (1998), pp. 173–87.

25 Simon H. Adamson, *Seaside piers* (London, 1977), pp. 74, 104; Fischer and Walton, *British piers*, p. 20.

26 Clunn, *Famous south coast pleasure resorts*, p. 46.

27 Fischer and Walton, *British piers*, p. 28.

28 Ibid., pp. 26, 53, 64, 96; Chase, 'The creation of place image in inter-war Clacton and Frinton', pp. 186–200.

29 Musgrave, *Life in Brighton*, p. 377; G. Young, *A history of Bognor Regis*, (Chichester, 1983) pp. 231–2.

30 G.J. Mellor, *Pom-poms and ruffles* (Clapham, 1966), p. 25.

31 Ibid.; Chapman and Chapman, *The pierrots of the Yorkshire coast.*

32 Chapman and Chapman, *The pierrots of the Yorkshire coast*, pp. 13–30, 82–99; Mellor, *Pom-poms and ruffles*, p. 29.

33 Chapman and Chapman, *The pierrots of the Yorkshire coast*, pp. 51, 57.

34 Cross, *Worktowners at Blackpool*, pp. 128, 135.

35 Ibid., Chapter 16.

36 Stafford and Yates, *The later Kentish seaside*, pp. 149–51; Walton, *Blackpool*, pp. 125–8; P. Bennett, *A century of fun* (Blackpool, 1996).

37 Edwin Corrigan, *Ups and downs and roundabouts* (Driffield, 1972), pp. 102–3.

38 Cross, *Worktowners at Blackpool*, Chapters 9, 12, 18; PRO HO45/16275/655652, notes on Blackpool Improvement Bill of 1935.

39 Walton, *Blackpool*, pp. 108–9, 129, 139; Cross, *Worktowners at Blackpool*, Chapter 20.

40 Cross, *Worktowners at Blackpool*, pp. 145–9.

41 *The official guide to Deal and Walmer* (Deal, 1949), pp. 10–11.

42 Clunn, *Famous south coast pleasure resorts*, p. 110.

43 Demetriadi, 'The golden years'.

44 Hough, *Where?*, pp. 12–13, 17, 26–7, 46, 51, 61, 66, 79–80.

45 Walton, *Blackpool*, Chapter 6.

46 Adamson, *Seaside piers*, pp. 87–115; Fischer and Walton, *British piers*, pp. 40–5 (photographs of the decayed West Pier at Brighton), 48 (the Triodome), 90–91 (Clevedon); Theroux, *The kingdom by the sea*; Nick Jones, 'Alive and kicking', *Guardian, Travel*, 7 August 1999, pp. 6–7.

47 Maurice G. Hope, *Castles in the sand: the story of New Brighton* (Ormskirk, 1982), pp. 25–8.

48 S.D. Adshead and H.V. Overfield, *The future development of Scarborough* (Scarborough, 1938), pp. 38–40.

49 Musgrave, *Life in Brighton*, pp. 292–5, 383–5.

50 Burchill, 'Off at the deep end', p. 3.

51 T. Gale, D. Botterill, M. Morgan and G. Shaw, 'Reconstructing the past: an analysis of landscape, brochures and local authority involvement in the seaside resort of Rhyl, 1945–97', *Concord*, 8 (1998), p. 33.

52 Ibid., pp. 29, 33.

53 *Lancashire Evening Post*, 7 May 1999, p. 9.

54 English Tourist Board website, 'Tourism professionals', tourism statistics for 1997.

55 Roger Tredre, 'Oh I don't like to eat beside the seaside', *Observer*, 15 June 1997, p. 16.

56 Chase, 'The creation of place image in interwar Clacton and Frinton', pp. 271–4; personal observation.

57 Theroux, *The kingdom by the sea*, p. 47.

5

Seaside environments

S easide resorts grew up as places which traded in access to and enjoyment of a particular kind of desirable environment, exploiting the perceived
health-giving properties and scenic beauties of sea, beach and coastline. Their
governors have therefore had a vested interest in protecting the amenities
which are their stock in trade, while taking account of the changing tastes and
expectations of their actual and preferred customers, whether holidaymakers
or (increasingly) more-or-less leisured residents. A particular concern has
been to manage environments and police boundaries so as to reconcile the
needs and aspirations of different visiting publics and of local interests, with
varying and changing degrees of power to shape and challenge the uses
made of desirable spaces and the images attached to them.[1] These problems
have been negotiated with varying degrees of success; and this chapter looks
at seaside environments in the twentieth century, assessing the ways in
which resorts have coped with reconciling growth in urban area and visitor
numbers (or in some cases stagnation and lack of resources), and changes
in image and visiting public, with their aspirations to providing a healthy,
attractive and competitive setting for the pursuit of recuperation, relaxation
and fun.

We begin with the meeting-point between the sea and the shoreline, whose
re-evaluation during the eighteenth century as a health-giving, romantically
alluring and aesthetically pleasing location was the foundation for the whole
great industry and complex of cultural practices that constitute seaside tourism.[2]
Bound up in this in England was an equation between the sea, patriotism and
national identity, or so the paintings of J.M.W. Turner and William Lisle Bowles
at the turn of the eighteenth and nineteenth centuries have been interpreted.[3]
But here we encounter the apparent paradox that the sea itself, for all its perceived
sacredness and mystique, has been allowed to become polluted and defiled by

matter out of place – by excrementitious matter, as the Victorians would have said, but also by industrial waste and the casual detritus of those who come to enjoy and leave their traces behind – to such an extent that on many stretches of British (and especially English) coastline the ascribed characteristics which made it so culturally desirable in the origins of seaside tourism have now become subverted and parodied.[4] Growing awareness of the state of the sea, a transformation brought about in part by the sheer numbers of its own votaries, has played a significant part in the decline of the British seaside in the late twentieth century.[5] And the state of the sea has had its own repercussions on the shoreline, where attempts at management and control have been extensive and sustained, but generically unable to resolve the contradiction between the containment of the sea, the protection of maritime property, and the sustaining of a clean, tidy, but 'natural' environment. The paradoxes at work are telling and require exploration.

Seaside resorts at the turn of the century, and long afterwards, continued to place the healthiness of their maritime setting (sea water and sea air) at the core of their allure, as part of a broader catalogue of climatic and health statistics, evidence on water supply and quality of subsoil, and efficiency of drainage systems. But the obsessive interest in sewage disposal did not extend to treatment, and this had consequences which were not discussed in the promotional material, and did not pose similar problems for the climatic and upland scenic resorts and the suburbs of large towns which were promoting their residential desirability according to a similar agenda.[6] What it meant, as a burgeoning scientific literature was already aware at the turn of the century, was that the resorts' sewage was being dispatched into the sea with ever-growing efficiency; and, of course, its volume was greatest in the summer months at the height of the holiday season.

W.J. Dibdin's treatise on sewage and water purification set out the current state of informed knowledge in 1903. He lamented that:[7]

> One of the favourite methods of disposing of sewage . . . is its discharge into sea-water, on the assumption that the enormous dilution effected would speedily bring about its disintegration and destruction . . . the universally considered panacea for the sewage difficulty at seaside towns was to run an outfall sewer as far as convenient out into the sea and to discharge the sewage at such time of the tide as was thought would effectually carry it away . . . [but] in some cases the flow of the tide has brought the sewage back to the point of departure, and in some cases right into the stretch of water used for bathing, so that visitors have had to postpone their 'dip' until the unsightly flood has drifted further on.

Dibdin went on to quote at length from the work of Arthur Newsholme, Brighton's Medical Officer of Health, who blamed the resort's remaining enteric fever cases on shellfish from beds contaminated by sewage; and he concluded that the discharge of crude sewage should be prohibited near shellfish beds and also 'within a considerable distance of any seaside resort. Two or three miles away is entirely insufficient, as the tidal flow will soon travel this distance, with, to say the least, a by no means pleasant result to those who look for pure-water bathing.' He argued that, in the light of recent developments in sewage purification technology, there was no excuse for contaminating food supplies and bathing water, and warned that, 'It will soon become recognised that certain seaside resorts do not employ proper and effective methods for purifying their sewage, and the resulting loss to the town by the abstention of visitors will far more than make up for the slight saving on the rates'.[8] This warning was to go largely unheeded, and its predicted consequences did not come to pass for many years.

This might be thought surprising. *Punch* had been alert to the problem of bathing-water pollution for many years, and the evidence presented to the Royal Commission on Sewage Disposal at the turn of the century provided scarifying examples of what might be thought to be obvious, tangible contamination of bathing beaches. The Commission identified several current problems, including 'washing up of faecal matter on the shore', 'formation of sludge banks', and 'objectionable contamination of bathing places'. The coasts of Kent and Essex were particularly polluted: in some places it was not unusual to find 'smellable' 'black slimy deposit' along the shoreline, although a witness felt that this did not worry working-class bathers: 'with eighteenpenny fares they would go anywhere, no matter what the state of the place was'. That this was over-simplified is indicated by the growing concern to extend outfall pipes out to sea, which posed additional problems for hard-pressed oyster and other fisheries without doing more than palliating the bathing-water problem. So long as this stopped short of generating an epidemic, and so long as visitors kept coming and believed the environment to be healthy, palliatives continued to suffice. The Local Government Board, which was tightening its control over these issues in the early twentieth century, put the cheap disposal of urban sewage ahead of environmental considerations involving fisheries and bathing water, and outfall extensions continued to be preferred to expensive treatment plants. The power of the assiduously propagated popular myths about the health-giving and purificatory powers of the sea is well illustrated in a Blackpool promotional publication of 1950, when worries about the possible consequences of continuing to increase the coastal discharge of untreated sewage had been widespread in municipal circles for over a decade: 'Blackpool sea water is specially beneficial to health. Sufferers from all kinds of ailments acknowledge this . . . Sea bathing improves the complexion. Be sure to have a salt water bath or swim each day you are on holiday.' The popular perceptions to which this pamphlet appealed were to prove difficult to dislodge, and in the post-war years they were still being reinforced by government scientists. As complaints about disgustingly polluted bathing water mounted and were publicised during the summers of the 1950s, and possible links with the current poliomyelitis epidemic were canvassed, the Public Health Laboratory Service took six years to produce a complacent report which demanded 'smoking gun' standards of proof that coastal sewage damaged health, and, on its publication in 1959, buried the issue in government circles until the early 1970s. This came as a relief to local authorities who did not want to incur the costs of treating their sewage, failing to follow the successful example of Bournemouth around 1960. It also made life difficult for the Coastal Anti-Pollution League, founded in 1957 by a couple who had lost their daughter to polio after she had swum in contaminated waters. It was obliged to highlight good beaches rather than attack foul ones, but from 1960 onwards its annual Golden Beaches list attracted extensive publicity. But it took the raised profile of environmentalism in the 1970s, and the EC's bathing water directive of 1976, to even begin to make a difference to ingrained and self-interested attitudes in local and national government.[9]

Meanwhile, even as resorts neglected to purify their sewage, they were busily engaged in managing their beaches and foreshores, erecting sea defences, extending and embellishing promenades and imposing official (and sometimes officious) standards of approved tidiness on fishermen and stallholders. This was already a very well-established set of themes by the beginning of the century, when an extensive literature had developed on the most effective ways of constructing sea-walls while minimising damage to the beach below them, and the best deployment of groynes to gather shingle and raise the level of the beach. Failure to allow for the set of wind, tide and currents could be very costly, and the struggle to preserve beaches, keep the sea at bay and prevent erosion was demanding and of uncertain outcome. The comfort and security of promenades and promenaders, as well as the owners of sea-front property (which at Hastings, for example, was liable to be damaged by shingle propelled at windows by fierce high tides), depended on successful solutions to these problems.[10] Even at the end of the century, the installation of groynes could have unintended consequences for the quality of the beach itself, as Minehead found

to its cost when its sand was washed away in 1998–99.[11] Moreover, the struggle to protect coastal property against ferocious erosion was sometimes a losing battle, especially on the east coast, as continuing slippage into the sea and
collapses of unstable cliffs regularly indicated. The property in question in the
1990s ranged from the prestigious Holbeck Hall Hotel at Scarborough, in a
dramatic and well-publicised incident in 1993, to unpretentious bungalows
near Winchelsea and Rye. Not all shorelines with vulnerable buildings could
be safeguarded at acceptable levels of expenditure, and incomplete sea defences
merely transferred the worst of the problem. The impossibility of winning
the 'battle of land and sea' on all fronts was becoming increasingly apparent
as the century waned, and global warming brought the prospect of renewed
flooding to match the North Sea inundation of 1953, when a storm surge
overwhelmed sea defences from Lincolnshire to Kent, killing more than 119
people in Essex alone and making more than 21,000 homeless in that county.
The worst carnage was at places below sea level with informal bungalow
settlement, as at Canvey Island, Jaywick and at the back of the sand dunes
between Hunstanton and King's Lynn in Norfolk, demonstrating that some
kinds of seaside settlement were a disaster waiting to happen. Swift rebuilding
and enhancement of sea defences followed in the mid-1950s, with financial
support from central government, but rising sea levels meant that dangers were
postponed and palliated rather than prevented.[12]

Rights of access to the shore might raise complex issues in themselves. As
Humphrey Baker put it in 1931:[13]

> Access to the seashore and the land immediately adjoining it is greatly prized by
> the people of these islands . . . There is . . . a conflict of interest, which unfortun-
> ately tends to become more acute, between people who wish to take the shortest
> cut everywhere to the shore and who regard the cliff path as morally . . . a public
> right of way, and the owners of seaside properties who like their premises to have
> direct access to the bathing beach and a monopoly of a section of the cliff.

This was an enduring set of issues. Local authorities had sought to preserve
access as well as to regulate behaviour on the foreshore in Victorian times, although
sometimes they had privatised stretches of sea-front and imposed tolls on promenades in the interests of selectness and decorum.[14] Access to the beach below
high water mark was guaranteed by convention rather than by law for all except
those who went expressly to fish, although, as Baker remarked, it was 'unusual,
though not unknown, for attempts to be made to interfere with the public use
of the beach itself'. Such attempts were known to be productive of controversy
and opprobrium, which helped to discourage them. The land behind the beach

was more vulnerable, though much of it could be defended against privatisation as common or waste; but the law here was a minefield, and it was very difficult to prove the dedication of access by public footpath unless a landowner had expressly granted it. Purchase by or for the National Trust provided the best security for public access, but overall it was remarkable how little the technical rights of private property were exploited to keep the general public away from coastal access. It happened, but it was unusual and controversial; and the reputation for power and embarrassment potential of public opinion must have played an important part in keeping British coastlines much more public than those in parts of (especially) Mediterranean Europe.[15]

These open and accessible shorelines had to be ordered morally, however, if the excitements of liminality were not to get out of hand, with the exuberance of some threatening the more sedate pleasures of others. Questions of control and responsibility on resort beaches had largely been resolved in favour of local authorities by the turn of the century, and we saw in Chapter 4 how bathing continued to be policed (against a backdrop of changing expectations about appropriate dress and behaviour) and other activities regulated. Stalls, donkeys, boats, Punch and Judy and other alfresco entertainments all came under the rule of by-laws (subject to parliamentary approval) and the gaze of the foreshore inspector, while tensions were reduced by the way in which most beaches had already acquired recognisable characteristics by the early twentieth century, so that those whose sensibilities might be outraged always had alternative destinations.[16]

Physical attempts to reshape the maritime environment through ambitious, extensive and fallible technologies, which extended to controversial estuarine barrage schemes at the end of the twentieth century, were accompanied by extensions to and widenings of that classic Victorian seaside institution, the promenade, which sought to subjugate nature by imposing straight lines or planned smooth curves and level surfaces on nature's irregularities in the interests of an aesthetic of balance and control, and to further the physical comfort of strollers and, increasingly, ease of passage for vehicles. There was no shortage of Edwardian investment of this kind, as the examples of Bournemouth's controversial Undercliff Drive and Blackpool's enormous widening and extension schemes (each of which also embraced vital investment in sea defences) illustrated at the top end of the resort league.[17] The high priority given to open-air amenities on the sea-front in the inter-war years ensured that expenditure on promenades would continue to feature strongly in local authority budgets. The three biggest spenders per head on highways (which included promenades and sea defences) among the large towns (defined here as county boroughs) between 1919 and 1939 were Blackpool, Brighton and Hastings. The figures for parks and open spaces, which were often associated with promenade planning schemes, were more dramatic: seaside resorts took eight of the top eleven places, with between eight and a half times (in Blackpool's case) and twice the national average. The three remaining places were occupied by Wallasey, which included New Brighton, and West Hartlepool and South Shields, which included resort areas within their boundaries.[18] The consequences of these interventions were not always welcomed. A New Brighton resident, looking back to the late nineteenth century before the local authority's promenade extensions imposed their 'geometrical shape' and 'the rough sandstone edges and straying sands were consumed by sea walls and esplanades', culminating in the 'protective mass of King's Parade' which 'suffocated the Noses' (a distinctive and attractive geological feature), expressed a sense of loss:[19]

> I just feel a bit sad, as I really do think the natural beauty of the town has been spoiled. All very well these Proms, bathing pools, boating lakes etc., but one can see these at any seaside place now . . . My mind goes back to the beauty of the plantation . . . the Red Noses, where one could go ever so far into the caves . . . Then when they started on the Promenade from New Brighton to Egremont, that was tearing another treasured part away. And so it has gone on and on, one beauty spot after another crushed and destroyed for ever. And what do we get in return? High rents and rates.

This is, perhaps, not mere nostalgia. A standard style of seaside planning did develop in the inter-war years, as municipal engineers (and their consultants, such as the ubiquitous T.H. Mawson and Thomas Adams, who were particularly powerful where, as at Clacton, no planning staff were employed locally) worked within recognisable idioms, though this did not prevent a measure of individuality. The concern to protect shorelines, ease access and promenading, and (relatedly, as in the purchase and demolition of New Brighton's own notorious 'Ham and Egg Parade' for sanitised promenade improvements) excise those elements of the raffish which might compromise morality, did tend to reduce distinctiveness and excitement as well as vulnerability, discomfort and danger. Thus was a distinctive version of the 'civilising process' imposed on resort shorelines, assiduously and at great expense, during the inter-war years.[20]

The inter-war years also brought new architectural styles to the seaside. The exotic eclecticism of the late Victorians and Edwardians, which had produced a distinctive pleasure architecture, helping to define the seaside as a desirable and different location in which constraints were relaxed, gave way to a growing preference for the smooth lines and flowing curves of what might broadly be described as Art Deco, although some of it aspired to the higher pretensions of International Modern. This was above all a development of the 1930s, although it began in the 1920s, and it found expression more in scattered buildings than in whole developments, and in recreational rather than domestic architecture. Its most impressive and enduring manifestations were the De La Warr Pavilion at Bexhill, a particularly confident expression of faith in the adaptability of the seaside, Joseph Emberton's Pleasure Beach casino at Blackpool, and the Midland Hotel at Morecambe with its Eric Gill murals, while new buildings on pier superstructures also displayed it in playful form. Laura Chase argues that, 'To the limited extent that modern architecture found favour in inter-war England, it attained its greatest popularity at the seaside resort. Nautical references such as porthole windows, curved walls, sun decks and railings all entered the vocabulary of Modern architecture in the twenties and can be found in seaside resorts throughout England in domestic, hotel and entertainment architecture.' But the latter prevailed: the new seaside semi-detacheds and (especially) bungalows which housed most of the resort population expansion of this period rarely displayed significant differences from their inland coun-terparts, with mock Tudor prevailing over maritime motifs, although porthole windows were perhaps slightly commoner at the coast and panelling from super-annuated ocean liners gave a touch of distinction to the internal arrangements of some Blackpool houses which looked quite ordinary from outside. The Frinton Park Estate, a rare attempt to create a 200-acre housing development in an uncompromisingly Modern style, using fashionable architects, fell foul of planning restrictions on materials and wall thicknesses, and consumer resist-ance to the unconventional and dangerously 'continental' appearance of this architecture of 'hygiene and modernity'. The developers retreated hastily into more familiar and reassuring styles.[21]

The commercial holiday camps of the later 1930s paid a more down-market homage to modernity. Butlin's advertised the pioneer Skegness and Clacton camps as 'AN EDEN-ON-SEA and . . . almost an Earthly Paradise', offering cool white buildings, glass doors, tanned faces and informality, and emphasising that the chalets were designed like little houses. At Skegness they featured 'electric light, running water, comfortable beds with interior spring mattresses', adding up to 'a luxurious home of your own'. The L.M.S. Railway's Prestatyn holiday camp was even more confident in the smooth and soaring lines of its central tower and the geometrical arrangement of the sur-rounding lawns and chalets. Some complained that these were mere barracks for the mass holidaymakers of a regimented future, but others celebrated them as expressions of the new democratisation of holidaymaking which holidays with pay were supposed to usher in.[22]

At the other end of the scale were the exclusive eccentricities of wealthy developers who sought to create desirable enclaves where the rich and prominent could indulge in sports and games without compromising their exclusivity. These developments were anything but 'modernist' in the architectural sense, but they represented an alternative way of celebrating the seaside life of sunshine and the pursuit of happiness through healthy outdoor activities. Thorpeness, just north of Aldeburgh in Suffolk, was a particularly eccentric example. Here G. Stuart Ogilvie turned a tidal mere into a boating lake and created a holiday village of eclectically archaic architecture, which eschewed popular commercial amusements while providing a golf course and constituting a haven of exclusivity for county society and London professional families, winning the approval of John Betjeman and even the Council for the Preservation of Rural England in the process. This was a self-described bungalow development which rejected modernism and democracy while using concrete and other contemporary building materials, and set itself up as a model of landscape protection and good taste when set alongside the 'tin tabernacle' buildings which were colonising neighbouring areas of Suffolk sand-dunes. It predated and in a sense anticipated the landscape campaigner Clough Williams-Ellis's Italianate venture at Portmeirion near Ffestiniog on the Welsh coast in the inter-war years.[23]

These proponents of 'tasteful' seaside development for a fashionable clientele would have hated to see their fantasies equated with the 'bungalow towns', whose proliferation became a source of serious concern to planners. Their drive towards a standardised rationality was confounded by the systematic rule-breaking these settlements exhibited, especially when even grid-plans were off the agenda and dwellings using various makeshift materials (including asbestos and galvanised iron) were scattered apparently randomly in colourful but untidy gardens and overgrown plots. These were not incursions into areas of outstanding scenic beauty as conventionally defined, but the buildings and their settings were greatly valued by occupiers and users who shared neither the cultural expectations of planners nor the aesthetics of the articulate apostles of 'unspoiled' countryside. There were issues of public health and access to services, of course, as well as aesthetic ones, especially where sewering was non-existent and cesspools were beginning to poison the land and threaten water supplies. Complaints and resistance began to multiply during the inter-war years, as the official emergence of a planning profession whose consensus derived from the public health and Garden City movements was reinforced by the different but overlapping priorities of the defenders of 'unspoiled' countryside against development of any kind. But throughout the inter-war years the planners' aspirations outran their powers. The Town Planning Act of 1925 allowed rural districts (within whose boundaries most of the 'bungalow towns' were developing) to prepare formal planning schemes, with a remit which included preserving natural beauty; and it also promoted regional planning schemes which brought emergent problems to light on a broader canvas. The Acts of 1932 and 1935 added little that was relevant, especially in dealing with established settlements. Even where the emotive issues surrounding preservation of the English countryside were involved, they had to struggle with equally entrenched presumptions about the rights of property-owners; and although administrative practices increasingly made it difficult to develop new 'bungalow towns', the existing ones remained unscathed. When Canvey Island acquired its own urban district council in 1926 its only controls were directed at 'the worst properties, such as old railway carriages and bus bodies'. In 1932 Lindsey (Lincolnshire) County Council obtained its own Act of Parliament to stop the further extension of recreational huts and shacks along its coastal sand-dunes, and by the mid-1930s it was imposing standard colour-schemes on what was already there; but this was an exceptional initiative. It was supported by the Commons Preservation Society, which saw these small-scale piecemeal enclosures as detracting from public access and enjoyment just as dangerously in principle and cumulatively as the more high-profile schemes of large landowners and big business. On the eve of the Second World War the 'bungalow towns' were less threatened by planners and redevelopment schemes than were the fishing quarters of established resorts, despite the latter's claims to picturesque qualities and associations with the maritime valour of fishermen who also manned lifeboats and the wartime Royal Navy. Despite their continuing immunity, it was clear that what were arcadias symbolising holiday freedom for some, were rural slums for others; and anxious, critical wartime surveys revealed the extent to which they had spread.[24]

Even when the Town and Country Planning Act of 1947 enabled local authorities to curb the extension of existing 'bungalow towns', the established settlements proved impossible to uproot: the best the advocates of tidiness and uniformity could hope for was a gradual upgrading of premises and the introduction of basic urban services, pushing owners away from idiosyncrasy and towards building a closer resemblance to an orthodox urban environment. Some of this was being done spontaneously during the 1930s, as urban services were extended, public health regulations required increased plot sizes and individual properties were upgraded. At Pagham, near Bognor, and Jaywick Sands near Clacton, as at Peacehaven, there was a recognisable road layout anyway, and the Jaywick residents were eager to come into the fold of officialdom by getting a reluctant local council to recognise their right to exist and provide both sea defences and the full panoply of urban amenities. The war led to the bulldozing of many bungalows for coastal defence purposes, and left a legacy of damage to the survivors; but as soon as restrictions on access were lifted the owners were back, rehabilitating their property and resisting attempts to prevent them. High officialdom and the courts treated them more sympathetically than the fishing families, and where properties were purchased it was usually at a fair valuation, involving procedures which were too costly for most councils to wage all-out war on settlements which some had always found picturesque, a view which the weathering of time was making more widely acceptable. Further development of this kind could not be tolerated in an era of 'mass' holiday-making, as the planners perceived it, which would swamp the whole coastline unless controlled and directed into approved, sanitised sites; but most of the existing developments enjoyed long-term survival, gradually merging into the broader conventions of seaside suburbia and losing most of their distinctiveness. The 'bungalow towns', on the coast as elsewhere (for there were riverside and rural variants), were tamed rather than being suppressed, and the 'Bohemian' aspects of the lifestyle that went with them gently withered away.[25]

Caravan sites were also tamed and regulated in the post-war years, although few could match Sidmouth's Dunscombe Manor Farm, which in 1957 was trying to resolve the incongruity of being a caravan site in this exclusive resort by offering forty-four acres for fifty caravans, claiming that it was 'not a commercial site, but the ideal for the discerning caravanner', with 'individual toilets' and 'views, privacy, seclusion, quiet, tonic air and all the beauty that is Devon'. It was all 'in keeping with the fair name of Sidmouth'.[26] At the other extreme were the coasts of Lincolnshire and Flintshire: flying northwards from Skegness in 1969 Anthony Smith was amazed that 'the view was all caravans at the start, with a thousand a mile for the first twenty miles': a rhetorical statistic which still conveys a sense of enormity. Almost all of this had happened over the past generation, and containing and concentrating caravans continued to exercise the minds of planners, who were constrained by the status of static caravans as nominally temporary and portable structures which resisted building by-law restrictions.[27]

At the opposite extreme aesthetically to the regimented rows of post-war caravans were the old fishing communities around and within which resort activities were developing, and which appealed to an aesthetic (both popular and 'artistic') of the nostalgic and picturesque, offering attractive untidinesses, while challenging the inter-war planners' obsession with cleanliness, airiness and light. By the 1930s, and sometimes earlier, the pendulum was swinging against the fishermen in several resorts. At Hastings the struggle between fishermen and local government for access to and use of the eastern Old Town beach and its surroundings can be traced through from the 1820s to beyond the Second World War, as successive attempts were made to move the fisher-men further eastwards and to deprive them of land for boat and net storage, and of effective sea defences. The local fishing industry declined steadily through the first third of the twentieth century, and from the mid-1920s a forceful Borough Engineer, Sidney Little, took up the town planner Thomas Adams's proposal for a new road to clear the 'slums' of the Old Town, while using its beach for day-tripper amusements. Fierce opposition from residents delayed the start of the redevelopment until 1938, just in time to leave the centre of the Old Town, with its vernacular buildings, 'derelict and devastated' during fifteen years of war and austerity. Meanwhile the beach had been acquiring a new car and coach park and the fishermen's oldest stade was lost to a boating lake, although they fought successfully to keep their capstans and winches, organising from 1937 in a Fishermen's Protection Society. In a final post-war push the local authority sought to demolish all the sea-front housing in the fishing quarter and place an amusement park on the site, luring the trippers away from the more genteel west end, but this scheme was rejected in 1946 after a public outcry, and the fishermen and the remains of the Old Town were preserved for devotees of the alternative aesthetic to enjoy. But bitter conflicts between the 'City Beautiful' at the seaside and older local interests were not con-fined to Hastings, although here they were part of a longer and deeper struggle.[28]

Examples of attempts to 'tidy up' fishing quarters by demolition and rede-velopment spanned England from Penzance to Scarborough, although with widely varying outcomes. When Penzance extended its boundary to include Newlyn, the local authority proposed to demolish most of the village (making room for an improved coastal road to Mousehole) and move the inhabitants to a new estate at the top of a one-in-five gradient. The Newlyn school of artists sup-ported the fishing community's resistance and brought in the town planning professor S.D. Adshead for an alternative report, while a petition against the scheme was taken up the Thames by fishing vessel for well-publicised delivery to the Ministry of Housing. This cut no ice, and it took the Second World War to stave off the redevelopment.[29] At Lowestoft, however, it applied the *coup de grâce* to a less picturesque fishing community. Here the Victorian flint and brick terraces known as Beach Village, which had played host to many impecunious holiday-makers, were evacuated and used by the Army for street-fighting practice and then demolished, the inhabitants being rehoused on council estates. When clearance was completed an industrial estate occupied the site, so this was a distinctive case; but it would be interesting to know more about why this district, in particular, was selected for sacrifice.[30]

Developments at Scarborough highlight the rise of a new set of attitudes. The planning consultants who reported in 1938 complained about the insensitivity of piecemeal redevelopment of parts of the 'Old Town' fishing quarter under the Housing Acts, and urged that the positive value of what remained should be safeguarded:

> The old village should be regarded not only as a collection of cottages for fishermen but also as a special feature of interest to Scarborough. As time goes on visitors to our seaside resorts are more and more attracted by the quaintness and beauty of these old relics of the fishing industry . . . it is important to retain as far as possible its original character, in particular the charming character of the eighteenth-century houses which in broken outline form the facade of the harbour.

The planners drew attention to current preservation work at Whitby, St Ives and Plymouth, and to the popularity with visitors of old fishing villages such as Polperro and Clovelly; and they made extensive and specific recommendations for the Old Town. Here was a developing and distinctive alternative planning perspective, marking a shift towards heritage tourism; but the authors were unable to resist a further twist. They proposed the replacement of the Ice Factory with a Fun Fair, which might:

> partake of the character of a street of old three-storey fourteenth-century wooden houses, with the open space formed by the removal of the old buildings between Tindall Lane and Parkins Lane made to look like an old English market place. This is a suggestion that would make the place attractive and at the same time preserve, in outward appearance at least, the character of the village.

This kind of compromise was to be a commonplace of the post-war years, as the tensions between preservation and commercial exploitation worked their way into practical synthesis and gift shops and amusement arcades penetrated the declining inshore fishing communities.[31]

The urge to redevelop along 'modern' lines, with little attention to seaside distinctiveness, resurfaced as soon as resources became available after the Second World War. Bognor Regis exhibited this tendency particularly strongly, though ineffectually. The 1960s were punctuated by schemes for the transformation of the area between the pier and the (itself controversial) new Butlin's camp, with a gradual retreat from plans for eighteen-storey tower blocks and decked promenades with escalator access to the beach (the 'Ocean Liner' look) to more modest proposals for motels and leisure centres. But it took twenty years and a change of local government system before the Bognor Regis Centre opened, and meanwhile the Urban District Council continued its inter-war policy of the piecemeal acquisition and demolition of the distinctive and emblematic buildings from the town's past. These were increasingly controversial issues, as local conservation movements gathered momentum in the 1970s, while the Ratepayers' Association kept a close eye on expenditure; and similar confrontations were the stuff of local politics in many other resorts, as we shall see. The outcome was the loss of much, though by no means all, of the architecture and arrangement of urban space that made the urban seaside distinctive and attractive.[32]

Tensions between the pursuit of modernity and the celebration of the past overlapped with the perennial question of whether and how to manage urban space and regulate behaviour so as to create an appropriate mix of freedom and security for preferred and attainable visiting publics. This applied in streets and parks as well as on the promenade and beach. By 1910 the Home Office had approved a long list of model by-laws which local authorities could adopt, including prohibitions on beating carpets, allowing dogs to bark (to the annoyance of any person, after being required to desist by a constable), ringing bells or sounding gongs or trumpets or other noisy instruments, begging, touting, lecturing or entertaining in public places. These were widely adopted at the seaside: in 1912, for example, Blackpool joined Eastbourne and Torquay in adopting the barking dogs clause.[33]

There was sustained pressure from resorts to extend most of these powers. Blackpool was particularly keen to restrain hawking in the streets, in a campaign which reached a climax on the eve of the First World War, when the Town Clerk told the Home Office that hawkers needed to be registered and badged because they obstructed the streets and annoyed visitors by selling inessential goods such as rock, matches and 'pictorial postcards of doubtful propriety', competing unfairly with established shopkeepers. The hawkers were 'people of bad character from other towns', whose habits were filthy and who often lived on the earnings of prostitutes; and they often used street selling as a cover for 'begging and thieving from railway stations'. These pleas cut no ice with the Home Office, where a civil servant minuted that Blackpool's rulers were 'extraordinary people' for thinking they could adopt the special by-laws of the City of London for their own purposes.[34] In 1934 Blackpool succeeded in adopting by-laws against loudspeakers, gramophones or amplifiers in public places 'so loud or continuous or repeated as to be or cause a nuisance to occupants . . . of any premises in the neighbourhood'. As the supportive correspondence sent to the Home Office shows, however, this was aimed less at the Golden Mile than at safeguarding the amenities of residential streets whose inhabitants poured out heartfelt complaints against inconsiderate neighbours.[35] Strict regulation aimed at popular holiday areas themselves was both less likely and more determinedly resisted from the centre: in 1936 an internal memorandum described the Home Office's 'worst reverse last year (or this year)' as occurring when Rhyl was allowed parliamentary sanction to forbid booths on private land (the important innovation) adjoining the promenade for commercial purposes. A strong case had to be made if free trade was to be impeded beyond the existing conventions.[36]

But sometimes, and perhaps increasingly by the 1930s, the traffic ran the other way. In 1932 several south coast resorts campaigned for extended public house opening hours at holiday time: what a Home Office memorandum described as a 'Brighter Seaside' movement in Kent and Sussex resorts, led by (of all places) Eastbourne, where wholesale extensions of opening hours had been granted over long weekends at Easter and during the summer, and enthusiastically supported in Margate. In part this initiative was directed against Continental competition: 'There has been a strong feeling that in the present crisis it is more patriotic to spend a holiday in a British seaside resort instead of going abroad'. But a movement for the relaxation of drink sales restraints argues for fears of undesirable visitor behaviour being comfortably outweighed by worries about lost trade through undue restrictions; and this sums up a general relaxation of social tensions at the coast during the inter-war years. The Home Office was more than willing to go with the flow.[37]

These more relaxed attitudes suggest that the politics of space, the concern to preserve certain desirable seaside environments for the decorously privileged which was a central theme of the British seaside in the second half of the nineteenth century, had faded from the limelight over most of the coastline by the inter-war years. Zoning systems, formal and informal, had become established by Edwardian times, and when transport innovations opened out new flexibilities to people with limited resources they tended to find their own levels of

shared preferences. Places which sought to sustain exclusivity amid increasingly democratic expectations, such as Frinton, Westgate and Thorpeness, still
experienced culture wars of familiar kinds, and we have seen the proliferation
of caravans and 'bungalow towns' provoked horror among lovers of picturesque
or simply empty landscape as well as among tidy-minded planners, in sometimes unprincipled coalitions. The growing restrictive power of planning
regulation in the post-war years reduced the sustained intensity of such conflicts without removing them; and the increased coastal holdings of the armed
forces, restricting access to 'unspoilt' coastline, also provoked protest at times.
The privatisation of coastal space through golf courses and chalet developments
was also a sustained theme, but conflicts over the use of established leisure space
increasingly had a generational dimension, prefigured in the antics of 'bright
young things' at inter-war Frinton but expressed in much more threatening
ways (especially when amplified through the media) by the beatniks of Brighton
in the late 1950s or the Mods and Rockers clashes of the mid-1960s. But most
people, most of the time, had learned what was accepted of them at the
seaside by the First World War: the grammar of where to go and how to behave,
and the shifting boundaries of the transgressive. The very qualified and self-
policing nature of this limited liminality made the tasks of resort regulators
easier, until the spread of seaside unemployment and the wildernesses of bedsit
drug culture began to invade old boarding-house areas from the 1980s.[38]

The 1980s brought renewed social and environmental problems to the
seaside, and they also brought a countervailing change in trend. These years
saw the rise of the 'heritage industry' and a polemic about the conversion of
Britain into a 'museum culture' as its older industries were allowed to wither
and decay; and within this framework some of the older resorts were beginning
to recycle and trade on their own history. Alongside the museums of mining
and manufacturing industries, the seaside holiday industry began to present
its own past as an article of consumption. Brighton, fittingly, was early in the
field, as amenity groups struggled with growing success to protect its Regency
architecture, which could then be used as the basis for a kind of cultural tourism
which celebrated the distinctive attractions of its built environment and fitted
in neatly alongside the growth of the conference trade and white-collar employment in service industries and higher education. The focus of Brighton's
tourist-related activities moved away from the sea-front, where the more
raffish and down-market of the older holiday activities were increasingly
discouraged and corralled, to the Pavilion, the antique-shop district of the Lanes
(which was given a 'heritage' makeover with cast-iron street furniture), and the

Georgian terraces. The piers were allowed to decay while, from the 1980s, an increasingly assertive and strongly promoted Brighton Festival invented traditions, promoted arts-appreciating tourism and self-consciously pushed the tourist trade up-market. Kevin Meethan sums it up thus: 'the appropriation of spaces for the traditional and boisterous, and for the more sensitive cultural pursuits, reveals that one tradition – the seaside holiday – is being superseded by the creation of another tradition – that of heritage and architectural conservation'. The preferred past for commercial exploitation was that of the Regency beau as *flâneur* in the civilised urban street, rather than the tripper and what had become the traditional seaside entertainment. Brighton was being remade as a resort, but one that only happened to be at the seaside. Meanwhile its poverty-stricken outer estates remained outside the charmed circle of investment, while a crowded and uncomfortable bedsitter land lurked behind the repainted facades of some of the Regency terraces.[39]

Brighton was not alone in turning its back on the sea. Something similar can be argued about Blackpool, where the waves lost their allure as awareness of the gross pollution of the Irish Sea along this coastline became more widely disseminated (an adverse report of 1988 from the Department of the Environment was being publicised as far away as Italy in the early 1990s); and the town's commercial entertainments, which had been important to its pulling power since the late nineteenth century, now became overwhelmingly dominant.[40] In 1993 the European Court ruled that all Blackpool's beaches had unacceptable levels of coliform bacteria in their bathing water, but the local MEP described the European standard as 'pretty silly', adding that, 'People who come to Blackpool don't come here to swim.' Promises of amendment through sewage treatment works were brought into public view on the promenade at the end of the decade. But this was a widespread set of problems, already prominent in the media by the 1980s as EC criticisms became widely disseminated, and extending to litter and debris as well as sewage contamination. By the mid-1990s campaigns by groups such as Surfers Against Sewage and the Marine Conservation Society (which absorbed the Coastal Anti-Pollution League in 1987) were puncturing the complacent rhetoric of officialdom and drawing attention to the aesthetic damage and threats to health presented by the continuing disposal of raw sewage, which was affecting up to a quarter of the English coastline and linked with hepatitis and a variety of other viral infections among bathers. Floating faeces and condoms, together with litter of less offensive kinds, were prevalent on rural Cornish beaches as well as in more populous resorts, and in 1994 seventy-one out of around five hundred English beaches failed to reach the

Marine Conservation Society's water quality standards, while about a hundred did not come up to the minimum EU bathing water requirements. The whole of north-west England, from Allonby to New Brighton, failed to meet the society's standards, as did (for example) Brighton, Eastbourne, Hastings and Great Yarmouth. Welsh bathing-water pollution was more localised, and much of Scotland had a clean bill of health, despite the horrors of Edinburgh's Portobello as graphically described by Anthony Smith in 1970; and despite promises of amendment from government and privatised water companies, investment in effective treatment technologies proceeded at glacial speed. The spreading awareness of the sea as health hazard, turning the expectations created in the eighteenth century on their head, was another damaging blow to the British seaside, in the guise of a loss of innocence and faith in relation to what had been taken-for-granted 'natural' attributes of the coastal environment.[41]

Degradation of the built environment also became an issue, as the new architecture of the 1960s onwards lost its seaside distinctiveness, while older emblems of seaside pleasures were demolished and redeveloped or allowed to decay, as we saw in Chapter 4. The most visible impact of redevelopment at Blackpool itself came along and behind what until the mid-1970s was the ramshackle and (some thought) engagingly scruffy 'Golden Mile' between the North and Central Piers, and in the pedestrianised shopping streets behind the Tower. Like most British seaside resorts north of London, there was very little development of sea-front flats, whether low- or high-rise, and the view from the promenade remained recognisably Victorian, in striking contrast to most European seaside resorts of similar vintage. Where development of this sort did occur, principally in up-market south-eastern retirement resorts like Hove and Eastbourne, it also reduced the visual sense of seaside place-identity. Such changes detracted from the sense that the seaside was a special, recognis-able kind of place with its own aesthetic, and reduced the options for resorts which might have wanted to follow Brighton down the 'heritage' trail. Penarth's sea-front was extensively redeveloped, for example, with a brutalist concrete car park, which might have been in Birmingham, occupying a key site near the pier. The subsequent restoration of the pier pavilion to its Art Deco splendour, and the rescue of the swimming-pool which faced it through a pub conversion, salvaged important elements of the sea-front townscape, but the surviving resort architecture was an isolated little group rather than an extended theme.[42]

Nevertheless, the end of the century saw renewed interest in the distinctiveness of surviving resort architecture, while investment in improved bathing-water quality seemed at last to be under way along with the potential for developing what was, in effect, the industrial archaeology of the holiday trades as the basis of heritage attractions. The surviving Victorian piers and pleasure palaces were being looked after, and new uses were being found for them, often with the help of European funding and lottery grants, although the sun-terraces, open-air cafes and bathing-pools of the inter-war years were often still decaying. The history of the British seaside was often more visible on the ground than that of continental counterparts, and tourism planners were beginning to realise, at locations from Weymouth to Morecambe, that this was an asset that could be turned to account in attracting middle-class readers of broadsheet newspapers. Marinas, indoor leisure centres and funfairs began to celebrate their surroundings rather than look just like their inland counterparts. Alongside the dereliction and decay, new shoots were sprouting; and many of the established visitors had never abandoned their old haunts in the first place. The death of the British seaside had been prematurely anticipated and greatly exaggerated, although its endemic problems (already apparent in its heyday) had not gone away. The analysis of seaside social structures and social problems in the next chapter acknowledges this, while taking note of changes over time and variations between places.

Notes

1 Kevin Meetham, 'Place, image and power: Brighton as a resort', in Tom Selwyn (ed.), *The tourist image: myths and myth making in tourism* (Chichester, 1996), pp. 179–96.

2 Corbin, *The lure of the sea.*

3 Geoff Quilley, ' "All ocean is her own": the image of the sea and the identity of the maritime nation in eighteenth-century British art', in G. Cubitt (ed.), *Imagining nations* (Manchester, 1998), Chapter 8.

4 See Mary Douglas, *Purity and danger* (London: Ark, 1984), for the concept of matter out of place.

5 *Guardian*, 22 April 1994, 13 May 1994.

6 Alan A. Jackson, *Semi-detached London* (London: Allen and Unwin, 1973).

7 W.J. Dibdin, *The purification of sewage and water* (3rd edn, London, 1903), p. 221.

8 Ibid., p. 232.

9 G.A. Parsons, 'Property, profit and pollution: conflict in eastuarine water management, 1800–1915', Ph.D. thesis, University of Lancaster, 1996, Chapters 7–8; L. Ash Lyons, *Blackpool bathing beauties souvenir 1950* (St Annes-on-sea, 1950), p. 3; John Hassan, 'Were health resorts bad for your health? Coastal pollution control policy in England, 1945–76', *Environment and History*, 5 (1999), pp. 53–73;

and for a coastal survey in 1970, Smith, *Beside the seaside*, which offers extensive descriptions of marine pollution.

10 W.H. Wheeler, *The sea-coast* (London, 1902), Chapters 4–6.

11 *Guardian*, 13 February 1999.

12 Hilda Grieve, *The great tide: the story of the 1953 flood disaster in Essex* (Chelmsford, 1959), pp. 86, 172–8, 356, 824–36.

13 Humphrey Baker, 'The public and the sea coast', *Journal of the Commons, Open Spaces and Footpaths Preservation Society*, 2 (1931), p. 72.

14 Walton, *The English seaside resort*, pp. 206–8.

15 Baker, 'The public and the sea coast', pp. 72–7.

16 Walton, *The English seaside resort*, Chapter 8.

17 Roberts 'The corporation as impresario' and Walton 'Municipal government and the holiday industry in Blackpool', in Walton and Walvin (eds), *Leisure in Britain*.

18 S.V. Ward, *The geography of inter-war Britain: the state and uneven development* (London, 1988), pp. 158–67.

19 Hope, *Castles in the sand*, pp. 21–3.

20 Chase, 'The creation of place image in inter-war Clacton and Frinton', pp. 90–112.

21 Ibid., pp. 126–33 (quotation from p. 126).

22 Bodleian Library, John Johnson Collection, Box 1 (Clacton and Skegness) and Box 3 (Skegness); Ward and Hardy, *Goodnight campers!*

23 A. Ogilvie de Mille, *One man's dream: the story behind G. Stuart Ogilvie and the creation of Thorpeness* (Dereham, 1996).

24 Hardy and Ward, *Arcadia for all*, Chapter 2; J. Sheail, 'The impact of recreation on the coast: the Lindsey County Council (Sandhills) Act, 1932', *Landscape Planning* 1977; 'Editorial Notes', *Journal of the Commons, Open Spaces and Footpaths Preservation Society*, 2 (1931), pp. 67–8.

25 Hardy and Ward, *Arcadia for all*, Chapters 3–4.

26 *Official guide and souvenir of Sidmouth* (Revised edn, Gloucester, 1957), p. 97.

27 Smith, *Beside the seaside*, pp. 35–6.

28 S. Peak, *Fishermen of Hastings: 200 years of the Hastings fishing community* (St Leonards-on-Sea, 1985).

29 John Corin, *Fishermen's conflict: the story of Newlyn* (Newton Abbot, 1988), pp. 113–17. There was no love lost between Penzance and Newlyn, which added spice to this dispute.

30 D. Butcher, *Living from the sea* (Sulhamstead, 1982), pp. 19–21.

31 Adshead and Overfield, *The future development of Scarborough*, pp. 29–36.

32 Young, *A history of Bognor Regis*, pp. 255–70.

33 PRO, HO 45/17966; HO 45/22722, T. Loftos to Home Office, 26 December 1912.

34 PRO, HO 45/22722, Loftos to Home Office, 4 December 1913, and minuted comments.

35 PRO, HO 45/22722, letters from Irvine Walsh, J. Smith and A. Johnson, June 1934.

36 PRO, HO 45/17966.

37 PRO, HO 45/21750.
38 Walton, *Seaside resorts of England and Wales*, Chapter 8; Musgrave, *Life in Brighton*, pp. 430–7.
39 Meethan, 'Place, image and power', especially p. 190.
40 Walton, *The Blackpool landlady*, Chapters 6–7; Severgnini, *Inglesi*, p. 143.
41 Stafford and Yates, *The later Kentish seaside*, p. 111; *Times*, 15 July 1993, p. 7a; *Guardian*, 22 April 1994, 13 May 1994; Smith, *Beside the seaside*, pp. 112–16; Hassan, 'Were health resorts bad for your health?', p. 69.
42 Personal observation, May 1999.

6

Seaside economies

At bottom the seaside resort is an industrial town, selling access to and enjoyment of a desirable environment, although with varying emphases and in different but overlapping senses. Its dominant employments involve servicing the needs of visitors and residents: building and maintaining accommodation, selling goods and entertainment, keeping up an attractive environment, sustaining a sense of security, moving people to and fro, and ministering to their daily needs. These employments are often ill-paid and seasonal, although seaside resorts also generate ample demand for professional services from doctors, lawyers and the professions associated with building and estate management. Seasonality makes for busy migration flows among workers as well as visitors, and resorts are places to seek a quick fortune or eke out a precarious living in the short term rather than secure economic environments which offer an abundance of long-term, regular employment. They attract small, vulnerable businesses with limited capital whose proprietors work themselves and their families hard when work is available. Some also have surviving traditional industries, especially associated with fishing, which have seasonal rhythms and insecurities of their own. Increasingly, the seaside has also attracted commuters and retirement migrants, not all of whom are straightforwardly prosperous and some of whom struggle to eke out their fixed incomes. Despite their prosperous appearance during the season (in many cases and for much of the century), and despite the presence of comfortably off business families and people of independent means in districts of impressive planned crescents and villas, seaside resorts have always experienced the economic problems that go with their distinctive occupational profiles and seasonal fluctuations; and this chapter explores the changing patterns of poverty and affluence in their various guises and settings through the twentieth century. We begin with the workers by hand, the people at the back of the stage who make the glamour, bustle and excitement of the season possible, and seldom get due acknowledgement from either their customers or from those who write about the seaside.[1]

The distinctive pattern of employment on offer to working-class people in seaside resorts throughout the twentieth century is encapsulated in F.C. Ball's description of 'Mugsborough, England', the Edwardian Hastings which Robert Noonan experienced as a working house-painter and which he wrote about so mercilessly under the name of Robert Tressell in *The ragged-trousered philanthropists*:[2]

> The town being entirely without factories and industry, the working classes lived off the Corporation (and men literally fought for jobs there), the public utilities, the railways (and horse-buses), shops and hotels (the two worst-paid occupations), and domestic service, or the 'kiss-me-Aunt' trades as they were referred to by an irascible elderly gentleman of my youth who used to carry the hod. And last of all there was the building.

This was, at the time, the worst trade of all, in a town which had reached its peak resident population at the turn of the century and was already shrinking, offering little new building work and requiring its small firms to subsist on extensions and renovations. This was unusual, especially as it was to continue for most of the century: most seaside resorts had thriving building industries until the 1950s. Also unusual was the sheer scale of Hastings' reputation for municipal corruption and intimidation: the corporation here was enduringly known as the 'Forty Thieves'. But otherwise this was a standard kind of seaside resort economy, with its small firms struggling to survive in cut-throat competition with each other, its low wages for workpeople who found it impossible to organise in an environment dominated by seasonal and sweated labour in which it was only too easy to blacklist troublemakers, and its legion of elderly widows and spinsters eking out a bloodless, etiolated, penny-pinching version of gentility on incomes from rents and dividends. Family earnings were at a premium in towns like this, as men, women and children took up whatever opportunities were available and moved from one kind of work to another as opportunity and the passing of the seasons allowed. Winter poverty was endemic. Hastings, like several other major seaside resorts, had a fishing industry which was in long-term decline through the twentieth century, but continued to interleave its own seasonal fluctuations with those of the holiday trades; while on the other hand sport and entertainment were to grow in importance as employers, in this setting as in others.[3] So were commuting and retirement populations. Seaside residence offered temptations to the enterprising, the retired and those who needed to look after their health, as in Noonan's own case (he

was to die of tuberculosis); but for most of those who took the bait provided
by busy summers and encouraging health statistics, it flattered to deceive.

The maritime activities which had been at the core of many original resort
identities from the eighteenth-century origins of commercial sea-bathing, provoking mixed responses from visitors who might be fascinated or repelled,
continued their nineteenth-century decline in all but a few distinctive settings;
and local government policies tended to reinforce the adverse economic trends,
preferring tidiness, symmetry and an appearance of cleanliness to the quaint
but smelly disarray of capstans, caulking, net-mending and fish-processing. We
looked at some of the campaigns to marginalise fisherfolk and tidy up their
communities in Chapter 5; and these were so important, and so hard-fought,
because fishing was particularly visible, emblematic and (often) controversial,
making a contribution to perceptions of resort identities out of all proportion
to its actual contribution to twentieth-century resort economies, basing itself
in distinctive communities with their own dialects, informal expertise and patterns of work, and focusing the attention of social reformers as well as seekers
after the picturesque. At Hastings, again, the number of fishermen operating
from a shrinking area of beach in front of the Old Town was in long-term
decline: there were still sixty-three boats in 1885, but only thirty-nine in 1903
(when three families dominated the industry), thirty-eight in 1923 (after prosperous years in the First World War which allowed investment in motor-boats),
and nineteen in the late 1930s. Censuses (particularly unreliable here) found
326 fishermen in 1911, 259 in 1921 and 147 in 1931. This was a common pattern in the larger resorts: Brighton's 150 fishing boats in 1862 had dwindled
to 88 in 1903 and 48 in 1948, when they were mainly used for pleasure trips
in summer. The industry at Hastings kept afloat after the Second World War,
however, and has increasingly been recognised as a tourist attraction, with its
distinctive net store buildings and fresh fish auctions. The larger Hastings
vessels might travel as far as Cornwall and Scotland for mackerel and herring,
and the more purely inshore fisheries declined earlier and more steeply. At nearby
Rye, for example, fishing practically disappeared between the wars, while
Sidmouth's sea-front, which had been a 'little Billingsgate', crowded with boats,
in the herring season in 1885, had only seven active drifters left on the eve of
the First World War as against more than twenty in the previous generation.
By the mid-1920s fishing had practically given way to pleasure boating. This
was not universal, and even Brighton kept its fish market on the beach until
1946; but by the post-war years inshore fishing was becoming a picturesque,
subsidised, minority activity in almost every resort, with the disappearance of

the pilchard shoals from Cornwall and the subsequent general decline of the herring fisheries contributing significantly to the process.[4]

The fishing seasons fitted in alongside other aspects of the resort economy, and the holiday season provided markets for the local catch while offering opportunities to boost incomes by catering for pleasure parties ('frights', or freights, as they were known in Edwardian Sidmouth). As the autumn herring season moved down the east coast it coincided with late holidaymakers at Scarborough and then dovetailed in just after the season at Great Yarmouth and Lowestoft, allowing the Scots 'herring lassies' (whose dexterity with the gutting knife made them a tourist attraction at Scarborough) to extend the lodgings season for the more unpretentious landladies. This is a reminder that most fishing families had complex household economies: men might supplement resources by beach-combing, working at local mines or quarries, or taking temporary work in local service industries by carpet-beating, cleaning or pushing a wheelchair. They could also be paid for membership of the Royal Naval Reserve. Women could do laundry work, take in seasonal lodgers, or find waitress or bar work in hotels and boarding-houses, as well as (in some parts of the country, such as North Yorkshire) playing their part in the fishing economy itself by mending nets, gathering bait and going out to sell the catch. Daughters away in service might send money home, and those who worked in lodging-houses might get left-over food as well as meals at the workplace. This range of resources was not available to younger families, and low incomes (estimated at an average of fifteen shillings a week over the year for Edwardian Sidmouth, or little better than the poorest agricultural labourers) tended to arrive in 'lumps' when fishing or pleasure boating was successful, making budgeting difficult. Problems were compounded by marketing difficulties, as fishermen were usually at the mercy of middlemen in dealing with distant markets; and these nominally independent traders suffered as much exploitation under the prevailing economic system as any factory worker. Meanwhile, they were expected to live up to the visitors' image of the 'old salt', deferential and full of picturesque lore and sayings, and viewed alternately as brave (especially in lifeboat contexts) and idle (when no work was to be had). The rise of the holiday industry offered new survival strategies, and no doubt helped to keep inshore fisheries going through income from visitors; but it also turned fishermen into service workers and objects of a version of the tourist gaze, as the presence of obtrusive observers changed what was observed, gradually, into a parody of its former self.[5]

The fisherman, as potential hero of the Royal Navy or the lifeboat crew, nevertheless had a legitimacy that other characteristic seaside workers might struggle to achieve. The reminiscences of George Meek, who became a bath-chairman at Eastbourne for nineteen years at the turn of the century, are coloured by his socialist politics and their accompanying rhetoric; but this perhaps merely made him more articulate in interpreting experiences which others endured in silence or obscurity. Meek's main trade was a highly visible resort occupation, casual and uncertain, with rent to be paid to the chair's proprietor and defer-ence due to the hirers, who might respond with regular employment and tips. In earlier years he was a steward at the Liberal Club and worked behind the scenes at a local theatre. 'I have tried window-cleaning, everything I could think of to fill in the blank hours, but always some one else has wanted the work and edged me out of it.' In the long run he was unable to make ends meet, even with the support of his wife's earnings as an ironer in laundries. When he obtained winter work navvying on Corporation relief schemes under the Unemployed Workmen Act of 1905, his body was unable to keep up with the demands of the work. Meek summed up his situation thus, pointing up the humiliations as well as the discomforts and fears surrounding casual work in a resort with heavy winter unemployment:[6]

> Eastbourne is one of the loveliest pleasure towns in England. It is the paradise of the idle and sometimes vicious rich, the rest-place of jaded well-paid workers; but it is a hell to the poor who try to live in it by casual labour . . . Many a time we have stripped the clothes off our backs and put away our bed for rent. So one gets low and shabby and disheartened. In a snobbish town like Eastbourne dress means so much. With little chance of a healthy night's sleep owing to the insect pests, little decent food, many unoccupied hours, much worry and often many disappointments during the day, it is no wonder one is driven to the abuse of alcohol . . . How we shall get through the coming winter I don't know. Still, some-how we seem to have kept on through the years . . . always on the edge of the abyss, never quite sinking into it.

These were recurrent Edwardian themes, which retained their force in the inter-war years and never quite went underground, reappearing strongly in the last quarter of the century. Bournemouth's Distress Committee dealt with 502 applicants for relief work, with 1,108 dependants, during the winter of 1906–7. This was only two per cent of the population, but a contemporary report pointed out that it was the tip of a large iceberg, in spite of Bournemouth's recent rapid growth and abundance of building work:[7]

> as a matter of fact, there are thousands of skilled mechanics and others who have the greatest difficulty making ends meet during the winter months, but who loathe the name Distress Committee to such an extent that they put off applying for

assistance until the last possible moment, and in some cases when driven to the Committee have absolutely refused to give the information required concerning what they consider their private affairs . . . The casual nature of the employment of a large number of the applicants seems to have become almost chronic, records of jobs lasting only a few weeks or months is the usual tale told . . . an army of casual workers, whose common lot is unfortunately one of acute nervous tension, and dread of the workhouse.

Thus did official sources confirm the testimony of Robert Noonan and George Meek, even in this most buoyant of Edwardian seaside economies. At Brighton the highest similar Edwardian total was 9,557 applicants and dependants in 1908–9, peaking sharply in the two months after Christmas. This was just over 7 per cent of the population. At Blackpool in 1909–10 the Chief Constable's relief fund, an altogether more convincing indicator of distress (while still leaving out the proud and determined), gave assistance in kind to 15.6 per cent of the inhabitants. Everywhere, most of the distressed families with male heads depended mainly on general labouring or the building trades. There were isolated examples of more specialised holiday occupations: Southport's applicants in 1906–7 included a golf caddie, a dog trainer, an ice-cream vendor and a bathing-van attendant, as well as someone mysteriously described as a 'band attendant'. But the seasonal trades were staffed mainly by seasonal migrants, which meant that the endemic competition for employment was sustained throughout the year, or by locals who moved into holiday occupations for the summer. Insecurity was indeed widespread to the point of being the norm among the seaside working class, in a setting where trade unions were very difficult to organise and sustain.[8]

The army of caterers for holiday crowds who gave colour and excitement to the streets and beaches were a small minority of resort populations. The pierrots were usually itinerant (and often impoverished, if tales of men who later became famous entertainers having to sleep under piers can be trusted), and so were many of the fortune-tellers, phrenologists, Punch-and-Judy men and other conjurers of seaside pleasure. The hawkers of postcards and hatguards, and the professional touts who advertised cafes and shows with leaflets and leather-lunged shouts, were presented as equally rootless and much more disreputable by local authorities, as we saw in Chapter 4. Ice-cream stall and donkey proprietors were beginning to acquire local addresses and ratepayer status in Edwardian times, at least in Blackpool; but here we are moving towards the ranks of small and medium-sized family businesses, from souvenir stalls to boarding-houses, which dominated the social structure of seaside residents. The emblematic figure here was the seaside landlady, whose status as matriarch and businesswoman made her the object of alarm and therefore ridicule as a powerful woman who dominated husband and guests alike. Her defensive need for rules and regulations, to safeguard visitor comfort, respectability and her own time for cleaning and sleep, was caricatured as dictatorial, and had to be relaxed when cheaper and more informal alternatives began to compete for her customers; but by the inter-war years many guest-houses were going up-market, relabelling themselves as private hotels and taking the extra profit which went with supplying full board to visitors who could now afford to pay for meals and escape from the old system of buying the food for the landlady to cook. The boarding-house buildings remained predominantly late Victorian and Edwardian, however, and it was to prove difficult to upgrade them to meet rising expectations in the post-war years. Meanwhile, however, most houses in the mainstream popular resorts took in visitors during the season, and resort social structures would look overwhelmingly lower middle-class if classified according to female occupations. Armies of servants and service workers, again largely supplied by seasonal migration, augmented the female predominance in seaside resort populations.[9]

Many of these smaller businesses were themselves volatile and vulnerable, and part of complex domestic economies in which children were pitched into paid or unpaid employment very early. The long winter months were difficult for small businesses trying to survive on three months' trade, as well as for wage-earners; and many people were self-employed in the season and sought what waged work they could get for the rest of the year. The seaside imposed versatility in a way that remained unfamiliar to people with steady year-round jobs, and its fluctuating and complex economy makes quantitative statements particularly perilous. But careful analysis of censuses and other official sources allows broad general comments to be made, with reservations, and at least about the spring population.

Key characteristics of the larger seaside resorts were in evidence in a ranking exercise based on the eighty-three English and Welsh county boroughs at the 1931 census. Several indicators of affluence saw the seaside resorts highly placed. The four county boroughs with the lowest ratios of people per room were (in order) Bournemouth, Great Yarmouth, Blackpool and Southport, with figures between 0.64 and 0.67; Eastbourne was seventh, Hastings tenth, and Southend two places further behind, at 0.72. Brighton, with its railway works and poverty-stricken terraces behind the sea front, was twenty-sixth, at 0.79. The median figure was Bolton's 0.85, the highest Gateshead's 1.23. An April census hid the inevitability of very different ratios in July and August, but the resorts showed equally impressively in the return for female domestic servants as a percentage of total population, with the top six places going to Eastbourne (12.3 per cent), Bournemouth, Blackpool (where boarding-houses contributed much more than private residents), Hastings, Southport and Brighton (8.6 per cent), while Southend was ninth and Great Yarmouth, with its important harbour and fishing interests, came fifteenth with 5 per cent. The median here was 3.3 per cent and the lowest figure 1.8 per cent. Even more impressive was the seaside resort dominance in a league based on the percentage of the local workforce being self-employed or in managerial posts: the eight seaside resort county boroughs swept the board, from Blackpool's 29.4 per cent to Brighton's 17.8 per cent, with Wallasey, a Liverpool suburb across the Mersey which included New Brighton, coming ninth and Bath tenth. Professional occupations showed a less spectacular profile, despite the ample scope for doctors and lawyers to make a good seaside living out of ailments, wills and property speculation; but here again, although Oxford took the lead, Hastings (8.1 per cent), Eastbourne and Bournemouth took the next three places, with Southport and Southend seventh and eighth, Brighton (4.9 per cent) eleventh, and Blackpool and Great Yarmouth (3.0 per cent) further back at seventeenth and twenty-ninth. But even these most plebeian of the large resorts came out strongly against a median figure of 2.3 per cent and a lowest level of 0.9 per cent. Unemployment, mean-while, was a below-average problem in most large resorts on these figures in this generally painful year, although by the time of the April census the pre-season quickening of the local economic pulse had pulled many of the seasonally idle back into the labour market, and we shall see that other indicators are less optimistic. Bournemouth (5.6 per cent recorded as 'out of work') and Eastbourne had the second and third lowest figures, Southend was seventh, Hastings eighth, Brighton twelfth, and Southport (8.6 per cent) fifteenth; but Blackpool and Great Yarmouth were again the odd ones out, bracketed just above the median rate with 14.7 per cent jobless.[10]

Elizabeth Brunner's broad thematic analysis of the 'holiday trades' at the seaside refines the unemployment figures for the 1930s and picks out addi-tional distinctive features of resort social structure through the 1931 census. She points out, using the 1938 statistics, that unemployment figures in six resorts were much lower during a June–September 'season' than for the rest of the year. The gap was widest in Blackpool, where the summer average was 11.6 per cent and that of winter 24.9 per cent, leaving 4,643 people 'seasonally affected', although the figure would be significantly higher in the depths of winter. The gap was nearly as wide at Great Yarmouth (11.7 and 22.5 per cent) and the specialised, smaller Isle of Wight resort of Sandown (3.2 and 12.6 per cent), but it was much narrower at Southend, with its large London commuter population (9.6 and 16.3 per cent), and especially at Brighton (8.5 and 10.7 per cent), where the holiday season was now only a small part of a complex urban economy, and in any case visitors also came in autumn and winter. More detailed monthly figures show that Blackpool's unemployment rate peaked at 29 per cent in November and December, when male unemployment passed 30 per cent, while at up-market Bournemouth the worst mid-winter figures failed to go beyond 10 per cent. So the seasonal unemployment phenomenon was general in outline, but variable in its impact.[11]

There were also seasonal influxes of labour. When the Ministry of Labour noticed this phenomenon in 1930 and alerted the Labour Exchanges, nearly 40,000 people (including over 31,000 women and girls) were found seasonal seaside work, mostly as domestic servants, waiters and waitresses; and nearly 16,000 of these were brought in from outside the resorts. This officially documented movement was certainly a small proportion of the whole, as many people continued to migrate on the basis of personal contacts or on the assumption that work was there for the finding. Blackpool, for example, attracted domestic servants from the coalfields of north-eastern England, where there was very little waged work for women. In the depressed years of the 1930s, growing numbers of summer migrants stayed at the seaside after the season finished, preferring the dole and relatively cheap accommodation in an off-season resort to the grimmer surroundings of industrial towns in which work was not forthcoming and the means test made families unwelcoming. In Blackpool many slept in the shelters on the promenade, discussing their circumstances vigorously and audibly, and generating fears of revolutionary contagion to add to the panics about sexual promiscuity which always swirled around these displaced groups, especially the young women.[12]

Seaside resorts were especially problematic because their economies fluctuated particularly sharply (most obviously in the more popular and specialised resorts which depended on the July–September season and had fewer affluent year-round residents or winter visitors) and because they concentrated a group of trades which were highly seasonal in themselves and whose fluctuations were exacerbated in this setting. Elizabeth Brunner divided these 'holiday trades' into primary (entertainment, sport and personal service), which were at the core of the resort economy as such, and secondary (commerce, finance, transport, utilities and building), which were 'stimulated by the tourist traffic . . . they provide the means to the end rather than the end of holiday-making. They are all necessaries in daily working life, but the man on holiday tends to consume much more of them so that the normal trade becomes swollen.'[13]

Employment in entertainment and sport was a small category, but it grew rapidly throughout the inter-war years. Between the 1921 and 1931 censuses it increased from 0.69 to 0.94 per cent of the occupied population, and this trajectory continued through the 1930s. In Blackpool in 1931 the location factor for these trades (the percentage of the occupied population working in them locally divided by the national percentage) was 4.9, reflecting the relative importance of these occupations in this high-profile setting even at an April census. At seven other important seaside resorts the corresponding figure fell between 2.5 (Sandown) and 1.4 (Bournemouth), with Brighton (2.4) and Llandudno (2.3) showing strongly. Much more numerous, and equally characteristic of the twentieth-century seaside, were personal services, employing between 198 per thousand of the occupied population (Southend, location factor 1.5) and 356 (Sandown, 2.8) among Brunner's eight sample resorts. This category involved work in private domestic service, lodging- and boarding-houses, restaurants, hotels, laundries and hairdressing, with particularly spectacular concentrations in lodging- and boarding-house work at Blackpool (110 per thousand, location factor 17.0) and Bournemouth (77, 12.0). This sector employed a very high ratio of women to men and, relatedly, tended to be undercounted in censuses which generically failed to record women's work which was often part-time and hidden behind other labels. It was also highly seasonal at the seaside, where an April census would miss many locals for whom the season had yet to begin, and migrants who had not arrived. But even these minimum figures are impressive.[14]

As might be expected, the secondary holiday trades showed less striking concentrations. Building showed up most strongly and consistently, not surprisingly given the buoyancy of resort growth in the inter-war years: location factors in the eight sample resorts ranged from 1.9 in Ramsgate to 1.2 in Llandudno. This was a seasonal industry with a different rhythm, suffering from bad weather in winter but also losing out to the demands of the holiday season in high summer. The utilities (gas, water, electricity) were important contributors to resort amenities, and location factors varied from Ramsgate's 2.0 to Bournemouth's 0.9, the only figure below the national average. Commerce and finance ranged between 1.7 and 1.1, and transport was altogether less convincing as a holiday trade within the resorts, with four of the eight location quotients dipping below 1.0. Travel to the coast employed large numbers of train crews, coach drivers and ancillary staff whose homes for census purposes lay elsewhere, of course.[15] Shops were also particularly important in seaside economies, although the census did not enable them to be counted accurately; but at Great Yarmouth in 1930 the distributive trades found work for one-fifth of the insured population, and Brighton had nearly 3,000 shops in the town centre in 1937, which added up to one shop for every forty-seven inhabitants. This was double the national density, and in 1946 the distributive trades employed one-sixth of Brighton's workforce. These were, however, regional as well as local and holiday trade shopping centres. Shop work also accounted for a disproportionate amount of total working hours, especially during the season, with early closing regulations suspended for the duration and up to ninety-one hours a week being worked in cooked food shops. This apart:[16]

> The longest seasonal overtime is found in confectioners' and fancy goods and toy shops. In confectioners' shops in Yarmouth and Southend . . . investigators found that 79, 77, 73 and 71 hours a week (exclusive of meal times) were common during the season, and in Yarmouth 78 hours were worked in a fancy goods and toy shop. Fruiterers and florists were open 8 a.m. to 10 p.m. seven days a week in the holiday season and in the holiday area, and work is continuous. The tourist certainly means a boom for the trade, but too often at the cost of its employees.

The seasonal fluctuations in demand which these patterns reflected did not deter multiple grocers and department stores from being attracted to the spending power of the larger and more residential resorts, especially on the south coast. Thus at the beginning of the twentieth century Sainsbury's first nine 'country' branches, beyond its London and suburban heartland, included Brighton, Hove, Eastbourne, Bournemouth and Folkestone though (perhaps significantly) not Hastings, Margate or Ramsgate. A little earlier Bobby's chain of department stores had similarly colonised the affluent residential south coast resorts, and these foundations were firmly built on in the inter-war years, when Bobby's departure from Margate was a striking indicator of its declining social tone.[17]

But the widespread seasonal exploitation of labour, especially in more down-market settings, which extended in less public ways into the hotel and boarding-house sectors (and included family members in family businesses among the rest), was the other side of the coin of the winter unemployment. Allen Hutt was grinding a Communist Party axe but also echoing Edwardian comments when, in 1933, he commented that, 'Unemployment and misery weigh no less heavily on the workers in the much-boosted holiday resort of Lancashire

[Blackpool, where a huge new hotel was planned] than on the workers in the factory town'; but his recognition that resorts were industrial towns, with their own distinctive specialisms and social problems, was telling and important.[18]

Nor were the retired people who continued to flood into some of the quieter resorts during the inter-war years necessarily comfortably off: there was plenty of scope for sinking into genteel poverty, isolated from relatives and old friends and with limited scope for building a new social life, on an emergent *Costa Geriatrica*. M.P. Fogarty identified problems in Sussex at the end of the 1930s, although he considered the overall outcome to be 'reasonably sound':[19]

> The influx of retired people, while providing a more stable demand for local services, had serious social disadvantages. One [Nuffield] Survey report comments on the existing population of pensioners along the East Sussex coast as 'an inert mass, the vast majority of whom neither could nor would participate in any developments of a social or industrial character . . .' Though many are wealthy persons, there are many more with small independent incomes, and if taxation rises . . . the presence of this aging mass of unoccupied persons, with ever-shrinking incomes, may present a serious social problem.

The dimensions of seaside retirement, which was already affecting age-structures on parts of the Sussex and south Devon coasts in Edwardian times, had indeed expanded considerably by the 1930s. The proportion of people of pensionable age in the population of Worthing was 9.2 per cent in 1901, 18.7 per cent in 1931 and 29.7 per cent in 1951. For Bexhill the corresponding figures were 6.3 per cent, 15.0 per cent and 28.0 per cent. Similar trends were evident elsewhere in Sussex and in the up-market south Devon resorts, as well as in northern retirement centres like Grange-over-Sands. This pattern was to spread to new places and become much more pronounced in the post-war generation.[20]

Not only was the seaside resort, as a kind of town, increasingly biased towards the elderly among its residents: it was also, and had long been, what V.S. Pritchett described (discussing Scarborough in 1934) as 'a woman-run town':[21]

> The boarding-houses are held very commonly in the woman's name; the place is the widow's or the spinster's gold mine; and if there are husbands and they are not shopkeepers or clerks in a town which has no other industry, they are pigeon-fancying, greyhound-racing idlers, meditative retired gentlemen. As the seaside resort becomes organised as an industry, the men, of course, creep back into public office. There are the gardeners, the inspectors, the amusement park staff, the dance hall attendants, bandsmen, the advertisers; their life is in the *business* of entertainment. They are the creators of the town's beauty parlour. But the substance of the industry is in the hands and in the pockets of the women; and the young men of a town like Scarborough leave the place when they grow up.

This portrayal is affected by Pritchett's (widely-shared) vision of seaside resorts as courtesans, trying to coax and charm money from visitors by seductive feminine wiles; and, as we have seen, it neglects the key masculine occupations of this kind of town. Even so, there is a fundamental truth in this perception.

This also brings out further aspects of the characteristic complexity of family economies in seaside resorts. Not only did many of the women run small businesses, so that a female occupational structure would be lozenge-shaped (concentrated into the lower middle class) while a male one would approximate more closely to the traditional pyramid (though with a shrunken skilled working class and broader-than-usual upper and lower strata); there was also a variety of seasonal expedients for augmenting incomes which were likely to be straitened in the winter months. The scriptwriter and comic performer Frank Muir illustrates this in his memories of childhood in the Kentish resorts of Ramsgate and Broadstairs during the 1920s. In early years his father, a marine engineer who had come ashore on marriage, did labouring jobs while his mother kept a sweetshop and helped out in her mother's nearby pub. A period of prosperity came when Mr Muir senior went to work in Selby, Yorkshire, for a large building firm, leaving his wife in Broadstairs (a common seaside expedient: resorts were inhospitable to skilled men seeking employment); but he had to return after a serious illness, and worked for his brother-in-law installing wireless sets (a reminder that, despite the high rates of mobility into and out of seaside resorts, family ties could be important contributors to survival strategies). The family moved to a rented bungalow with scope for taking in visitors (always a key goal: such houses commanded higher rents), and the extra income went partly into carpeting the house throughout, a remarkable luxury at the time. As the young Frank grew older he was able to make a little money by selling programmes on the esplanade and beach, meshing in (though in a relatively amateurish way) with the unofficial summer juvenile labour market which remained characteristic of seaside life. Other memoirs of the period demonstrate the common threads which link this account with many others, forming kaleidoscopic patterns of shifting incomes as pressures and opportunities waxed and waned among the working and lower middle classes in these difficult settings.[22]

The inter-war years brought increasing recognition, both by journalists and social scientists, of the distinctive nature and problems of seaside resort society. Some aspects, such as seasonal unemployment, gender and the problems associated with seaside retirement, became more pronounced than hitherto and more visible to outsiders. The Second World War brought temporary changes, as resorts became unwontedly full of young men in training, manning coastal defences or, by 1944, awaiting the Normandy landings. They brought a cosmopolitan character to many resorts, as Blackpool welcomed Black American servicemen to its flourishing wartime entertainments and Bognor Regis played host to Canadians and Norwegians, whose preference for the King's Beach Hotel at Pagham led to its being rechristened 'Little Norway'.[23] Where civil servants and the military took over hotels and places of entertainment, as at Blackpool, Brighton and on the north Wales coast, it often took several post-war years to return them to holiday use. Bomb damage and the disruption caused by the closure of extensive areas of coastline for military purposes also caused enduring problems, and an eloquent description of Margate in 1943 emphasised the prevailing neglect and decay of gardens and other amenities, while only a handful of the hotels and boarding-houses were open in August. What is remarkable is the speed of the post-war recovery, even here, fuelled as it was by unprecedented demand; but old problems resurfaced, sometimes in new guises, as normality returned.[24]

The post-war holiday boom did not bring universal sustained prosperity to resort economies, with problems becoming apparent early in some of the smaller northern centres after the immediate rush to the sea in the late 1940s had worked itself out. Despite optimistic projections of future demand in 1950, the middle of the decade found Whitby, the subject of a survey by a group of geographers, already in difficulties. J.W. House summarised the problems which had taken 635 bed-spaces out of the market between 1951 and 1956, leaving just under 5,000, while several properties lay empty. Here as elsewhere, many boarding-house proprietors had bought at inflated wartime prices from a previous generation who were ready to retire, but they soon had to cope with a scarcity of seasonal labour (whose cost was boosted by the Catering Wages Act), high levels of local taxation and interest rates and a decline in both the length of the season and the social status of holidaymakers, which made it even more difficult to raise prices which had long been pegged by inter-war deflation. Meanwhile, retailing was stagnating, apart from the shops and cafes that catered for the growing day-tripper motor-coach trade. The local authority had limited resources with which to boost entertainments or advertising. House suggested that Whitby was failing to adjust as effectively as some of its regional competitors, and that in general 'for the future, the outlook for the holiday industry in Northern England seems fairly bright'. Over the next decade or so he was right about the north as a whole, and Whitby itself was able to stabilise and consolidate, although caravans and apartments, which generated less direct employment, increased in popularity at the expense of hotels and boarding-houses. In 1967 Whitby's 56,000 staying visitors were said to contribute £581,000 to the local economy, of which more than half went directly on accommodation, at a time when the gross turnover of the town's retail shops was said to be around £2.5 million. At the same time Scarborough's 446,000 staying visitors allegedly contributed £7 million, a quarter of which went on the amusements which were much more in evidence here. Here, as at Blackpool (on a much larger scale) and Morecambe on the opposite coast, the holiday industry was still an important contributor to local economies at this least-favoured end of the country, even at the end of the post-war generation. New Brighton's collapse was still exceptional.[25]

The scarcity of seasonal labour was a general issue in the post-war period of full employment. In about 1950 the future television scriptwriter Johnny Speight went to Clacton for a summer, scraping a living at first by playing in a jazz group in a pub, and sleeping in unused Butlins staff accommodation until it was occupied and he and his friend Peter took to a bus shelter and the beach. But finding work was absolutely no problem, disreputable as he must have seemed:[26]

> We didn't have to bum around the beach at night for long, nor in the day time ... We all got a job in a small guest house ... We were still playing in the pub at night but during the day I was head cook and bottle washer in this guest house; Peter was my assistant and both Connie and Ivy were chambermaids. We had things very much our own way in this guest house, the people who owned it could hardly find anyone to work in it, they could hardly find anyone to stay in it either. The food under my culinary regime was good, wholesome and reasonably cooked – if you ate in the kitchen with the staff. What was served in the dining room was a different matter.

Apart from what this romantic but plausible reminiscence says about the post-war seasonal labour market, it also suggests that under such circumstances the workers had a measure of agency, even power, within a workplace that desperately needed them. This was something new.

It was also only part of the story. The old problems of seasonal unemployment and low-wage poverty never disappeared entirely, even during the relatively affluent 1950s and 1960s. Between 1952 and 1964 Blackpool had winter unemployment peaks which took its average for the year to higher levels than most north-western industrial towns, with winter peaks of 8 per cent in 1952 and 7.5 per cent in January 1959. These were much lower than corresponding figures for the 1930s or 1980s, and the 1952 figures followed the closure of an aircraft factory which had offered more stable manufacturing work than was usual at the seaside, where industry had been discouraged ostensibly through fear of pollution but (it was often alleged) also because its presence might pull wages up in the holiday industry, to the disadvantage of local politicians. Scarborough in 1949 had maximum unemployment running at just under 3 per cent of total population (as opposed to insured workforce), and it also had persisting slum clearance problems. Brighton also had 'very high' unemployment in January 1950, and the urban pathology of the seaside was generally resistant to the most optimistic post-war trends. The best that could be said for low unemployment levels inland was that they reduced competition for summer jobs and allowed Johnny Speight to flourish in Clacton.[27]

The post-war generation also saw a sharp decline in the hotel and boarding-house sector, as rising costs met the loss of middle-class custom and the trend to shorter and more flexible domestic holidays (leaving beds unoccupied in mid-week) in a pincer movement. The strongest trend was evident at the top of the market, as large hotels in Thanet, Clacton and Ilfracombe (for example) went out of business, and hardly any new ones were built to take their place. Only a few up-market resorts, such as Bournemouth and Torquay, were able to update their five-star hotels and keep an appropriate clientele. Lower down the scale the decline from the 1950s is harder to measure, and the census figures clearly exaggerate; but the seaside landlady was coming under increasing pressure, alongside an entertainment industry which could not satisfy an appetite for radio and especially television stars who commanded ever-increasing fees. As these aspects of the by-now traditional holiday industry came under increasing pressure, the balance of resort economies began to change in earnest.[28]

A key trend of the post-war generation was the new impetus given to sea-side retirement, which developed particularly rapidly in the 1960s and brought in growing numbers from the lower middle and upper working classes to more mainstream resorts closer to population centres than hitherto. By 1971 thirty-five resorts with census populations over 15,000 had more than 20 per cent of their population above pensionable age (sixty-five for men, sixty for women), when the national figure was 16.1 per cent. Several percentages stood at more than twice the national norm: Bexhill led the field with 44.2 per cent (from 37 in 1961); then came Worthing 38.8 per cent (36.3 in 1961); Clacton 36.4 (29.2); Herne Bay 36.1 (33.8); Hove 33.6 (30.8); Eastbourne 33.4 (29.8); Broadstairs 32.7 (29.4); Colwyn Bay 32.3 (29.1); and Lymington 32.2 (27.1). Some remarkably high net migration rates among the older age-groups lay behind these figures, and in several smaller resorts more than two-fifths of the April residents were eligible for state pensions: Grange 45.5 per cent, Sidmouth 44.3, Southwold 43.5, Budleigh Salterton 43.0, Seaton 42.2, and Frinton/Walton-on-the-Naze 40.8. These were remarkable figures, especially when we bear in mind that over large areas of (especially) bungalow estates well over 80 per cent of the population might be 'elderly'.

As Valerie Karn pointed out, these statistics had implications for the nature of resort society, especially in the upper-crust retirement resorts of south-west England where class and age distinctions coincided to create a 'social gulf', across which upper-class retirers sometimes treated home helps like 'lackeys'. Karn's detailed studies focused on Bexhill and Clacton, which could not match the high social standing of the older-established retirement centres of south Devon or indeed of Eastbourne, whose prices had been out of the reach of many of her sample. Bexhill, however, was significantly more up-market than Clacton, drawing on affluent south London suburbs whereas Clacton's retirers came more from the capital's north-eastern districts, often closer to the city centre. Sixty per cent of the Bexhill sample had retired from professional or managerial posts, and 24 per cent from lesser white-collar jobs, as compared with 25 and 18 per cent in Clacton, where more than half the retirers had been manual workers. In some places, such as Littlehampton, the working-class presence was boosted by the Greater London Council setting up its own seaside bungalow estates. What these retirers wanted, above all, was a healthy climate, sea air and quiet-ness, especially escape from traffic congestion and noise. Many chose their destination partly because friends were already in the area, and club member-ships flourished, though much more in Bexhill (which had a Cat Club with 300 members, but also a Philosophical Society) than in Clacton. But there was heavy dependence on companionate marriages, and some admitted to loneliness. Karn was guardedly optimistic about the overall outcome: coastal retirement was 'not . . . an unqualified success for the people concerned', but 'for most retired people the move turned out a satisfactory one'. These developments did pose problems in the retirement areas, however, as retirers' savings and pensions failed to keep pace with inflation and they preferred to use up savings rather than claim benefits to which they were entitled, while the South-East Economic Planning Council in 1967 provided a broader economic analysis:

> As a result of labour shortages, the staffing of some essential services is becoming difficult; the pattern of amenities and entertainment suited to old people is less attractive to holidaymakers; and because of the high incidence of low and fixed incomes, rate income and consumer spending in these towns is not rising as else-where in the region.

Thus the accentuated volume of seaside retirement fed into other economic and social problems of the resorts during this time of relatively full employment, storing up problems for the future. Karn accurately predicted that, 'In a few years Clacton will find there is a major problem of poverty, particularly in relation to the upkeep of owner-occupied houses'. As her evidence showed, there were significant variations between places in the social composition and behaviour of seaside retirers; but the overall themes were strongly delineated across broad stretches of coastline, especially in south-eastern England.[29]

Seaside resorts might have distinctive economies and age-structures, but in terms of religion and ethnicity they were less remarkable, although an early tendency for all preferences within the Church of England to be accommodated, making sure that no portion of the respectable middle-class market was discouraged, carried its influence through into the new century. As befitted their liminal status the larger resorts were perhaps more likely to house an unusually wide range of fringe religious groups, as in the tendency for Christian Scientists and spiritualists to congregate in resort settings, which John Gay ascribes to the large number of elderly migrants in the populations, without making the connection stick. What counted here, perhaps, was a search for stability, certainty and sociability in later life, among people who were away from old friends and relatives and in need of new communities; but even this assumes that eccentric religious adherence was acquired at the seaside rather than imported in the cultural baggage of the migrants themselves. More significantly, the twentieth century saw the growth and consolidation of some of the strongest Jewish communities in Britain in seaside settings. Blackpool, Brighton, Southend and Southport all had thriving Jewish communities before 1930, and the new wave of Jewish immigration during the 1930s boosted a second group of settlements, especially in Bournemouth (with perhaps 2,500 Jewish residents in the late 1960s) and Margate (with a concentration in Cliftonville), but also elsewhere along the south coast and in north Wales. Philip Oakes remembered the regrets of his rabidly anti-semitic uncle at buying a bungalow at Westcliff in the late 1930s, too close to Southend which he described as 'the new Jerusalem' and 'Little Palestine', full of an imagined plethora of Jews 'driving around in their flashy cars, stuffing themselves in the best hotels'; and novels about seaside entertainment and its entrepreneurs made use of such caricatures, rarely affectionate, though usually without this admixture of bile and hatred. These resorts not only had Jewish hotels which provided kosher food and observed the religious festivals; they also became attractive centres for commuting and retirement among comfortably-off Jewish families from London, Liverpool and Manchester.[30]

The seaside was capable of providing niches for other ethnic and religious minorities. After the Second World War Great Yarmouth, for example, became the centre of perhaps the largest British Greek Cypriot community outside London. By the mid-1990s there were perhaps 150 families, many of whom had followed classic migration chains from the village of Eptakomi, operating family-run restaurants and guest-houses in a tight little area around Regent Road, at the heart of the resort area between the piers. This is an illustration of how promising seaside territory can be for small businesses and communities of interlinked families, and the Yarmouth Cypriots even have their own church, passed on by the Church of England and renamed St Spyridon's.[31] Italian communities have also found their niches at the seaside, centred on similar activities to those they made their own elsewhere. They went busily into fish and chips and ice-cream, dominating the best pitches on Blackpool beach, and setting up successful cafes all around the coast from the turn of the century onwards. Charles Forte's catering empire was firmly founded in his father's and uncles' ventures in coastal resorts across southern England from Weston-super-Mare to Bournemouth, Worthing and Brighton, where he himself gained experience and access to capital.[32] This was more than merely replicating activities inland, for the resort outlets were crucial to the inter-war development of the business; but in the absence of detailed research it seems that the post-war waves of Chinese, Indian, Italian and more exotic restaurants which also colonised the seaside were more like the mixture as elsewhere. What should be stressed, however, is the lack of 'minority ethnic groups' recorded in the 1991 census across a wide area of resort coastline in south-west England and East Anglia, along with Scarborough, where they accounted for at most 0.6 per cent of the population, and the unwillingness of Asian settlers in the old industrial towns of Lancashire and Yorkshire to move across and set up small businesses in the resorts.[33]

Another characteristic feature of some of the larger seaside resorts came to be their hospitality to gays, as both residents and visitors. Brighton and Blackpool had reputations as centres of regional gay communities and as containing safe venues for making contacts for many years, although until recently it has been difficult for outsiders to find evidence on the extent and nature of the gay presence. By the 1990s it was becoming more visible, and increasingly acceptable to tourism promoters. When the British Tourist Authority began a marketing drive to attract gay tourists from the United States in 1999 it highlighted Blackpool, Brighton and Bournemouth. Blackpool had a spectacular array of gay night-spots, including local entrepreneur Basil Newby's Flamingo and his drag cabaret Funny Girls, and a growing list of gay or gay-friendly hotels and guest-houses, some of which perpetuated the resort's general reputation for cheapness. Blackpool already had a May Queen ceremony for drag queens at Lucy's Bar in about 1960, when Pepe's was another gay venue; but it was not until 1980, when Newby (the son of a Blackpool landlady) bought the Flamingo and founded his business empire, that the scene really began to develop. Already in 1991 there were around 150 guest-houses catering mainly for gays, concentrated into the unpretentious terraced streets around both North Station and the main gay night-clubs. When Funny Girls opened in 1994 its success in bringing together the most mixed of audiences, and extending the town's central entertainment area northwards, set the seal on Newby's business respectability and personal acceptability. The setting helped: Blackpool's kitsch and ribald traditions (the comic postcard, the jokes about landladies and strong women, and so on) gave it a camp appeal of its own, reinforced by its reputation as a centre for theatrical aspiration; and the widespread gay obsession with bingo added to its attractions. At Brighton, 'the gay capital of the south' and even 'of Europe', (a title to which Blackpool also laid claim), with its specialised bars and accommodation and August gay pride festival (and plans in 1999 for a gay-themed day at the racecourse), gay men and lesbians were said to account for between one in four and one in five of the population, although these speculative statistics were perhaps more a public relations exercise than a plausible piece of demography. But it is less arresting to find this image being celebrated at this classically liminal and culturally diverse site than at ostensibly proletarian Blackpool. Bournemouth's gay image was older and more sedate, as befitted other aspects of its traditional reputation. Here was an aspect of seaside social structure which chimed in well with aspects of the celebration of 'otherness' in seaside entertainment, from the minstrels of the Victorian years to the celebrations of the strange and exotic on Blackpool's inter-war 'Golden Mile', but which had been hidden from the uninitiated until it dared to speak its name in public at the end of the century.[34]

Blackpool's embrace of the 'pink pound' was encouraged most seductively by a local entrepreneur, returning to traditions of social mobility from modest origins through entertainment and related businesses which harked back to the turn of the century. This stood out all the more in a setting where control of the entertainment industry had been passing first to national, then to international, big business combines, for whom their seaside holdings had to be looked at dispassionately alongside the rest of the investment portfolio. Rescues from closure by voluntary bodies, such as Blackpool's Friends of the Grand

Theatre, were more significant as underlining the capacity of resorts for generating powerful and determined residents' groups than as a major reversal of this tide. The business history of seaside entertainment would provide an additional window on the debate over resort decline, but it also illustrates the growing difficulty of advancing through resort social structures as markets became tighter and competition fiercer. There is scope for interesting research projects on all these themes. Meanwhile, the declining social status of most resorts in the late twentieth century was only too apparent.

A telling illustration of this loss of comparative affluence and status is the seaside resorts' apparent failure to share in 'the resurgence of demand for domestic labour in Britain through the 1980s' among the prospering middle classes, although this is partly a demographic matter, given that much of this new demand was for the care of pre-school children while resort populations were increasingly elderly. Employers were heavily concentrated into middle-class London, suburban Surrey and the rest of the affluent south-east, which included the coastal counties of Kent and West Sussex but without any particular emphasis on their resorts. At the beginning of the century a high incidence of domestic service had been a prominent feature of seaside resort populations. By the 1980s this distinguishing feature, with all its connotations of affluence and status, had practically disappeared.[35]

The distinguishing features that counted, indeed, were increasingly concentrated at the other end of the social scale by the late twentieth century. Even as its tourism planners pursued gentrification and the 'cultural tourism' of architecture and 'heritage', picking out the bits of the past that suited it, Brighton was also reasserting its equally long tradition of poverty and overcrowding. By the mid-1980s it featured in the worst 10 per cent of urban areas on most of the Department of the Environment's criteria, in superficially refurbished Regency flats as well as on the council estates of the periphery. Blackpool's central wards were in worse case. Even Newquay, one of the beneficiaries of the diversion of domestic holiday demand to the far south-west in the 1950s and 1960s, had fallen on hard times in the late 1990s. It was still the most popular Cornish holiday resort, with more than a million visitors per year; but its unemployment rate was the highest in Britain, two and a half times a national percentage which had been steadily shrinking for six years, without this benign trend making much impact here. January unemployment ran at 12 per cent in 1999, still much less than comparable resort figures in the depressed winters of the 1930s, but cause for concern when coupled with extremely low wages and a common pattern of young people doing menial catering jobs in summer and living off the dole in winter, attracted by the surfing opportunities.[36] More-cambe was still enduring an even worse press at this time: despite its attempts at refurbishment and re-invention, it was labelled 'a town in sad decline' by the 1999 edition of the *Lonely Planet* guide to the UK, which also savaged other British seaside resorts, and came top of an unenviable league table as the English health authority which issued the most anti-depressant drugs per capita. Press coverage of this statistic summed the town up thus: 'the bed-and-breakfasts are full of benefit claimants, drugs are rife, the Grand Hotel is being pulled down and the tourists have fled to the Med'. The issue of small boarding-houses giving up the holiday trade and taking a year-round income from benefit claimants on what the tabloid press called the 'Costa del Dole' was contentious from Morecambe to Margate in the 1990s, and at the end of the century the strug-gling accommodation industry of the latter resort was also playing host to equally controversial asylum seekers (Albanians, Kurds, Afghans, Kosovans) whom the locals professed to find disturbingly 'other'. Here were perceived pathologies of the declining seaside, shading over in places and at times into something approaching moral panic.[37]

Analyses of the 1991 census showed a more complex picture. Out of 366 local authorities in England, two resorts featured in the fifty which experienced the worst social deprivation, based on a scale which incorporated unemploy-ment, single parenthood, single pensioners, long-term limiting illness and dependency. These were Blackpool, which came thirtieth, immediately behind fifteen Inner London boroughs, various old industrial centres and the Scilly Isles, and Thanet, fifteen places behind. A material deprivation index, based on the proportion of the population living at more than one to a room, coupled with the percentage of households without cars, central heating and basic amenities, captured four major resorts in the top fifty: Blackpool again at twenty-first, followed by Hove at twenty-seventh, Brighton at thirty-third and Bournemouth at forty-fifth. Hove might be thought a striking inclusion, and Bournemouth even more so; and the areas of affluence within all these towns were sufficient to ensure that the impoverished wards would have to be in dire circumstances to counterbalance them. At the other extreme, Christ-church and East Dorset (especially) featured among the fifty least deprived districts. Moreover, there was evidence of economic recovery by the end of the 1980s in some less obviously dynamic resorts, although it was concentrated into sectors other than the holiday industry. On the West Sussex coast unem-ployment had fallen by nearly 60 per cent by December 1988 (an interestingly off-season month) from its early 1986 peak, and in the Worthing commuter belt the 3.8 per cent receiving benefit allegedly 'represented little more than people hard to employ or in the process of changing jobs'. Even Brighton's commuter belt had only 5.6 per cent unemployment by this time, against a national figure of 8.3 per cent. Problems focused on skill shortages and recruitment problems in an area where house prices were 'relatively low for the region' and 'the workforce is large, growing and adaptable'. But growth was in business services rather than tourism: the coastal hotel trade was in decline, and growth in this sector was now in 'the countryside and inland towns' within the county. The seaside here was recovering prosperity, but for new reasons in which the maritime location was at best incidental.[38]

Certain resorts appeared prominently in lists of deprived areas on particular measures: Blackpool, Scarborough and Torbay for lack of central heating, Blackpool and Brighton for low levels of car ownership, Hastings for single-parent households, Blackpool for limiting long-term illness (a product of large numbers of retirement migrants from the old industrial working class), and Thanet for unemployment. Positive indices stand out much less, and no resorts featured among the fifty authorities with the most prosperous residents (Blackpool and Thanet appeared at the other end of the scale). The only unequivocally positive characteristic to stand out, on most assumptions, was a high level of home ownership, with a string of Sussex and other south coast districts hovering around 80 per cent along with the Fylde (genteel Lytham St Annes) and, more surprisingly, Cleethorpes. A corollary of this was the prevailing low levels of council housing, with ten resort areas in the bottom fifty, from Blackpool's 10.2 per cent of the housing stock to Christchurch's 2.8. These absences put stronger pressure on working-class living standards. More generally, prosperity was not an identifying feature of the English seaside as the century's end approached.[39]

By this time, too, population growth at the seaside was concentrated into a narrow band of locations (although on some coastlines saturation point had been reached long before). Among the twenty fastest-growing places between 1981 and 1991 were East Dorset (13.5 per cent), Teignbridge and North Cornwall in the south-west (where almost every coastal district was in the top or second quartile), Suffolk Coastal, and more arrestingly East Yorkshire and East Lindsey (Lincolnshire). At the other end of the scale Brighton shrank by 5 per cent. Attractive, semi-rural seaside locations were still pulling in migrants, but the older resorts were stagnating.[40]

Resorts displayed distinctive demographic traits which were entirely compatible with this evidence. Above all, the outcomes of the trend to seaside retirement were still very much in evidence, most obviously along the south coast. Seaside resorts completely dominated the tables showing pensioners as percentage of population, and resident population over 75 years old, in the 1991 census. Pensioners made up 24 per cent of Eastbourne's population, 23.4 per cent of Worthing's, and more than one-fifth in Arun, Christchurch, Hove, East Devon, West Somerset and Thanet. These were actually less striking figures than those for the seaside retirement boom years of the 1960s, but they still stood out comparatively. Fourteen highly specialised resort districts had more than 10.8 per cent of their inhabitants over 75, underlining the growth of the retirement home industry during the 1980s. Resorts also featured prominently towards the foot of tables showing households with young and growing families, and at the top of the single-person households league (bedsitters as well as pensioners). This overshadowed the traditional importance of self-employment and work in the building trades and the service sector, although self-employment stood out in certain south-western resort districts. An interesting feature of these areas, which was shared with Thanet and especially Dover, was a high proportion of the workforce reporting working hours of over forty per week. But above all, by the end of the century, what characterised seaside resorts in economic and demographic terms was the elderly and economically inactive sectors of their populations, along with high incidences of poverty concentrated into the older, larger and more down-market centres.[41]

The characteristic seaside resort combination of the middle-aged and elderly, with transient youthful seasonal workers and pockets of poverty, has marked out an urban culture in which the needs of the holiday industry have been in tension with the priorities of retired residents, the former needing subsidies and a measure of liveliness, the latter preferring low levels of local taxation and a quiet life. Where holiday businesses and retired residents coincided, until the 1990s, was in a dominant preference for Conservative politics, although the most visible fault-lines in terms of policies cut across party labels. This is an important set of issues, and questions of power, resources and conflict in seaside resorts will be pursued further in the next chapter.

Notes

1 Walton, 'Seaside resorts and maritime history'; and see Neale, *Bath*, for pioneering attention to such concerns.

2 F.C. Ball, *One of the damned: the life and times of Robert Tressell, author of The ragged-trousered philanthropists* (London: Weidenfeld and Nicholson, 1973), p. 32.

3 Peak, *Fishermen of Hastings*.

4 Ibid., pp. 61, 81–2; *A hand-book and history of Sidmouth, from the Triassic period up to 'Now'* (London, 1885), p. 12; Mate's Illustrated Guides, *Sidmouth* (Sidmouth, 1905), unpaginated; Harold Wright (ed.), *Letters of Stephen Reynolds* (Richmond, Surrey, 1925), p. 64; Gilbert, *Brighton, old ocean's bauble*, p. 247.

5 J.K. Walton, 'Fishing communities 1850–1950', in D. Starkey (ed.), *History of the fisheries of England and Wales* (London: Chatham, forthcoming, 2000); and see especially Stephen Reynolds, *A poor man's house* (London, 1908).

6 *George Meek, Bath chair-man*, pp. 177, 215, 287, 293.

7 London School of Economics, Webb Local Government Collection, Vol. 302 (Bournemouth).

8 Ibid., Vols. 335 (Brighton), 310 (Southport); Walton, *Blackpool*, p. 98.

9 Walton, *The English Seaside resort*, Chapter 4; Walton, *The Blackpool landlady*; Walton, 'The Blackpool landlady revisited', *Manchester Region History Review*, 8 (1994), pp. 23–30 for discussion of the problems of measuring actual numbers in this period.

10 S. Davies *et al.*, *County borough elections in inter-war England* (Aldershot, 1999), Vol. 1, Appendix 2–6.

11 Brunner, *Holiday making and the holiday trades*, pp. 40–43; Fogarty, *Prospects of the industrial areas of Great Britain*, p. 214.

12 Brunner, *Holiday making and the holiday trades*, p. 42; Gurney, ' "Intersex" and "Dirty Girls" '.

13 Brunner, *Holiday making and the holiday trades*, p. 25.

14 Ibid., pp. 26–30; Walton, 'The Blackpool landlady revisited'.

15 Brunner, *Holiday making and the holiday trades*, p. 26; Gilbert, *Brighton, old ocean's bauble*, p. 250.

16 Brunner, *Holiday making and the holiday trades*, pp. 36–8.

17 Bridget Williams, *The best butter in the world: a history of Sainsbury's* (London, 1994), p. 51; and see Bill Lancaster, *The department store* (Leicester, 1995).

18 Allen Hutt, *The condition of the working class in Britain* (London, 1933), p. 70.

19 Fogarty, *Prospects of the industrial areas of Great Britain*, pp. 404–5.

20 Walton, 'Seaside resorts of England and Wales', p. 40.

21 V.S. Pritchett, 'Scarborough', in Cloud (ed.), *Beside the seaside*, pp. 213–14.

22 Frank Muir, *A Kentish lad* (2nd edn, London, 1998), pp. 17–18, 27–8, 42–6.

23 Walton, *Blackpool*, Chapter 5; Young, A history of *Bognor Regis*, p. 242.

24 Stafford and Yates, *The later Kentish seaside*, pp. 156–7.

25 Daysh (ed.), *A survey of Whitby*, pp. 183–95; Lavery, *Patterns of holidaymaking in the Northern region*, pp. 28, 33; and see above, Chapter 2, for New Brighton.

26 Johnny Speight, *It stands to reason: a kind of autobiography* (London, 1973), p. 157.

27 N. Essafi, 'Some aspects of poverty in Blackpool, 1945–60', MA dissertation, Lancaster University, 1990; Scarborough Reference Library, Annual Reports of the Medical Officer of Health, 1950, pp. 3–5; Musgrave, *Life in Brighton*, p. 416.

28 Demetriadi, 'The golden years', pp. 59–69.

29 Karn, *Retirement to the seaside*, pp. 33–5, 47–59, 65, 83–91, 107–13, 127–8, 183, 250–3, 362 n. 1.

30 J.D. Gay, *The geography of religion in England* (London, 1971), pp. 187–90, 214–20, 319, 323–4; Philip Oakes, *From middle England: a memory of the 1930s and 1940s* (Harmondsworth, 1983), pp. 60, 183–4; D.L. Murray, *Leading lady* (London, 1947).

31 Dave Hill, 'New Britons: Great Yarmouth', *Observer, Life*, 4 February 1996, pp. 20–1.

32 Charles Forte, *Forte: the autobiography of Charles Forte* (London, 1987), pp. 23–9; J.K. Walton, *Fish and chips and the British working class 1870–1940* (Leicester, 1992), for the Clyde coast.

33 Forrest and Gordon, *People and places*, p. 63.

34 Walton, *Blackpool*, pp. 146–7; Lisa Jolly, 'Interview with Basil Newby', appendix to 'Blackpool: a seaside sex capital?'; *Guardian*, 27 March 1999, p. 16; *The Observer*, Sport section, 18 April 1999, p. 13.

35 Nicky Gregson and Michelle Lowe, *Servicing the middle classes: gender and waged domestic labour in contemporary Britain* (London, 1994), pp. 47–50.

36 Meethan, 'Place, image and power', pp. 191–4; Walton, *Blackpool*, pp. 159–61; Charlotte Denny, 'Sand, sea and social security', *Guardian*, 22 April 1999, p. 26.

37 *Observer*, 2 May 1999, p. 16; *Guardian*, 24 August 1999, p. 7.

38 Forrest and Gordon, *People and places*, pp. 58–61; West Sussex County Council, *The West Sussex Coastal Districts*, second review, April 1989 (B.L. YC.1990.b.2529), pp. 10–11, 23–4.

39 Forrest and Gordon, *People and places*, pp. 7, 11, 19, 21, 29, 33, 55; D. Gordon and R. Forrest, *People and places 2: social and economic divisions in England* (Bristol, 1995), p. 85.

40 Forrest and Gordon, *People and places*, p. 39.

41 Ibid., pp. 25, 27, 47, 49, 53; Gordon and Forrest, *People and places 2*, pp. 23, 25, 31.

Seaside politics

The seaside economy generated its own distinctive kind of politics, which responded to the preoccupations of and conflicts between the contending interests whose fortunes ebbed and flowed, and whose capacity for gaining representation and influencing policies did not always match their numbers or articulacy. In party political terms the Conservatives were dominant almost always and almost everywhere, until their widespread collapse in seaside resorts as elsewhere during the rapidly changing circumstances of the 1990s. Enduring Conservative strength reflected the over-representation of the middle classes and the elderly at the seaside, the mixture of deference-generating service occupations and highly competitive small businesses which dominated the lower end of the labour market, the cultures of patronage and dependence which arose in casual and seasonal occupations which set a premium on good relations with bosses and foremen, and the lack of large-scale manufacturing industry to provide a purchase for trade union organisation and support for the Labour Party, which generally found the seaside to be inhospitable territory. The Liberals, meanwhile, sustained a strong presence wherever nonconformity was powerful among traders and a concern for respectability remained good business; but, parliamentary elections apart, the politics of seaside resorts usually took the form of internecine struggles between interest-groups within Conservative-dominated local authorities. The contests over image, resources, local taxation and the policing of contested spaces, which were what mattered most to resort residents, were played out within the municipal arena with little overt reference to official party programmes. This did not mean that they were either half-hearted or unimportant; and their outcomes affected the nature of resort development and the ability of seaside towns to sustain and expand their markets against proliferating competitors at home and abroad.

Local government was particularly important in seaside resorts.[1] Their spokesmen liked to present them as bastions of free enterprise, but they depended on collective endeavours to provide those amenities, for residents and increasingly for visitors, that private firms felt unable to supply at an adequate profit in a highly competitive, seasonal setting. Promenades and parks were important here, and so were the great bathing-pools of (mainly) the inter-war years, with their extensive spectator accommodation. But many local councils in resorts also had to intervene to subsidise, or even to operate directly, more conventional entertainments associated with ailing piers, winter gardens, theatres or other shows whose profitability over a short season was insufficient to sustain or attract private enterprise; and this was over and above the municipal orchestras which enhanced the up-market attractions of several genteel watering-places. Advertising the resort as a whole, as opposed to the separate promotion of competing businesses within it, became increasingly a municipal responsibility, and the key issues of public health and public order, both vital to the image, identity and competitive power of resorts, were firmly in the hands of the local authority. Finding an appropriate level of regulation of visitor behaviour, combining a suitably relaxed atmosphere with a sense of security for the persons, property and sensibilities of the preferred visiting public, was a vitally important local government role, even in that majority of resorts which did not control their own police forces. Putting everything together, and bearing in mind that for much of the period many of the larger resorts also had municipally run utilities (gas, electricity, water, transport, markets) as well as libraries and art galleries, we find that local government was at the core of seaside resort economies. Its importance was such that the politics of where to site amenities (or activities like sewage farms which everyone needed but nobody wanted as a neighbour), how much to charge for essential services, how much to spend on resort as opposed to residential services (pitting commuters and the retired against the holiday industry), and the appropriate level of local taxation generated conflicts which were the very stuff of resort political life. The high level of municipal involvement in resort economies might be better labelled 'municipal capitalism' than 'municipal socialism', as has been argued, because the aim was to represent the ratepayers as if they were the shareholders of a great limited company in competition with others, and to organise resources practically in pursuit of this goal, rather than to redistribute resources and create a fair, satisfying civic life for local citizens as a matter of principle.[2] The local state was highly active, but with distinctive assumptions and motives; and wherever local government boundary changes altered the importance of resort interests within local authorities, especially through the local government reorganisation of 1974, the results were likely to be particularly contentious.[3] The resulting struggles in local politics created contested narratives and sustained dramas whose working out through press and public meeting helped to forge the collective identities which made resorts what they were. This is therefore an important chapter.

We begin, however, with parliamentary politics. Their outcomes helped to create resort images in their own important ways, and to set the tone and expectations which provided the language of political debate at Town Hall level. In terms of parliamentary elections, seaside resorts were dominated by the Conservative party until the remarkable 'New Labour' landslide of 1997, when the tide flowed as overwhelmingly in this setting as anywhere else in the country. It might be argued that Labour had to become indistinguishable from the Toryism of an earlier generation to succeed at the seaside: it had certainly made little headway previously. E.W. Gilbert remarked on the Conservative tradition in resorts at mid-century, pointing out that the fourteen largest inland and seaside watering-places, with eighteen parliamentary seats in 1951, formed a solid bloc of Conservative MPs. The majorities (in October 1951) ranged from 24,296 in Hove to 4,610 in Southend East. Eleven of these towns were at the seaside: Hove, Southend, Worthing, Eastbourne, Southport, Bournemouth, Blackpool, Torquay, Brighton, Hastings and Poole. 'Thus the health resorts together form a Conservative stronghold just in the same way that the coalmining areas are solid supporters of the Labour party', although the former have had much less attention from historians. Gilbert ascribed this outcome to 'the comparatively small size of organized labour and industry, the high average level of incomes and the dormitory element in the population, . . . (and) the large proportion of elderly retired persons'[4] In the Labour landslide of 1945, seven seaside constituencies (Bournemouth, Blackpool, Brighton, Hastings, Hythe, Southend and Southport) collectively produced a 54 per cent Conservative vote, matched only (outside Northern Ireland) by the 'residential and business' districts of London (55) and the non-borough constituencies of southern Surrey and Sussex, the latter of which included several resorts which did not elect their own MPs as separate boroughs. Southend was interestingly out of step, with a Conservative vote share of 44.7 per cent, but Bournemouth provided the only Conservative majority of over 20,000 at this election, and the swing to Labour in Gilbert's seven seaside resorts was only 8.5 per cent as against 12 per cent nationally.[5] A subsequent classification of parliamentary constituencies, as revised in 1971, isolated a 'family' of 'rural areas and seaside resorts' within which there was a 'cluster' of 'resorts and retirement areas' which was marked by 'an aged population with residents of high socio-economic status, and with local employment "mostly in services" '. These characteristics helped to generate a continuing predominance of Conservative voting, a pattern which endured right through to its sudden dissipation in 1997.[6]

Such blanket Conservative dominance had not always been in evidence; indeed, Gilbert himself pointed to Brighton's older radical traditions. Not only had it harboured a strong Chartist presence: between 1832 and 1880 it returned twenty-two Liberals (many of them Radicals) and eight Conservatives, fortified by bad housing conditions and the presence of organised labour at the railway works. But from 1885 until mid-century only three Liberals breached the Conservative monopoly: one at a by-election in 1905 and two at the famous election of 1906 which ushered in the last great reforming Liberal government. Inter-war Brighton was solidly Conservative; but some cross-currents can be found elsewhere.[7] The inter-war years saw Liberal victories at Blackpool and Southport in 1923, although in each case the triumph was short-lived, while Great Yarmouth, whose economy was more diverse than those of Gilbert's ideal-type resorts, had a full-scale Liberal tradition which held good in 1922, 1923 and 1929, giving way to the Conservatives through the National Government after 1931. It was here, in 1945, that Squadron-Leader E. Kinghorn became Britain's first Labour M.P. for a seaside resort. Great Yarmouth's inclusion in Gilbert's lists would have dented his generalisations without overturning them.[8] Bournemouth, Brighton, Hastings and Southend were all solidly Conservative, with (interestingly) Labour almost always taking second place, but in the two-member Brighton constituency in 1945 Labour's share of the poll in a straight fight was a mere 19.3 per cent. At Hastings and Southend in the same year the proportion was more than double, which is a reminder that in a good year nearly 40 per cent of those who voted, even here, were capable of preferring Labour. Conservatives might dominate at the seaside, but the opposition was seldom negligible.

The post-war pattern from 1950 onwards was, if anything, more strongly marked. The only exception to the overwhelming rule of Conservative parliamentary dominance was Brighton Kemptown, which Labour won twice during the Wilson years, by seven votes (and to general astonishment) in 1964, and by 831 votes in 1966, before a Liberal intervention tilted the balance back to the Conservatives in 1970.[9] Attempts to explain the apostasy of Kemptown from what seemed to be the natural order of things focused on the 'carefully planned political activities of the left-wing . . . staff and students' of the recently founded University of Sussex, whose members (however conspiratorial) were still far too few to deserve this accolade.[10] The continuing reputation for Conservatism which clung to seaside parliamentary seats made the eventual collapse of the walls at the sound of New Labour's trumpet in 1997 seem all the more apocalyptic. Labour made a clean sweep of Blackpool and Brighton, and a poignant moment on election night came when Tony Blair was told that Hove had fallen. His reported response was, 'Don't be ridiculous. You'll be telling me we've won Hastings next.' They did; but the exchange provides a further illustration of perceptions of the armour-plated Conservatism of resort electorates; and in this case the stereotype outweighed the current evidence. Hastings, like Blackpool, had already become practically a Tory-free zone in local government. Where Labour failed, the Liberal Democrats might take their place, as at Weston-super-Mare, Southport and (by the narrowest of margins) even Torbay. A few redoubts looked down uneasily on the swirling tide, as at Bournemouth and Folkestone; but this long-delayed revolution reflected broader long-term changes in resort society, which had come to a head in the late twentieth century, and had already been sending shock-waves through local government for several years.[11]

Tory domination in seaside local government had a varied pedigree, and the picture was always more complicated than in the parliamentary arena. In some resorts, like Blackpool, Conservative control went back to the earliest days of the Corporation, with party political labels being introduced at the first borough elections and the Conservatives ruling practically unchallenged for over a century.[12] Others, like Southport, had strong Liberal traditions, and there were many in which political labels and formal organisation were kept at bay until after the Second World War, or went into abeyance and were then revived. Bournemouth is a good example, governed as it was by 'Independents', with a small Labour minority concentrated into two and then three wards with a working-class presence, throughout the inter-war years, after the 'Progressives' had carried the banner of municipal investment and enterprise through the turn of the century. The Liberals had won the parliamentary seat in 1906, but the ostensible 'Independents' brought together Liberals and Tories against the common enemy that was emergent Labour, and the Liberals lost their separate identity in the process. Torquay is another well-documented case: in 1945 its council had thirty-five Independents and a single representative of Labour, and it was in belated response to Labour's initiative, which had begun in the inter-war years, that the Tories began to put in officially labelled candidates in 1947. The Liberals also began to organise and win seats from 1958 onwards, while Labour became moribund; and on the eve of the local elections of May, 1964, there were still twelve Independents alongside fifteen Conservatives and nine Liberals. The word 'alongside' is carefully chosen: most of the Independents were clearly of a Conservative frame of mind, but chose to run in this guise in acknowledgement of a 'strong anti-party attitude among councillors and the electorate', which led even some Tory candidates to espouse a policy of 'no politics in local government'. What this really meant was the furtherance of a middle-class consensus, on a council which was overwhelmingly dominated by the owners and managers of local businesses; and we shall return to this issue.[13]

In some of the more rural resort-dominated municipalities this pattern persisted into the 1970s and beyond. This was the case in the post-1974 local government districts of East Devon (which included Budleigh Salterton, Exmouth and Seaton), North Devon (Ilfracombe and Lynton as well as Barnstaple), South Wight (Sandown, Shanklin and Ventnor), North Norfolk (Cromer, Sheringham, Wells-next-the-Sea, North Walsham) and West Somerset (Minehead and Watchet). The rise of overt party politics brought in Conservative dominance in East Devon by 1980 and in South Wight by 1983, but in North Devon the Liberal Democrats became the beneficiaries during the 1980s and in the other two authorities the Independents remained the largest group into the 1990s. What this might mean in terms of policies and conflicts as opposed to labels is a different question. More usual was the persistence of strong Tory dominance, sometimes (as at Bournemouth as well as Torbay) involving the relabelling of Independents. In 1973 the Conservatives ran local government in (for example) Torbay, Bournemouth, Brighton, Hove, Dover, Thanet, Blackpool, Great Yarmouth, Bognor Regis and Worthing. This list excludes places where resort interests were subsumed into larger local authorities (which raised important issues, as did the combining of resorts with different visitor profiles and identities under the same administration); but, interestingly, there were exceptions. Weymouth and Portland had a narrow Labour majority (which it soon lost, becoming an enduringly 'hung' council); Eastbourne was Liberal, and oscillated thereafter between Conservatives, Liberals in their various incarnations, and no overall control; Hastings lacked a controlling party, and reverted to this condition in 1980 after a spell of Tory dominance; Southend showed a similar pattern; and Adur (embracing Bognor and Littlehampton, and with a high Liberal representation), along with Cleethorpes and Scarborough (which included Filey and Whitby) where Independents remained important, also lacked a single governing party. These cross-currents persisted into the 1980s, and seaside local government, though predominantly Conservative, did not sustain the uniform political coloration which might have been expected from reputation and parliamentary voting, even during the years of greatest Tory dominance nationally: an outcome which may have reflected widespread awareness of the importance of local government in resorts and the dangers presented by the curbs on spending power and local autonomy which were at the core of the Thatcherite project.[14]

Even in the Conservatives' most entrenched seaside strongholds, the tide began to ebb from the late 1980s onwards, and in the 1990s control began to pass to Labour or the Liberal Democrats, paving the way for the sea-change in the parliamentary electoral landscape in 1997. Brighton itself had become a Labour municipality by 1988, as campaigns on tourism, housing and welfare policy which had begun in the early 1970s began to make their mark. Blackpool was also early in the field, responding to crises in the local welfare state, to a newly visible Conservative incompetence in managing the holiday industry (which had been a key claim to legitimacy), and to revived hints of municipal corruption in a resort with a long history of such allegations. The Conservatives lost overall control for a time after the 1987 elections, before being beaten comprehensively in 1991 and giving way to Labour. 1995 saw them reduced to a rump of a mere two councillors. Blackpool's municipal government had been Conservative-run since incorporation as a borough in 1876, with a brief Liberal interlude in 1958–59. This was unusually spectacular, but there were similar seismic shifts elsewhere. Thanet, which 'by some measures has the second-highest unemployment in the country' in 1997 and had been in steady economic decline since the 1970s, saw Labour become the main opposition party for the first time in 1992 and take control of the council in 1995. Hastings, 'not quite the comfortable place it once was . . . it has become a place where local authorities dump their homeless', had rejected the last of its Tory councillors by the mid-1990s, even though fourteen of the thirty-two seats were still Conservative in 1992, as Labour fought it out with the Liberal Democrats.[15] At this point (for example) Labour held Dover and (since 1990) Great Yarmouth, while the Liberal Democrats were running North Devon, the two Dorset coastal authorities, Eastbourne and Worthing, and the Conservatives had lost control of classic fiefdoms such as Christchurch and the Fylde (which was dominated by the elderly gentility and comfortable commuter estates of Lytham St Anne's). Trends in Scotland cannot be isolated so readily, but in England the 1999 municipal elections saw the Conservatives regain ground, reappearing on Hastings council (with two seats) and winning back some of their more improbable losses. The political analyst Professor Anthony King put matters in perspective with a tart comment: 'I never thought I'd sit in a TV studio and hear the chairman of the Conservative Party boast about retaking Worthing. That is how far they have fallen.' This remark also gave further, academic reinforcement to the historically emblematic status of seaside resorts, which had been assumed to be natural Conservative spheres of influence and beyond the hopes or aspirations of rival parties.[16]

The ostensible political coloration of resort local government was important in terms of image, but for most of the twentieth century political labels masked the real patterns of conflict, which (with the successful sidelining of class issues) were about conflicts of interest which transcended party divisions and brought together shifting coalitions of antagonism on particular issues, a situation which helped to legitimate the ideal of the independent councillor. Recurring themes, across time and between places, can be discerned in these conflicts; and the lack of purchase for class-based issues in towns where big industrial employers were practically absent was not as inevitable as (for example) Brian C. Smith suggests. His comment that, 'Few political issues divide Torquay along class lines', together with the close juxtaposition of the ideas that 'Most council work is non-partisan in character . . . The Labour Party is not represented', presents as explanatory something that needs to be investigated. But the dogs that did bark need to be examined first.[17]

A class-related issue that dominated the politics of some important resorts in the early twentieth century, and remained significant beyond the Second World War in places, was the declining role of the landed estate in local decision-making processes. David Cannadine has charted the transition 'from feudal lord to figurehead' which was especially common in those seaside resorts where landed estates had been instrumental in promotion, planning and even funding essential services and amenities. There was a common pattern of conflict between local government and landed estates at the turn of the century, as municipal corporations began to flex their muscles and sought to buy up landowners' utility companies and to acquire land for sea defences, promenades, parks and pavilions; and this was often tied in with Liberal campaigns for leasehold enfranchisement, the right of tenants holding long (usually 99-year) leases to buy out their freeholds and become outright owners. This proved to be a passing phase, and at Eastbourne, Southport and Bournemouth, to take three high-profile and well-documented examples, the interests of estates and local government were successfully reconciled early in the new century. Eastbourne welcomed successive Dukes of Devonshire to ornamental mayoralties, benefiting from the publicity which came from the opulent festivities and royal visits which the Cavendishes could provide, putting up prominent statues to the seventh and eighth Dukes and publicly acknowledging the estate's contribution to the town's up-market attractions. But such cosiness was made possible by the abdication of landed families and their agents from positions of power in local politics, and such developments recognised the transition from aristocratic rule in this important minority of resorts to the vesting of power in the hands of elected members of (overwhelmingly) the local middle classes and their professional advisors. At Bournemouth, where several landed estates were important to the town's development, the advent of a new generation of landowners, more aware of new balances of power and political realities and more emollient in their public utterances, helped to ease the transition; but it was a general theme.[18]

Alongside the political transition ran a longer-term economic one, which reached a peak in the aftermath of the First World War and was given an additional push by the consequences of the Second World War. In a climate where their powers were being systematically eroded, especially by the Town Planning Act of 1909, and where their estate revenues and (at death) values were being taxed with increasing severity, landowners began to divest themselves of the management problems and responsibilities of urban estates. The hard-pressed Haldon family at Torquay had begun this process as early as 1885 and completed it before 1914; and a lesser, but significant, form of disengagement came when the Earl of Radnor and Earl de la Warr ceased to be resident in Folkestone and Bexhill. At Eastbourne the ninth Duke of Devonshire struggled to escape from his loss-making Parks and Baths Company during 1912–13, although its most conspicuous problems arose from the cost of the orchestra which his predecessor had introduced as recently as 1907. In 1913 he also leased out his Eastbourne mansion, Compton Place.[19]

In most resorts, however, actual land sales were precipitated by the First World War. Cannadine comments that, 'At the seaside, the great families were especially quick off the mark'. He cites, between 1920 and 1926–27, Lord Radnor's sales at Folkestone, the Gilberts (Eastbourne's 'other' landed family) selling their manor house in 1923, Sir George Tapps-Gervis's sales of ground-rents at Bournemouth, where the Earl of Malmesbury also sold off his 600 acres, and the Scarisbricks' and Heskeths' wholesale retreat from Southport landownership.[20] The snobbish Thanet resort of Westgate-on-Sea, which since 1884 had been owned by Coutts' Bank after the previous proprietors absconded, was also managed like a particularly exclusive aristocratic estate, as befitted the status of its corporate owner, a private bank which also found the post-war economic climate difficult; and extensive property and land sales in 1919 were followed by the transfer to the local authority of private roads and open spaces. Most of the property, ironically, went to a local builder, the son of a carpenter, who pursued similar policies to those of his predecessors.[21] These withdrawals were part of a wider pattern, but it was not quite so simple. At Eastbourne itself the Cavendishes became regular visitors to Compton Place again in the inter-war years, and the estate remained important in the town's life. Even after the Second World War, although the remnants of the Devonshire Park Company were sold to the Corporation between 1946 and 1957, the Cavendish family remained a major shareholder in the Water Works Company, which had never been municipalised, through the 1970s; and in 1975 its Trustees provoked fierce controversy by their proposals to develop the Crumbles estate. At Southport Colonel Roger Hesketh bought back an estate on the fringe of the town after his father's land sales and did what he could to influence development and 'preserve [its] architectural integrity', serving as Conservative M.P. between 1952 and 1959 and contributing extensively to local charities. Even the Scarisbricks, who had never taken on the paternalist trappings of the conventional landed estate and were eager to liquidate their resources in the mid-1920s, kept hold of Southport's foreshore until 1978, when it was compulsorily purchased as a nature reserve after threats to drain and develop it had provoked outrage from conservation bodies. The Earl of Radnor opened an extensive amusement centre at Folkestone in the mid-1920s, and the Earls of Scarbrough hung on to most of their Skegness ground-rents until death duties forced extensive sales in the late 1940s and again after 1969. The retreat of Sidney Sussex College, Cambridge, from its involvement in Cleethorpes was likewise a long-drawn-out process. So the decline of aristocratic influence at the seaside was no sudden thing, despite the general loss of political power at the turn of the century: it was a gradual process of adjustment, punctuated by crises, which was still incomplete a generation after the Second World War.[22]

The transfer of power and ownership from the landed aristocracy and gentry to the local middle classes was an important theme in an interesting minority of resorts. A more general and enduring pattern of conflict, with a shifting balance of power in most resorts, took place within the middle class, pitting the holiday industry and its component businesses against the residential and retired groups, the owners of rented houses, and those who serviced their needs. On one side were the disciples of municipal investment in the holiday industry, through the provision and upkeep of amenities, the promotion of the resort through advertising and the attraction of excursions and conferences, and the rescuing of ailing entertainments which private enterprise was unable to sustain at an appropriate profit. Their opponents were concerned above all to keep local taxation to a minimum, objecting to high levels of municipal spending in support of what they tended to describe as a minority with its own special interests; and they were especially anxious to discourage initiatives to promote the popular side of the holiday industry, which they saw as lowering the tone and dignity of their surroundings and disturbing their sedate existences with unseemly ribaldry. Occasionally some of the residential interest might support subsidies for 'high-class' entertainments, especially municipal orchestras, but generally their top priority was protecting their pockets and their sensibilities. This theme in seaside politics was inherited from the Victorians, but in many cases conflicts were stoked up in the twentieth century as retired and other residential interests became more prominent and the finances both of themselves and of local government became more precarious.[23]

At one extreme, in resorts like Westgate, or Frinton, or Sidmouth, the residential interest always had the upper hand. Westgate had been developed in the manner of a high-class London suburb, by builders who were experienced in that setting; and from the beginning it was primarily an exclusive residential resort, geared up to families summering in and husbands commuting from large houses whose privacy was secured by gated estate roads. As the upper middle class family presence declined in the new century, Westgate became a 'place for schools', and the assertive headmaster/proprietors of its boys' preparatory schools, some of which had strong Eton connections, were active in local government and fiercely opposed to the provision of entertainments which might increase local taxes and attract 'common' holidaymakers, especially from nearby Margate. As a holiday season developed, and as shops, hotels and boarding-houses created a holiday interest, campaigns began for some limited measure of public entertainment. There had been a town band since 1887, although the small bandstand provided by public subscription in 1903 was controversial. From 1910 the Town Hall, a private speculation rather than a public building, offered dancing and other attractions; but in 1922–23 holiday industry representatives began to agitate for a pavilion and concert party in the wake of the banning of Punch and Judy in 1921. After fierce opposition from schools and sea-front residents, a small pavilion opened in 1925; but that was as far as the holiday interest could go. The town's dominant faction took pride in excluding tramways and charabancs, and it was not until the late 1930s, after incorporation into Margate, that Westgate's Carnivals began to offer more boisterous amusements alongside bathing and sport. But the nature of the contested territories was itself significant, and the balance continued to be tilted in favour of the residential interest.[24]

Larger and less tightly controlled resorts like Folkestone, Torquay and Eastbourne offered more leeway to the holiday interest. Torquay is a particularly interesting case, as a fashionable Victorian winter resort with many 'villa residents' which acquired a more plebeian summer season during the twentieth century, and in which the party of development won out in the long term despite losing some battles on the way. Morgan divided its municipal political factions into four groups in the early 1930s, all with deeper roots, and only one of which was part of the conventional tripartite national political system: a party of investment and development geared to promoting tourism, with the local Hoteliers' Association at its core and often labelled the 'Hotel Party'; the party which prioritised low rates and financial retrenchment for the residential interest; the advocates of a select and genteel holiday season, who were closely linked to the residential interest; and the Labour group, whose main distinctive policy was the extension of municipal trading. Despite the historic and continuing strength of the second and third groups, what is remarkable through most of the century is the success of the development interest, despite opposition from successive Ratepayers' Associations and a similar body founded in 1930 and dignified by the title of the Citizens' League, which had 800 members in 1931 and the sustained support of the *Torquay Times*. There was sustained heavy expenditure on acquiring and 'improving' open spaces as parks and gardens during the 1920s, and this was continued in the next decade, despite severe temporary cuts in the depths of the depression in 1931. A rate rise of sixpence (2.5p) in the pound was tolerated in 1936 to cope with spending on cafes, gardens, promenade improvements and an extension to the 'sun lounge', and two years later a controversial plan for a band enclosure and Pavilion was approved. The 1960s saw extensive investment in redevelopment and the conference trade, against a backcloth of continuing conflict between tourism and residential interests; but a new revival of tourism from the early 1980s, against the trend, owed much to innovative Corporation advertising policies. None of this went unchallenged, and there were regular victories for the opponents of popularisation (a vote against Sunday rail excursions in 1927; rejection of fish and chip stalls in the harbour area and even of a children's miniature railway in the post-Second World War decade); but it is arguable that Torquay's competitive success as a resort owed much to the ability of its holiday interest, which accounted for around one-third of local trade directory entries in the inter-war years, to take a dominant role in local politics against entrenched and well-organised opponents.[25]

Folkestone exhibited similar patterns of conflict. In 1920 opposition to spending £10,000 on improving the Leas and Cliff pleasure grounds was clearly marginal, and the opening of the Lea Cliff Hall in 1927, an attempt to bring the town's facilities into line with competitors like Bournemouth, was a celebration of municipal initiative. The introduction of a full-scale municipal orchestra followed; but the 1930s saw its personnel and salaries steadily eaten away under pressure from the Folkestone Ratepayers' Association, to protests from both the local newspapers, which stressed the importance of a permanent orchestra to attract residents and year-round visitors. Such conflicts reappeared in the late 1950s and early 1960s, showing, as Nigel Yates remarks, 'the tensions that existed in all the major English seaside resort towns' at this time. The refusal to appoint an additional senior officer in 1957, dividing the Entertainments and Publicity portfolio, despite strong evidence of need; the failure of the summer show at the Pleasure Gardens in 1960, with pressure from the Hotel and Catering Association on the Corporation to step in and fill the gap; and the challenge from the Ratepayers and Residents Association when the Corporation proposed to buy or lease the Pleasure Gardens Theatre to keep shows going for the visitors in 1963, all brought home the nature of the tensions. The Ratepayers and Residents Association made their position abundantly clear: 'at a time when the cost of essential services was rising yearly, the efforts of the Council should be directed to ways and means of keeping the rates as low as possible by eliminating all unnecessary and speculative spending, however desirable it appeared to be in the interests of certain sections of the community'. The Corporation's executive committee professed itself in complete disagreement with these sentiments, but the constant agitation and reputation for power of such bodies must have had its cumulative effect in limiting the range of possible policies open to municipal politicians.[26]

The power and appeal of residential lobbies was greatly enhanced by the seaside retirement boom which affected so many resorts from the 1960s, as we saw in Chapter 6. Valerie Karn explained why local property taxation was such an emotive issue in this context. Most resorts had low average incomes (due to retirement and service employment, often seasonal), and relatively high rateable values were attached to retired residents' houses, especially in Sussex where London's proximity pushed up the estimated rentals on which these were based. Resorts had little industry, and agricultural land was de-rated, so a relatively high proportion of local expenditure fell on residential property. Local government reorganisation eased the situation from 1974, wherever resorts were combined with differing neighbouring economies, and rate rebate schemes from central government also helped; but accelerating inflation during the 1970s worked the other way. Contrary to some rhetoric, resorts were not heavy spenders on social services, and their age-structures together with the prevalence of private schools gave them low education costs; but the high-profile conflicts tended to focus on holiday trade support expenditure, where passions ran higher than the relatively trivial sums involved really justified. The symbolism was what mattered.[27]

Some resorts coped with such problems much better than others. Scarborough, which lacked large estates and a strong residential retirement interest, was able to pursue active, expansive municipal policies much more securely after late Victorian conflicts over marine drives, entertainment centres and the pioneering bathing pool had been resolved at the turn of the century. Resistance came more from populist defenders of working-class interests, like Councillor Briggs who argued for the postponement of the South Sands bathing pool in 1913 because his impoverished constituents paid rates and would not benefit from the pool, than from the penny-pinching residential interests of Torquay or Folkestone. But Scarborough had the talismanic figure of Alderman Meredith Whittaker, whose motto 'Develop Scarborough majestically' carried the voters along, as 'The attitude of the ratepayers as a whole towards big expenditures on improvement schemes underwent a transformation under the educational process afforded by the success of bold schemes, many of which have proved to have great revenue-earning capacity'.[28] This frame of mind was expressed by Councillor Boyes, Mayor-elect in 1921, who emphasised the by-now conventional wisdom that, 'After all, they did not want to stand still. A policy of progress meant success, and a "stand still" policy meant decay'. Thus was developed a succession of parks, gardens and special attractions along the North Bay, culminating in the purchase of the *Hispaniola* of Walt Disney's *Treasure Island* film to act as a floating aquarium and stimulate piratical fantasies.[29]

Scarborough was unusually successful as a second-rank resort whose popularity expanded faster than its population under an interventionist municipal regime. The largest and fastest-growing resorts, with their rapidly expanding local taxation bases, were the best-equipped to overcome the tensions which bedevilled many of their lesser rivals and sustain a policy of investment in entertainments and amenities, especially as private enterprise was more likely to make profits under these conditions and there was therefore less need for controversial municipal subsidies to ailing concerns, or ventures into the wilder shores of municipal trading. The trick was to sustain the growth and dynamism that kept this magic carpet in the air. Bournemouth and Blackpool are cases in point. The former's 'Progressives' had beaten off challenges to ambitious schemes for Undercliff Drives to east and west of the town centre before the First World War, as the Undercliff Drive and Pavilion League overcame the resistance of the Bournemouth Residents Association, although the Pavilion which became a symbol of municipal commitment to tourist development was delayed until 1929 after meeting a series of legal problems. But this set the tone for enduring expansionist policies, territorial as well as economic, which were interrupted by episodes such as the retreat from running a symphony orchestra in the mid-1950s, but underpinned and were underpinned by Bournemouth's continuing growth and popularity.[30] Blackpool's dominant municipal faction, the 'municipal capitalists' who presided over its overwhelmingly Tory council, were even more effective at marginalising opposition and pressing on with their project to use municipal enterprise to attract visitors who would bring prosperity to local businesses. The value of an entrepreneurial approach to investment in amenities had been demonstrated by the success of the promenade-building project as early as 1870 and defied effective challenge thereafter. Occasionally Blackpool's rulers had to watch their backs: in 1952 they secured explicit parliamentary powers to spend money on the famous autumn Illuminations in case there was a challenge to their slightly dubious legality. Counsel for the Corporation in 1969, when they sought parliamentary sanction to operate (among other things) a zoo, a hoverport (near their existing airport), a golf course and a roller-skating rink, expressed the prevailing assumptions very clearly in response to objections from amusement park proprietors and the drink interest, who feared competition and were (along with the neighbouring borough of Lytham St Annes) the only objectors: 'The whole object of the exercise is to attract business into the town for the benefit of the amusement park proprietors, for the hotel industry, and for the shopkeepers. This is the whole purpose of the thing and it would be quite pointless for the Corporation itself to generate business merely for its own direct benefit.'[31] The Corporation was much less interested in providing amenities and high-quality services for the local working class: there was nothing idealistic or philanthropic about its penetration of the local economy, and any redistribution of resources went towards the holiday industry. Blackpool and Bournemouth shared the distinction, in the early 1930s, of being the lowest-rated county boroughs in the country; and Blackpool's borough treasurer defended it against accusations of cooking the books by valuing properties unduly highly to enable it to levy low levels of property tax per pound of gross estimated rental. He also emphasised the high levels of services which had to be maintained for an enormous seasonal influx of people who were not considered in census-based calculations. This expansionist politics was held up for a time by government financial restrictions and increasing housing and other social services commitments during the decade or so after the Second World War: here as in Brighton, the will was there but not the resources. But it was not until the late twentieth century, as the residential interest flexed its muscles even here while the local authority lost services to the county (after 1972), to central government and to privatisation, and failed to adapt to changing conditions in the holiday industry, that the mould of the old politics was broken.[32]

Resort politics were also expressed across party lines in the resources allocated to advertising and the pursuit of the increasingly lucrative (and often off-season) conference market. At the start of the century only Blackpool had substantial powers to advertise itself out of local taxation: in 1879, by what was clearly an oversight, parliament had permitted the Corporation to levy a rate of 2d (0.83p) in the pound for advertising purposes, and it had responded enthusiastically, using the money for an extensive poster campaign supplemented by guide-books and publicity stunts.[33] Rival resorts campaigned unavailingly for similar treatment, and before the Health and Watering Places Act of 1921 concessions were few and minor, as publicity had to be left to railway companies, Chambers of Commerce and *ad hoc* committees disbursing funds made available by the legal fiction of a mayor's salary. The Act allowed local government to apply the profits from municipal trading in amenities or recreation for visitors to advertising through a variety of conventional media, provided that expenditure never exceeded the proceeds of a penny (0.42p) in the pound rate on assessed property. Enthusiasm varied, but according to Nigel Yates, 'Most resorts advertised at railway stations or in the national press and many appointed professional publicity officers'. Within Kent, Ramsgate already had an information bureau and co-ordinated booking service by the early 1930s, while Folkestone did not even take over the publication of the local holiday guide from the Chamber of Commerce until 1946.[34] The resort guide-book projected the preferred images to information-seekers, and by the late 1920s the larger centres were following in Blackpool's footsteps by publishing opulent volumes, usually well-supported by advertising, especially from the accommodation sector. Morecambe's official guide in 1926 featured the town's name and crest on a plain cover with scallop-shell border, and placed particular emphasis on outdoor activities: almost all the illustrations were of pretty rural places in the excursion hinterland, and motoring, cycling and the Lake District were highlighted. Chapter headings included 'A famous water supply' and 'The "Mecca of the Bronchitic"'. One and a half pages of a thirty-six-page text were devoted to 'Indoor amusements and pleasure palaces', while a whole page set out and named the panorama of Lake District hills visible from the Promenade.[35] Three years later Southport's much fatter guide promoted 'Sunny Southport – England's seaside garden city', with full colour illustrations, a great emphasis on parks and gardens, and a very similar overall agenda.[36] Torquay's aspirations were aggressively respectable in 1932, when it tackled 'The question of "Tone"' head-on:[37]

> Vulgarians whose idea of a holiday is compounded of Big Wheels, paper caps, donkeys and niggers [minstrels], tin whistles, and generally a remorseless harlequinade, turn their backs on the town . . . The residue, the thoroughly normal, healthy and educated people who are the backbone of the nation, love Torquay as few other towns are loved, and it is they who throng its pleasant ways the whole year round.

This is a reminder that there was a politics of the official guide, and that deviation from an emphasis on health, sport and outdoor activities might bring opposition from the vocal guardians of 'social tone'. Even Blackpool's publicity followed this overall model, with only two double-page spreads on commercial entertainment in the official guide for 1938, although those who enjoyed the Tower and Pleasure Beach were, of course, presented as happy pleasure-seekers rather than vulgarians.[38]

Some of the more popular resorts, like Ramsgate, were already shifting towards swimsuited examples of female beauty to allure visitors by the early 1930s, building on an interest in the female form (an extension of the vogue for the healthy outdoor life) which encouraged the widespread development of beauty contests during the decade, which could themselves be used to promote resorts; but a concentration on landscape and amenities remained dominant for much longer in more up-market settings. In many smaller resorts the guide became trapped in a set of conventions which were increasingly outdated, but which it was difficult to change without incurring controversy. During the 1960s the bathing belles themselves became stereotyped, and attempts were sometimes made to combine them with visual references to heritage attractions. When Torquay resorted to allusive, almost abstract images which sought to convey a sense of sunny sophistication in the 1980s, there was fierce short-term criticism until the new imagery had proved itself; and in general the problems faced by many resorts from the 1960s were compounded by a conservative approach to publicity.[39]

The entertainments and publicity officers in the larger resorts were soon engaged in seeking conference bookings, which were particularly useful during the 'shoulder' weeks on either side of the main season. This was already an established trade in places like Blackpool at the beginning of the century, but it grew rapidly as competition became fiercer after the Second World War. Folkestone trebled its conference numbers in five years during the mid-1950s, but increasingly the second-rank resorts lost out as places like Margate and Clacton lost their big hotels and chose not to invest in new conference centres. Blackpool, confident in the resources of its privately run pleasure palaces, also took this route. In 1968 it welcomed about a hundred conferences, with between 100 and 6,000 delegates, and including Labour, the Conservatives, Rotary International and the National Union of Teachers. A facetious barrister pointed out that the list included the Licensed Victuallers and Alcoholics Anonymous (both at the same time), the Cremation Society and the National Union of Blastfurnacemen.[40] This catholic embrace meant that public figures had to be careful about what they said, especially when Tory mayors welcomed Labour or TUC conferences: resorts had to try to project an anodyne political image, and this helped to explain why they often chose to represent their local government as apolitical. Within local politics, however, the decision whether or not to invest in an expensive purpose-built conference centre was a hot potato. Blackpool was suffering from rejecting this option at the end of the twentieth century, with 'New' Labour threatening to sever its relationship with the town even as its mayors became potentially more friendly. Brighton, on the other hand, faced fierce opposition from the Left after making the opposite choice, as the campaigning group QueenSpark denounced the new conference centre, which on the group's calculations accounted for 31 per cent of the rates by 1982 (an increase from 1 per cent in 1975) and (it was alleged) symbolised a policy of concentrating on attracting the rich while running down the traditional holiday trade and local services.[41] The benefits of directing resources towards these prestigious and high-profile aspects of the tourist trade, which projected a desired resort image but seemed to divert expenditure from the residents at large without producing visible 'trickle-down' effects to justify the expenditure, were increasingly open to challenge.

The pursuit of 'progress' and image enhancement also entailed expansionist attitudes to municipal boundaries, the politics of which were very important to resorts, in terms of both territorial extension and amalgamation, affecting as they did both identities and policies. This was already a strong theme before the First World War, as (for example) Birkdale resisted incorporation into Southport until sewering problems in Ainsdale (which Birkdale in turn had swallowed up in 1905) made the takeover inevitable.[42] All the largest resorts developed imperialist designs towards their neighbours, seeking to extend territory and control by swallowing them up. Brighton, Bournemouth and Blackpool all looked outwards in this way, with little internal opposition, stirring up debate in the coveted districts between those who preferred the visibility of a better-known name and the promise of improved services, and those who feared the loss of a distinctive identity and the imposition of higher local taxes. Brighton was particularly expansionist in the inter-war years, as Sir Herbert Carden, its answer to Alderman Whittaker, presided over land purchases and boundary extensions to protect the water catchment area and preserve the scenic beauty of the Downs against development. He was also a staunch advocate of the corporation's electricity, telephones, housing estates and road improvement schemes, which marked Brighton's self-confident municipal politics in the 1920s and 1930s.[43] Where the annexed territories saw themselves as socially superior to their imperialist neighbours, opposition and resentment festered. Nowhere was this more in evidence than at Westgate, where from the late 1920s Margate's designs on a proudly exclusive resort which had until recently been separated from it by undeveloped coastline produced intransigent opposition from a parish council which had long sought, and been denied, its own formal urban status. The advocates of seclusion and exclusiveness campaigned furiously, bombarding the Minister of Health with letters from residents who were acquaintances or even members of his Club, throughout 1934, when the issue came to a head; but advocates of expenditure on the holiday season were more open to Margate's seductions, and in 1935 the amalgamation went through. Margate celebrated with an elaborate processional ceremony to beat the bounds of the newly expanded borough, and improved services were soon noted; but the apostles of selectness and refinement objected so strongly to locally posted letters bearing a 'Come to sunny Margate' postmark that the issue was discussed in the House of Commons. Questions of status and perceived 'social tone' remained at the core of the politics of resort identity.[44]

While the larger places sough to expand their empires, while suffering from the transfer of important responsibilities to the counties under the Local Government Act of 1972, smaller places saw their holiday industries threatened by the dilution of resort identities in the larger municipal units which became fashionable in the early 1970s. The local government reorganisation of

1974, by amalgamating neighbours into larger units, threatened the autonomy, identity and tourism investment policies of established resorts, some of which (like Whitby, which was subsumed into Scarborough and an extensive rural area), were quite substantial. In some places the relationship between a resort and the wider municipal district of which it formed part had long been a source of conflict. New Brighton's problems were worsened by its status as a single ward of the borough of Wallasey, where it was the plaything of rival groups on the local council, on which pro-resort Conservative control was usual but precarious, and Conservative policies of encouraging the holiday industry were tempered by Liberal advocacy of a switch to suburban residential development and Labour suspicion of resort interests. Thus was perpetuated into the post-war generation a fault-line of conflict familiar from elsewhere, which dated from the resort's earliest days, inheriting the battle-lines between 'The Residents' Party – supported largely by retired people and invalids – still long(ing) for a seaside Buxton, becalmed with bathchairs and potted palms, while the Recreational Party – tough tradespeople and ambitious businessmen – argued in favour of theatres, marinas and Amusement Parks like Blackpool'. These familiar entrenched positions, even more so than elsewhere, continued to prevent the adoption of coherent policies.[45]

The 1974 settlement created analogous patterns of conflict in many other resorts. The Lancaster Regionalism Group illustrated the outcome of Lancaster's amalgamation with adjoining Morecambe, whose tourist trade was just moving into crisis:

> A strong Lancaster versus Morecambe split developed in local politics. Issues became 'territorial' rather than 'partisan'. Lancaster councillors argued for spending on jobs and industry, while Morecambe councillors wanted infrastructural spending on tourist-related projects in Morecambe and vehemently opposed plans to develop Lancaster's tourist potential.

This created a climate of conflict in which, responding to a new Lancaster Plan in the mid-1980s which envisaged retail expansion in Lancaster, a separate political party, the Morecambe Bay Independents, was formed and won seats in the municipal elections, remaining an electoral force for more than a decade.[46] Rhyl was amalgamated with Prestatyn and the nearby inland town of Rhuddlan, which gave its name to the new authority; and on the eve of amalgamation Rhyl Urban District Council, to 'tie up loose ends', abandoned the Pier and Pavilion Theatre, which had been central to its identity and publicity.[47] Meanwhile the creation of Thanet District Council in 1974 brought together the contrasting resort traditions of Ramsgate, Margate, Broadstairs, Westgate and Birchington, creating a cocktail of political conflict. Ramsgate's port gave it industrial interests, a more interventionist brand of dominant Conservatism and a more active labour movement; Westgate (which had unsuccessfully resisted incorporation into Margate in the 1930s, as we saw) and Birchington had retired residents who favoured Independents in local elections; and Margate and Broadstairs were dominated by a more Thatcherite brand of Toryism. The economic stresses of the 1970s and 1980s brought crises over expenditure on Ramsgate harbour and the running of Margate's Winter Gardens, which split the Conservative Party down the middle and brought about a 'hung' council.[48]

Such battles were still being fought at the end of the millennium. The amalgamation between Brighton and Hove which was being mooted in 1995 distilled the ancient rivalries between self-consciously contrasting resorts: Brighton cosmopolitan and raffish, Hove aloof and refined, an extension of what novelist Alan Kennington described as Brighton's western 'colonel country, with a stiff outcrop of widows who play bridge and girls who beagle'. Amalgamation had been proposed, and rejected, at regular intervals in the past: it seemed logical enough to outsiders, when the resorts formed one continuous built-up area along the sea-front. In 1948 Hove's council insisted that it was 'opposed to amalgamation with Brighton in any shape or form', and the division survived the 1974 local government reorganisation. In 1995 Alex Bellos of the *Guardian* summed up the current state of mutual distaste, with a little journalistic licence:

> To show its distaste for 'dirty Brighton', when the Hove mayoral limousine drives over the border the driver locks all the doors. Its tourist slogan – Hove, Actually – is a bitchy aside to its neighbour . . . Brighton can give as good as it gets. 'Why should we merge with doddery old Hove with its blue-rinsed attitudes and stuck-up residents? Let Hove preserve itself like the sour gherkin it is', an angry Brightonian wrote recently in the local newspaper.

There was also a party political dimension, as Brighton's Labour Left local government tradition clashed with Hove's Tory monopoly and threatened to submerge it by superior numbers. There was a green angle: Brighton sought to discourage cars, Hove to encourage them. And Steve Bassam, Brighton's Labour leader, enjoyed winding up his neighbours with an expressed desire to 'create a socialist seaside city for the millennium'.[49] Just as the Conservatives feared, Labour won the first post-amalgamation municipal elections in 1995, with a string of narrow victories in Hove itself, and pursued its green transport policies on both sides of the old boundary. It also followed a 'New Labour' agenda of collaboration with the private sector for a £50 million redevelopment of the

Brighton Dome complex and a £20 million expansion of the Brighton Marina, boosting the tourist industry as well as local amenities, but occupying terrain which (as we saw) had been hotly contested by local socialists for two decades. In 1999 the amalgamated borough was being viewed as a touchstone for national trends in the local elections, as a key indicator of any possible Tory revival. As it happened, the tide did not rise this far; but the town's new identity as a (New) Labour fiefdom, however transitory, would have been unthinkable earlier in the century.[50]

Brighton and Hove also constituted a crucible of conflict over resort identities as expressed through architecture, as redevelopment plans threatened the fabric of the original resort and brought heritage defence campaigners into action, in a pattern of confrontation which overlapped with those between (especially) the popular holiday industry and the genteel residential interest, and which recurred in other resorts. The timing of this process was crucial. Bournemouth had lost its early Victorian villas to commercial redevelopment on either side of the First World War, and a 'vast block of flats' was erected on the old vicarage site in 1936, but the town's librarian could refer to this and the demolition of the Victorian Winter Gardens simply as 'progress' in 1957.[51] Brighton and Hove were a different matter, as huge concrete blocks of flats began to intrude among the Regency terraces during the 1930s, arousing mixed reactions. Sir Herbert Carden celebrated this version of modernity, advocating that the whole sea-front be rebuilt in this way; but others were bitterly critical, and when redevelopment resumed after the Second World War and Hove Corporation proposed to replace an extensive area of Regency housing in Hove with 'skyscraper blocks of flats' and a car park, the opponents organised their resistance through the newly founded Regency Society of Brighton and Hove, which defeated the planners at an appeal to Quarter Sessions. This architectural pressure group kept a close and protective eye on subsequent developments, pioneering the notion that seaside architectural heritage was an asset worth protecting. Conflicts between preservationists and developers, which have often split Conservative party memberships, subsequently became endemic in resorts as pressure for development mounted, although Brighton's combination of particularly attractive and evocative architecture and articulate artistic professionals who wanted to defend it could not quite be matched elsewhere. The case of Bognor, which lost almost all of its earlier resort architecture as its local authority failed to define its character and made a series of planning blunders, was closer to the norm than that of Brighton, where Regency terraces eventually came to look like good business.[52]

As the QueenSpark group argued forcefully, however, some kinds of seaside space were being privileged over others. The Regency terraces all too often hid rotting bedsitters and, in unfashionable parts of the town hidden from tourists, by the 1970s some of the inter-war council estates (the best of which had been presented as models of the planners' art when first built) were falling into decay. The ruling Conservatives could respond to the pleas of lovers of formal classical architecture within their own ranks, but the local working class was cast aside. The QueenSpark group grew out of a campaign to rescue the old German Spa building (historic, but not the 'right' sort of history) and use it as a nursery school for a deprived area. After winning this fight (after a six-year campaign), QueenSpark moved on to focus on the proposed closure of the Black Rock bathing pool, a product of the expansive 1930s which had been extensively used by local people. Its fate – handed over to a private leisure company which increased the prices beyond the pockets of the local unemployed – was symptomatic of a wider pattern: 'Public assets are run down and then let to private developers'. This particular pattern of conflict, which was not peculiar to Brighton (it was part of the indictment of Blackpool's Corporation in the late 1980s and early 1990s, for example), reminds us that class issues were not absent from the lived politics of the seaside, even if they failed to make a direct impact on the balance of power in local government or parliamentary elections. Nor was this a novelty in the 1970s.[53]

We saw in Chapter 6 that seaside resort economies generated and sustained significant pockets of poverty, insecurity and seasonal unemployment. The municipal franchise meant that lodgers, servants and many seasonal workers were unable to make their presence felt at the ballot box; but that did not make them unimportant. Even before the First World War socialist and Labour candidates were beginning to find their way on to local councils, from Eastbourne to Blackpool, and populist Liberals and Independents like Scarborough's Councillor Briggs swelled the ranks.[54] It might be difficult to rouse the sweated workers in Hastings' building trades, but even in Sidmouth the fishermen were beginning to identify a kind of kinship with visiting workers from inland towns.[55] The last years of the First World War and the immediate post-war years saw successful strikes by improbable groups of seasonal workers such as waiters and scene-shifters, and local election gains by the Labour Party.[56] These gains were not sustained, but the General Strike was widely observed in several of the larger resorts, especially Brighton, where 'the stoppage was . . . the most complete of any town in the south of England', and the railway workers were backed up by unemployed miners who had moved south in search of work. The climax of the strike was 'the Battle of Lewes Road', where a crowd of several thousand people outside the tram depot was dispersed violently by police supported by mounted volunteers ('farmers, sportsmen, hunting men and retired cavalry officers') carrying shillelaghs.[57] The increasing investment in council housing and in amenities for locals as well as visitors in the Brighton of the 1930s, and the concern for social amelioration in the post-war generation, should perhaps be seen partly in this perspective. Class dimensions to local politics were not absent just because they did not dominate press reporting of election campaigns. These were, after all, industrial towns in which employers exploited wage-labour, albeit mostly in small and often seasonal businesses.[58]

The clearances and attempted clearances of old fishing quarters which were discussed in Chapter 5 should also be seen in this context. In the sanitised world of the planned resort, especially in the inter-war years, these settlements were matter out of place. They had their defenders, offering a rhetoric of tradition and defence of the picturesque, and even an appreciation of the commercial possibilities of the fishing quarter, which could be seen surfacing in the late 1930s at (for example) Newlyn and Scarborough. All this illustrates the complexities of the patterns of conflict, continuity and change, cross-cutting between class, culture, space and identity, which made up the experience of British seaside resorts and their visitors during the twentieth century. The final chapter pulls these threads together.

Notes

1 Walton, *The English seaside resort*, Chapter 6; Walton, 'Blackpool', in Walton and Walvin (eds), *Leisure in Britain*; Cannadine, *Lords and landlords*, Chapters 20–4; Liddle, 'Estate management and land reform politics' in Cannadine (ed.), *Patricians, power and politics in nineteenth-century towns*; Morgan, 'Perceptions, patterns and policies of tourism'; Demetriadi, 'The golden years'.

2 P. Cooke (ed.), *Localities* (London, 1989), Chapter 5; L. Murgatroyd *et al.*, *Localities, class and gender* (London, 1985).

3 Urry, *Holiday-making, cultural change and the seaside*.

4 Gilbert, *Brighton, old ocean's bauble*, pp. 238–9.

5 R.B. McCallum and Alison Readman, *The British general election of 1945* (London, 1947), pp. 263, 293 and Appendix IV (facing p. 292); *The Times, House of Commons 1945*, p. 66.

6 Murgatroyd *et al.*, *Localities, class and gender*, pp. 60–3.

7 Gilbert, *Brighton, old ocean's bauble*, pp. 236–8, 240.

8 F.W.S. Craig, *British parliamentary election results 1918–1949* (Glasgow, 1969), pp. 93, 138, 246; *The Times, House of Commons 1945*, p. 51.

9   F.W.S. Craig, *British parliamentary election results 1950–1973* (Chichester, 2nd edn, 1983), p. 98.

10 Musgrave, *Life in Brighton*, p. 443.

11 Walton, 'Seaside resorts and maritime history'; *Guardian, G2*, 30 May 1999, p. 3.

12 Walton, *Blackpool*, pp. 161–3.

13 Davies *et al.*, *County borough elections in inter-war England*; Brian C. Smith, 'Torquay', in L.J. Sharpe (ed.), *Voting in cities: the 1964 borough elections* (London, 1967), pp. 210, 216, 218–20.

14 Evidence on local authorities extracted from C. Rallings and M. Thrasher (eds), *Local elections in Britain: a statistical digest* (Plymouth, 1994).

15 B. Cathcart, *Were you still up for Portillo?* (Harmondsworth, 1997), pp. 125–8.

16 *Guardian*, 7 May 1999 p. 1; 8 May 1999, pp. 18–19.

17 Smith, 'Torquay', p. 210.

18 Cannadine, *Lords and landlords*, Chapter 22; Liddle, 'Estate management and land reform politics', and Roberts, 'Landed estates and municipal enterprise', in Cannadine (ed.), *Patricians, power and politics in nineteenth-century towns*, pp. 157–63, 197–204.

19 Cannadine, *Lords and Landlords*, pp. 348–51, 421.

20 Ibid., p. 421.

21 Dawn Crouch, 'Westgate on Sea 1865–1940', Ph.D. thesis, University of Kent, 1999, pp. 41–2.

22 Cannadine, *Lords and landlords*, pp. 421, 426; Liddle, 'Estate management and land reform politics', pp. 163–6; Stafford and Yates, *The later Kentish seaside*, p. 119.

23 For Victorian antecedents see Walton, *The English seaside resort*, Chapter 6.

24 Crouch, 'Westgate on Sea', pp. 222–5.

25 Morgan, 'Perceptions, patterns and policies of tourism', p. 60 and Chapter 4.

26 Stafford and Yates, *The later Kentish seaside*, pp. 136–7, 140–47, 165–9.

27 Karn, *Retiring to the seaside*, Chapter 17.

28 S. Foord, 'Scarborough: records of interesting events and the development of Scarborough as a resort' (typescript, Scarborough Public Library, 1970); *Scarborough Mercury*, 23 May 1913, 13 November 1931.

29 *Scarborough Mercury*, 11 November 1921; 'A trip to Scarborough', *Picture Post*, 9 August 1952.

30 Young, *The story of Bournemouth*, Chapter 9.

31 LRO, CBBl 118/2 and 118/3, minutes of evidence, Blackpool Corporation Bill, 1969.

32 'Wonderful Blackpool', *Blackpool Gazette and Herald*, New Year supplement, 7 January 1933, Blackpool Public Library LE02(P), p. 21; Walton, *Blackpool*, Chapter 6; Musgrave, *Life in Brighton*, pp. 410–23.

33 J.K. Walton, 'The social development of Blackpool, 1788–1914', Ph.D. thesis, University of Lancaster, 1974, Chapter 7.

34 Stafford and Yates, *The later Kentish seaside*, pp. 109–10.

35 Advertising Committee of Morecambe Corporation, *The official guide to More-cambe* (Morecambe, 1926).

36 Southport Corporation, *Sunny Southport*.

37 *Torquay, the English Riviera: official guide* (Torquay, 1932), p. 10.

38 Blackpool Corporation Publicity Committee, *Blackpool*.

39 Stafford and Yates, *The later Kentish seaside*, pp. 103, 106, 111, 127, 172; Morgan, 'Perceptions, patterns and policies of tourism', Chapter 6.

40 LRO, CBBl 118/3, Day 1, p. 30; Day 3, p. 17.

41 QueenSpark Rates Book Group, *Brighton on the rocks: monetarism and the local state* (Brighton, 1983), pp. 104, 116–22.

42 Seed's *Southport and district directory*, pp. xxv–xxvi.

43 Gilbert, *Brighton, old ocean's bauble*, pp. 222–5; Musgrave, *Life in Brighton*, pp. 390–1; Young, *The story of Bournemouth*, pp. 153–6; Walton, *Blackpool*.

44 Crouch, 'Westgate on Sea', pp. 69–74.

45 Samuels, 'Research to hlep plan the future of a seaside resort', pp. 65–6; Hope, *Castles in the sand*, p. 17.

46 P. Cooke (ed.), *Localities* (London, 1989), pp. 153–4.

47 Gale *et al.*, 'Reconstructing the past', p. 33.

48 Cooke (ed.), *Localities*, pp. 187–94.

49 *Guardian*, 24 March 1995, p. 6; 30 April 1999, p. 12; Gilbert, *Brighton, old ocean's bauble*, p. 236.

50 Meethan, 'Place, image and power', p. 193; Walton, *Blackpool*, pp. 162–3.

51 Young, *The story of Bournemouth*, pp. 173–5.

52 Musgrave, *Life in Brighton*, pp. 412–13; Young, *A history of Bognor Regis*, Chapters 24–7.

53 QueenSpark, *Brighton on the rocks*, pp. 18–19, 36, 56; Gilbert, *Brighton, old ocean's bauble*, p. 226.

54 Walton, *Blackpool*; Cannadine, *Lords and landlords*.

55 Tressell, *The Ragged-trousered philanthropists*; Walton, 'Fishing communities'.

56 Walton, *Blackpool*, Chapter 6, and articles cited there.

57 Musgrave, *Life in Brighton*, pp. 313, 380–2.

58 Walton, 'Seaside resorts and maritime history'.

Conclusion:
the seaside in perspective

The resilient popularity of the British seaside needs explaining, and not only when it is set against Mediterranean or long-haul competition to provide similar services under more attractive climatic conditions. After his tour of the whole British coastline, Anthony Smith commented in 1970:[1]

> I believe the British to be more idiotic about their seaside than the citizens of any other country. Of course Italians and Greeks bask torpidly in their summer sun, but the British will attempt to do so beneath layers of cumulus and a personal coating of whitened flesh, goose-pimpled and rigid with cold. In Britain it is thought sinful not to take children to the beach, as if denying them Vitamin C or love, and yet each annual excursion can be a violent experience . . . Seaside first aid posts give statistics each season – jelly-fish stings, donkey bites, deckchair entanglements, tin cuts and bottle cuts, stomach disorders . . . and even sunstroke . . . We have meals out of doors when any polar explorer would be in his tent. We also have tenacity, because each generation of adults inflicts the same old games on children who . . . absorb the tradition and pass it on a couple of decades later . . . What is so magnificent about a front of concrete set beside the sea when there are fields and heather and woodland not too far away? Why piles of sand-hopping seaweed when there is bracken?

What indeed and why indeed? Viewed from this angle, the pioneering rise and sustained importance of the seaside in British (and especially English) economy, society and culture might be made to seem even stranger and more exotic than the rise of the cotton industry, with its distant sources of raw material and far-flung markets; but the seaside has proved more enduring than the original factory industry, which emerged as such at about the same time, peaked earlier, declined sooner and had practically disappeared by the time the British seaside was weathering the storms of the 1970s and 1980s.[2] The seaside's significance and capacity for survival have yet to generate a historiography to challenge that of cotton; but that is not for want of importance or scope for posing big questions. Rather, it reflects the enduring preoccupation of economic historians with production rather than consumption, the predominance of class conflict in manufacturing industry among the chosen themes of social history, and the condescension of the political history establishment towards popular culture. Only in the last two decades have the orthodox agenda been seriously challenged, and this book is a product of those times.

Perhaps, then, we should be trying to explain the British seaside's survival (and the indications of its incipient revival) rather than lamenting what might be made to seem a decline as inevitable as that of cotton. Taking this route requires examination of the deep cultural roots which the seaside had struck in popular consciousness, especially and tellingly in relation to children, by the early twentieth century, and the capacity of that attachment for accepting the changes which were made as resorts reinvented themselves in response to changing tastes and expectations, and (perhaps) sometimes ahead of them. Displaying and articulating those cultural roots, and the ability of their perennial flowers to mutate with changing circumstances, was the main mission of the first chapter. As the book's themes have unfolded it has become apparent that seaside resorts adapted well to the changes in visitor taste in the inter-war years, in many cases anticipating their full expression and helping to mould them, with local government well to the fore in this process. Matters were made easier by the variety of experiences and environments available, which was still expanding during the inter-war years as new kinds of coastal leisure settlement proliferated, and enabled most tastes to be catered for somewhere without the problems of mixing markets and culture, which had been so pressing in the late nineteenth century, getting in the way to the same extent.[3] So the seaside adjusted relatively painlessly to the cult of sun, freedom and the outdoors, and the rise of the crazes for dancing, jazz and fairground thrills. This was when the big resorts reinvented themselves without losing their old customers, with markets still expanding except at sophisticated middle- and upper-class levels, so that the logic of the product cycle in its seaside incarnation could be defied.[4] On these assumptions the real problems came after the Second World War, with new trends which really tested the resilience of the cultural assumptions which had sustained the seaside.

Cannadine has argued that, as visitors and residents experienced it, the seaside changed relatively little during the first half of the twentieth century and that the key watershed was the Second World War.[5] The argument of the previous paragraph, and of (especially) Chapter 4, is that there were, in fact, very important changes, but that the resorts dealt with them successfully. Moreover, to take the Second World War as watershed is to oversimplify. What is remarkable is how quickly the seaside resorts, even the fortified, damaged south-eastern centres for whom occupation by billeted Allied troops was nearly as traumatic as an external invasion force, resumed 'business as usual' and recovered their old patrons, their numbers boosted by paid holidays and their leisure spending boosted by the rationing of essentials. The key changes came later, with the new youth cultures of the 1950s and 1960s (much more divisive than in the inter-war years) and the gradual opening out of alternative holiday destinations within and beyond Britain which undermined the hegemony of the British seaside. Cannadine's is perhaps too Eastbourne-centred a view, although the diversity of the British holiday coasts might lead others to argue that my own depends too heavily on Blackpool, Scarborough and Brighton. But the problems emerged after the war rather than as a direct result of it.[6]

Critics of the post-war seaside might plausibly argue for entrepreneurial failure on the part of businesses and local government, which responded to the years of plenty in the post-war generation by taking profits without renewing plant, investing in innovations or identifying and catering to the spending power of a new generation. This would be too simple a critique, although the exceptions would be found disproportionately in the larger and more popular resorts; and it needs to take account of the mounting financial and political pressures which seaside local government faced in inflationary times, with declining financial autonomy and increasing opposition to holiday season expenditure from residential groups. These issues are dealt with in Chapter 7. The resurgence of conflicts over access to and use of desirable space which accompanied the rise of a confrontational youth culture, with its own music and values, also made it difficult for local government or private enterprise to sustain effective policies of leisure provision, especially when fashions like the one for ten-pin bowling came and went with bewildering rapidity. It was also difficult for the small businesses which dominated seaside accommodation to find the capital for complex improvements, especially in plumbing and the provision of en-suite accommodation, still less to expand provision and develop upwards on their cramped sites. This helped to discourage the importation of continental styles of sea-front flat development, and so did the relatively limited demand for second homes. The most damaging trend of all, perhaps, was a tendency for what new development and redevelopment there was, usually in

central retailing districts, to follow nationwide patterns of architecture and provision, undermining the distinctive sense of place which had made the seaside
attractive, and damaging the aura of the resort as an alluring destination.[7]

Nor had older conflicts over 'social tone' vanished, as resorts with mixed or
changing visiting publics agonised about evidence of going down-market, and
the articulate residents' groups became particularly vitriolic. The extended conflict
over the development of a Butlin's camp at Bognor in the late 1950s and early
1960s, or the battles over the provision and removal of 'tripper' amusements
on the Brighton sea-front, are early illustrations of the revived potency of this
theme.[8] It had never gone away, of course, as the struggles of Westgate and
Frinton to keep their exclusive status illustrated in particularly strong form;
and it revived in earnest in the late twentieth century, especially where the young
unemployed were colonising bed-sitters and boarding-house proprietors were
being attracted by the guaranteed year-round rents provided by housing benefit
towards the end of the century. Such developments were fiercely resisted by
the remaining bastions of the established holiday industry, in Blackpool, Margate
and elsewhere.[9]

Despite all the pressures and problems of the later twentieth century, however, it could be argued that the British seaside has been remarkably resilient.
Not only has it kept a strong share of an expanding holiday market, it has also
maintained its power as a cultural referent, and is beginning to market itself
in post-modern, ironic ways, inviting visitors to share the jokes about seaside
kitsch and enjoy a distinctive experience which is also sold as part of the heritage tourism boom. After the difficult years of the 1970s and 1980s there is
real evidence of a recovery of nerve and attractiveness, widespread although
far from universal, which has been gathering momentum during the writing
of this book and affecting my own perspective on the issues. The British seaside has been reinventing itself again, with a focus on clubs, shopping, heritage
and environment which is sharp enough to promote niche markets (many of
which were never threatened) and broad enough to offer benefits to most kinds
of resort. If Sidmouth can cope with the expansion of an English Folk-
Dancing and Song Society gathering into a full-scale folk festival, with all the
associated noise, drinking and alternative lifestyles, then there is scope for regen-
eration everywhere. There is still plenty of life in the enduring and reinvented
traditions and the continuing openness to innovation of the British seaside
holiday, despite the problems and conflicts which have been so prominent in
the foregoing chapters. The fate of the cotton industry is proving to be a false,
though useful, analogy.

Notes

1 Smith, *Beside the seaside*, pp. 20–1.

2 M.B. Rose (ed.), *The Lancashire cotton industry: a history since 1700* (Preston, 1996).

3 Walton, *The English seaside resort*, Chapter 8.

4 B. Goodall, 'Coastal resorts: development and redevelopment', *Built Environment*, 5 (1992) pp. 5–11; G. Priestley and L. Mundet, 'The post-stagnation phase of the resert cycle', *Annals of Tourism Research*, 25 (1998).

5 Cannadine, *Lords and landlords*, pp. 380–1.

6 D. Fowler, *The first teenagers* (London, 1995) gives more emphasis to inter-war developments; and see Demetriadi, 'The golden years'.

7 Urry, 'Cultural change and the seaside resort', in A. Williams and G. Shaw (eds), *The rise and fall of coastal resorts* (London: Pinter, 1997) pp. 102–13.

8 Young, *A history of Bognor Regis*; Musgrave, *Life in Brighton*, pp. 410–11.

9 Walton, *Blackpool*, p. 160.

Select bibliography

Manuscript sources

British Library, St Pancras   Typescript reports of local authorities and planning organisations, 1960–1989

Public Record Office, Kew   HO 45, Home Office correspondence

Bodleian Library, Oxford   John Johnson collection: ephemera dealing with resorts and publicity

Library, London School of Economics and Political Science   Webb Local Government Collection

Lancashire Record Office, Bow Lane, Preston   CBBl, Blackpool County Borough Records

Blackpool Public Library   Miscellaneous pamphlets and reports in local history section

Scarborough Room, Scarborough Public Library   Miscellaneous pamphlets and reports on aspects of the history of Scarborough

Newspapers

Blackpool Gazette
Guardian
Independent
Independent on Sunday
Observer
Scarborough Gazette
Scarborough Mercury
Times
West Lancashire Evening Gazette

Printed primary sources

Adshead, S.D., and Overfield, H.V., *The future development of Scarborough* (Scarborough: Scarborough Corporation, 1938)

Baker, Humphrey, 'The public and the sea coast', *Journal of the Commons, Open Spaces and Footpaths Preservation Society*, 2 (1931), 72–7

Barker, Nicola, *Wide open* (London: Faber and Faber, 1998)

Bennett, Arnold, *The card* (Harmondsworth: Penguin, 1975; first published 1911)

Blackpool Corporation Publicity Committee, *Blackpool: Official Guide* (Blackpool: Corporation, 1938)

Board of Trade, *An industrial survey of the North East Coast Area* (London, 1932)

Brown, Ivor, *Summer in Scotland* (London: Collins, 1952)

Brunner, E., *Holiday making and the holiday trades* (Oxford: Oxford University Press, 1945)

Bryson, Bill, *Notes from a small island* (London: Black Swan, 1995)

Burgess, Anthony, *Little Wilson and Big God* (Harmondsworth: Penguin, 1988)

Carter, Ella, ed., *Seaside houses and bungalows* (London: Country Life, 1937)

Cathcart, Brian, *Were you still up for Portillo?* (Harmondsworth: Penguin, 1997)

Chew, Doris N., ed., *The life and writings of Ada Nield Chew* (London: Virago, 1982)

Cloud, Yvonne, ed., *Beside the seaside* (2nd edn, London: The Bodley Head, 1938: first edn 1934)

Clunn, Harold, *Famous south coast pleasure resorts: past and present* (London: T. Whittingham and Co., 1929)

Common, Jack, *Kiddar's luck* (Newcastle: Bloodaxe, 1990; first published 1951)

Craig, F.W.S., *British parliamentary election results 1918–1949* (Glasgow: Political Reference Publications, 1969)

Craig, F.W.S., *British parliamentary election results 1950–1973* (2nd edn, Chichester: Parliamentary Research Services, 1983)

Cyclists' Touring Club, *Handbook and guide 1930* (London: C.T.C., 1930)

Daysh, G.H.J., ed., *A survey of Whitby* (Windsor: Shakespeare Head Press, 1958)

Deal and Walmer Corporation, *The Official Guide to Deal and Walmer* (Deal: Deal Corporation, 1949)

Dibdin, W.J., *The purification of sewage and water* (3rd edn, London: The Sanitary Publishing Co., 1903)

Dougill, W., 'The British coast and its holiday resorts', *Town Planning Review*, 16 (1935)

Fogarty, M.P., *Prospects of the industrial areas of Great Britain* (London: Methuen, 1945)

Forrest, R., and Gordon, D., *People and places: a 1991 census atlas of England* (Bristol: SAUS, 1993)

Forte, Charles, *Forte: the autobiography of Charles Forte* (London: Pan, 1987)

Fuller, Roy, *Souvenirs* (London: London Magazine Edns., 1980)

Goldring, Douglas, *Northern lights and southern shade* (Boston, Mass. and New York: Houghton Mifflin, 1926)

Golfing in Scotland at 100 holiday resorts (2nd edn, Cheltenham: J. Burrow, n.d., c. 1930 (Anon))

Goodsall, Robert H., *On holiday with a camera: at the seaside, in the country* (London: Fountain Press, 1939)

Gordon, D., and Forrest, R., *People and places 2: social and economic divisions in England* (Bristol: SAUS, 1995)

Graves, Charles, *-And the Greeks* (London: Cassell, 1930)

Greene, Graham, *Brighton rock* (London: Heinemann, 1938)

Greenwood, Walter, *Love on the dole* (Harmondsworth:, Penguin, 1969; first published 1933)

Gregory, Alfred, *Blackpool: a celebration of the '60s* (London: Constable, 1993)

Haggart, S.M., and Porter, D., *England on $5 and $10 a day* (New York: Arthur Frommer, 1969–70 edn)

Hornsby, M., *'The Queen' newspaper book of travel: a guide to home and foreign resorts* (London: Horace Cox, 1907)

Hough, S.B., *Where? An independent report on holiday resorts in Britain and the Continent* (London: Hodder and Stoughton, 1964)

Hutt, Allen, *The condition of the working class in Britain* (London, 1933)

Ilfracombe Joint Advertising Committee, *Ilfracombe: Official Guide* (Ilfracombe, 1969)

Jones, D. Caradog, ed., *The social survey of Merseyside* (3 vols., Liverpool: Liverpool University Press, 1934)

Kirkup, James, *A child of the Tyne* (Salzburg: Institut fur Anglistik und Amerikanistik, 1996)

Lavery, P., *Patterns of holidaymaking in the Northern Region* (Newcastle: University of Newcastle, 1971)

Laycock, Arthur, *Warren of Manchester* (London: Simpkin, Marshall, n.d. (*c.* 1906))

Lyons, L. Ash, *Blackpool bathing beauties souvenir 1950* (St Annes-on-sea: L. Ash Lyons, 1950)

Mawson, T.H., *The life and work of an English landscape architect* (London, 1927)

(Meek, George), *George Meek, Bath Chair-man, by himself* (London: Constable, 1910)

Morecambe Corporation, *The official guide to Morecambe* (Morecambe: Advertising Committee of Morecambe Corporation, 1926)

Muir, Frank, *A Kentish lad* (London: Corgi, 1998)

Murray, D.L., *Leading lady* (London: Hodder and Stoughton, 1947)

Murt, Eddie, *Downlong days: a St Ives miscellany* (St Ives: The St Ives Printing and Publishing Company)

Norman, Philip, *The skaters' waltz* (London: Hamish Hamilton, 1979)

Norris, P., Crewe, I., Denver, D., and Broughton, D. (eds), *British Elections and Parties Yearbook 1992* (Hemel Hempstead, 1992)

Oakes, Philip, *From middle England: a memory of the 1930s and 1940s* (Harmondsworth: Penguin, 1983)

Perkin, H.J., 'The "social tone" of Victorian seaside resorts on the north-west', *Northern History*, 11 (1976), pp. 180–94

Pinney, R.G., *Britain – destination of tourists?* (London: Travel Association of the United Kingdom, 1944)

Pontin, Sir Fred, *My happy life, always . . . Thumbs up!* (London: Solo Books, 1991)

Priestley, J.B., *English journey* (London: Heinemann, 1934)

Rallings, C., and Thrasher, M., eds, *Local elections in Britain: a statistical digest* (Plymouth: Local Government Chronicle Elections Centre, 1994)

Reynolds, Stephen, *A poor man's house* (London: London Magazine Edns., 1980; first published 1908)

Richards, Frank, *Billy Bunter at Butlin's* (London: Cassell, 1961)

Saleeby, C.W., *Sunlight and health* (London: Nisbet, 1923)

Seed's *Southport and district directory* (Preston: R. Seed, 1914)

Sidmouth Urban District Council, *Official Guide and Souvenir of Sidmouth* (Gloucester: British Publishing Company, 1957)

Smith, Anthony, *Beside the seaside* (London: Allen and Unwin, 1972)

Southport Corporation, *Sunny Southport: official guide 1929–1930* (Southport: Southport Corporation, 1929)

Speight, Johnny, *It stands to reason: a kind of autobiography* (London: Michael Joseph, 1973)

The Times, House of Commons 1945 (London, 1945)

Theroux, Paul, *The kingdom by the sea* (Harmondsworth: Penguin, 1984; first published 1983)

Thomas, Dylan, *Miscellany Two* (London: Faber and Faber, 1966)

Thorne, Matt, *Tourist* (London: Hodder and Stoughton, 1998)

Torquay, the English Riviera: official guide (Torquay: Torquay Publishing Co., 1932)

Tressell, R., *The ragged-trousered philanthropists* (London: Panther, 1965; first published 1914)

Wells, H.G., *The history of Mr Polly* (London: Pan Books, 1963; first published 1910)

W.H. Wheeler, *The sea-coast* (London: Longmans, 1902)

Wodehouse, P.G., *The heart of a goof* (London: Herbert Jenkins, autograph edn, 1956; first published 1926)

Woodruff, William, *Billy boy: the story of a Lancashire weaver's son* (Halifax: Ryburn, 1993)

Wright, Harold, ed., *Letters of Stephen Reynolds* (Richmond, Surrey: L. and V. Woolf, 1925)

Secondary sources: books

Adamson, Simon H., *Seaside piers* (London: Batsford, 1977)

Addison, Paul, *Now the war is over: a social history of Britain 1945–51* (2nd edn, London: Pimlico, 1995)

Anderson, R.C., and Frankis, G., *History of Royal Blue express services* (Newton Abbot: David and Charles, 1970)

Bailey, Peter, *Popular culture and performance in the Victorian city* (Cambridge: Cambridge University Press, 1998)

Baker, Michael H.C., *Railways to the coast* (Wellingborough: Patrick Stephens, 1990)

Ball, F.C., *One of the damned: the life and times of Robert Tressell* (2nd edn, Lawrence and Wishart, 1979; first published 1973)

Barke, M., *et al.*, eds, *Tourism in Spain: critical perspectives* (Wallingford: CAB, 1996)

Battilani, P., *Vacanze di pochi, vacanze di tutti: breve storia del turismo* (Bologna: Il Mulino, 1998)

Bennett, Tony, Mercer, Colin and Woollacott, Janet, eds, *Popular culture and social relations* (Milton Keynes: Open University Press, 1986)

Bingham, R., *Lost resort? The flow and ebb of Morecambe* (Carnforth, Milnthorpe: Cicerone, 1991)

Burdett Wilson, R., *Go Great Western: a history of GWR publicity* (Newton Abbot: David and Charles, 1970)

Butcher, D., *Living from the sea* (Sulhamstead: Tops'l, 1982)

Cannadine, David, *Lords and landlords: the aristocracy and the towns 1774–1967* (Leicester: Leicester University Press, 1980)

Cannadine, David, ed., *Patricians, power and politics in nineteenth-century towns* (Leicester: Leicester University Press, 1982)

Carr-Saunders, A.M., Caradog Jones, D., and Moser, C., *A survey of social conditions in England and Wales* (Oxford: Clarendon, 1958)

Chapman, M. and B. Chapman, *The pierrots of the Yorkshire coast* (Beverley: Hutton Press, 1988)

Cooke, P., ed., *Localities* (London: Unwin Hyman, 1989)

Corbin, A., *The lure of the sea* (Cambridge: Cambridge University Press, 1992)

Corin, John, *Fishermen's conflict: the story of Newlyn* (Newton Abbot: David and Charles, 1988)

Corrigan, Edwin, *Ups and downs and roundabouts* (Driffield: Ridings Publishing, 1972)

Cracknell, B.E., *Canvey Island: the history of a marshland community* (Leicester: Leicester University Press, 1959)

Crosby, A., ed., *Leading the way: a history of Lancashire's roads* (Preston: Carnegie, 1998)

Cross, Gary, *Time and money: the making of consumer culture* (London: Routledge, 1993)

Cross, Gary, ed., *Worktowners at Blackpool* (London: Routledge, 1990)

Davies, Andrew, *Leisure, gender and poverty* (Buckingham: Open University Press, 1992)

Davies, S., *et al.*, eds, *County borough elections in inter-war England*, Vol. 1 (Aldershot: Ashgate, 1999)

De Mille, Ailsa Ogilvie, *One man's dream: the story behind G. Stuart Ogilvie and the creation of Thorpeness* (Dereham: Nostalgia Publications, 1996)

Elleray, D.R., *Worthing: aspects of change* (Chichester: Phillimore, 1985)

Fearon, M., *Filey: from fishing village to Edwardian resort* (Beverley: Hutton Press, 1990)

Fischer, R., and Walton, John K., *British piers* (London: Thames and Hudson, 1987)

Fisher, Stephen, ed., *Recreation and the sea* (Exeter: University of Exeter Press, 1997)

Fiske, John, *Reading the popular* (London: Unwin Hyman, 1989)

Fowler, D., *The first teenagers* (London: Woburn, 1995)

Garrad, L.S., *A present from . . . Holiday souvenirs of the British Isles* (Newton Abbot: David and Charles, 1976)

Gay, J.D., *The geography of religion in England* (London: Duckworth, 1971)

Gilbert, Edmund W., *Brighton, old ocean's bauble* (2nd edn, Hassocks: Flare Books, 1975; first published 1954)

Green, Benny, *I've lost my little Willie* (London: Arrow, 1976)

Gregson, Nicky, and Lowe, Michelle, *Servicing the middle classes: gender and waged domestic labour in contemporary Britain* (London: Routledge, 1994)

Grieve, Hilda, *The great tide: the story of the 1953 flood disaster in Essex* (Chelmsford: Essex County Council, 1959)

Halliwell, Leslie, *Halliwell's film guide* (7th edn, London: HarperCollins, 1990)

Halsey, A.H. (ed.), *Trends in British society since 1900* (London: Macmillan, 1972)

Hardy, Dennis, and Ward, Colin, *Arcadia for all: the legacy of a makeshift landscape* (London: Mansell, 1984)

Hemingway, A., *Landscape imagery and urban culture in early nineteenth-century Britain* (Cambridge: Cambridge University Press, 1992)

Holm, P., *Kystfolk: kontakter og sammenhaenge over Kattegat og Skagerak ca. 1500–1914* (Esbjerg: Fiskeri-og Sofartsmuseet, 1991)

Hope, Maurice G., *Castles in the sand: the story of New Brighton* (Ormskirk: G.W. Hesketh and A. Hesketh, 1982)

Hudson, John, *Wakes Week: memories of mill town holidays* (Gloucester: Alan Sutton, 1992)

Humphries, Steve, *A secret world of sex* (London: Sidgwick and Jackson, 1989)

Jackson, A.A., *The middle classes 1900–1950* (Nairn: David St John Thomas, 1992)

Joyce, Patrick, *Visions of the people* (Cambridge: Cambridge University Press, 1991)

Karn, V., *Retiring to the seaside* (London: Routledge, 1977)

King, A.D., *The bungalow: the production of a global culture* (London: Routledge, 1984)

Lancaster, Bill, *The department store* (Leicester: Leicester University Press, 1995)

Laurence, A.E., with Insole, A.N., *Prometheus bound: Karl Marx on the Isle of Wight* (Newport, Isle of Wight, n.d.: Isle of Wight County Council)

Le Roy Ladurie, E., *Carnival: a people's uprising at Romans* (New York: Scolar, 1979)

Lencek, L., and Bosker, G., *The beach: the history of paradise on earth* (London: Secker and Warburg, 1998)

Lindley, K., *Seaside architecture* (London: Hugh Evelyn, 1973)

McCallum, R.B., and Readman, A., *The British General Election of 1945* (London: Oxford University Press, 1947)

Marshall, J.D., *Old Lakeland* (Newton Abbot: David and Charles, 1971)

Marshall, J.D., and Walton, John K., *The Lake counties from 1830 to the mid-twentieth century* (Manchester: Manchester University Press, 1981)

Mellor, G.J., *Pom-poms and ruffles* (Clapham via Ingleton: Dalesman, 1966)

Murgatroyd, L., Savage, M., Shapiro, O., Urry, J., Walby, S., Warde, A., with J. Mark-Lawson, *Localities, class and gender* (London: Pion, 1985)

Musgrave, C., *Life in Brighton* (London: Faber and Faber, 1970)

Neale, R.S., *Bath 1680–1850: a valley of pleasure or a sink of iniquity?* (London: Routledge, 1981)

Norris, S., *Manx memories and movements* (Douglas: Norris Modern Press, 1941)

North, Rex, *The Butlin story* (London: Jarrolds, 1962)

Nuttall, Jeff, *King Twist* (London: Routledge and Kegan Paul, 1978)

O'Connell, S., *The car in British society: class, gender and motoring 1896–1939* (Manchester: Manchester University Press, 1998)

O'Connor, B., and Cronin, M., eds, *Tourism in Ireland: a critical analysis* (Cork, 1993)

Pahl, R.E., *Divisions of labour* (Oxford: Blackwell, 1984)

Parry, Keith, *Resorts of the Lancashire coast* (Newton Abbot: David and Charles, 1983)

Payton, Philip, ed., *Cornwall since the war* (Redruth: Institute of Cornish Studies, 1993)

Pearson, L.F., *The people's palaces: the story of the seaside pleasure buildings of 1870–1914* (Buckingham: Barracuda, 1991)

Peak, S., *Fishermen of Hastings: 200 years of the Hastings fishing community* (St Leonards-on-Sea: NewsBooks, 1985)

Perkin, Harold, *The age of the automobile* (London: Quartet, 1976)

Pertwee, B., *Pertwee's promenades and pierrots* (Newton Abbot: David and Charles, 1979)

Pimlott, J.A.R., *The Englishman's holiday: a social history* (2nd edn, Hassocks: Harvester Press, 1976; first published 1947)

QueenSpark Rates Book Group, *Brighton on the rocks: monetarism and the local state* (Brighton: QueenSpark, 1983)

Richards, Jeffrey, *The age of the dream palace* (London: Routledge, 1984)

Richards, Thomas, *The commodity culture of Victorian England* (London: Routledge, 1991)

Rose, M.B., ed., *The Lancashire cotton industry: a history since 1700* (Preston: Carnegie, 1996)

Russell, Alice, *The growth of occupational welfare in Britain* (Aldershot: Avebury, 1991)

Severgnini, Beppe, *Inglesi* (Milan: Biblioteca Universale Rizzoli, 1992)

Shaw, Gareth, and Williams, Allan, eds, *The rise and fall of British coastal resorts* (London: Pinter, 1997)

Shields, Rob, *Places on the margin: alternative geographies of modernity* (London: Routledge, 1991)

Simmons, Jack, *The railway in town and country 1830–1914* (Newton Abbot: David and Charles, 1986)

Smith, David Norman, *The railway and its passengers: a social history* (Newton Abbot: David and Charles, 1988)

Stafford, F., and Yates, N., eds, *The later Kentish seaside* (Gloucester: Alan Sutton for the Kent Archives Office, 1985)

Soane, J.V.N., *Fashionable resort regions: their evolution and transformation* (Wallingford: CAB Publications, 1993)

Taylor, Harvey, *A claim on the countryside: a history of the British outdoor movement* (Edinburgh: Keele University Press, 1997)

Towner, John, *An historical geography of recreation and tourism in the western world 1540–1940* (Chichester: Wiley, 1996)

Travis, John, *The rise of the Devon seaside resorts 1750–1900* (Exeter: University of Exeter Press, 1993)

Urbain, J.-D., *Sur la plage* (Paris: Payot, 1994)

Urry, John, *Consuming places* (London: Sage, 1995)

Urry, John, *Holiday-making, cultural change and the seaside* (Lancaster: Lancaster University Regionalism Group, 1987)

Urry, John, *The tourist gaze* (London: Sage, 1990)

Urry, John, and Rojek, Chris, *Touring cultures* (London: Routledge, 1997)

Walton, John K., *Blackpool* (Edinburgh: Edinburgh University Press, 1998)

Walton, John K., *The Blackpool landlady: a social history* (Manchester: Manchester University Press, 1978)

Walton, John K., *The English seaside resort: a social history 1750–1914* (Leicester: Leicester University Press, 1983)

Walton, John K., *Fish and chips and the British working class 1870–1940* (Leicester: Leicester University Press, 1992)

Walton, John K., and Walvin, James, eds, *Leisure in Britain 1780–1939* (Manchester: Manchester University Press, 1983)

Walvin, James, *Beside the seaside* (Harmondsworth: Penguin, 1978)

Ward, Colin, and Hardy, Dennis, *Goodnight campers! The history of the British holiday camp* (London: Mansell, 1986)

Ward, S.V., *The geography of inter-war Britain: the state and uneven development* (London: Routledge, 1988)

Williams, Bridget, *The best butter in the world: a history of Sainsbury's* (London: Ebury, 1994)

Young, David S., *The story of Bournemouth* (London: Robert Hale, 1957)

Young, Gerard, *A history of Bognor Regis* (Chichester: Phillimore, 1983)

Secondary sources: articles and chapters in edited collections

Bandyopadhyay, P., 'The holiday camp', in Smith, Michael A., Parker, Stanley and Smith, Cyril, eds, *Leisure and society in Britain* (London: Allen Lane, 1973)

Bowman, G., 'Fucking tourists: sexual relations and tourism in Jerusalem's Old City', *Critique of Anthropology*, 9 (1992), 77–93

Built Environment, special issue on coastal resorts, 18 (1992)

Butler, R.W., 'The concept of a tourist area cycle of evolution', *Canadian Geographer* 24, 5–12

Durie, A., 'The development of the Scottish coastal resorts in the Central Lowlands, *c.* 1770–1880: from Gulf Stream to golf stream', *Local Historian*, 24 (1994), 206–16

Durie, A., and Huggins, M., 'Sport, social tone and the seaside resorts of Great Britain, 1850–1914', *International Journal of the History of Sport*, 15 (1998), 173–87

Gale, T., Botterill, D., Morgan, M., and Shaw, G., 'Reconstructing the past: an analysis of landscape, brochures and local authority involvement in the seaside resort of Rhyl, 1945–97', *Concord*, 8 (1998).

Gurney, P., ' "Intersex" and "Dirty Girls": Mass-Observation and working-class sexuality in England in the 1930s', *Journal of the History of Sexuality*, 8 (1997), 256–90

Hassan, John, 'Were health resorts bad for your health? Coastal pollution control policy in England, 1945–76', *Environment and History*, 5 (1999), 53–73

Huggins, M., 'Social tone and resort development in north-east England', *Northern History*, 20 (1984), 187–206

Jones, S.G., 'The Lancashire cotton industry and the development of paid holidays in the 1930s', *Transactions of the Historic Society of Lancashire and Cheshire* 135 (1986), 99–115

Lewis, R., 'Seaside holiday resorts in the United States and Britain', *Urban History Yearbook* 1980, 44–52

Meethan, Kevin, 'Place, image and power: Brighton as a resort', in Tom Selwyn (ed.), *The tourist image: myths and myth making in tourism* (Chichester: Wiley, 1996)

Meller, Helen, 'Nizza e Blackpool: due citta balneari agli inizi del Novecento', *Contemporanea* 4 (1998), 651–80

O'Neill, C., 'Windermere in the 1920s', *Local Historian*, 24 (1994), 205–16

Richards, Jeffrey, 'Cul-de-sac England', in Jeffrey Richards and Anthony Aldgate, eds, *Best of British* (London: Routledge, 1998)

Samuels, J.A., 'Research to help plan the future of a seaside resort', in S. Riley, ed., *Proceedings of the 12th marketing theory seminar* (University of Lancaster: Department of Marketing 1974), 63–77

Shaw, G., and Williams, A., 'From bathing-hut to theme park: tourism development in south-west England', *Journal of Regional and Local Studies*, 11 (1991), 16–32

Sheail, J., 'The impact of recreation on the coast: the Lindsey County Council (Sandhills) Act, 1932', *Landscape Planning* 1977

Simmons, J., 'Railways, hotels and tourism in Great Britain 1839–1914', *Journal of Contemporary History*, 9 (1984)

Smith, Brian C., 'Torquay', in L.J. Sharpe (ed.), *Voting in cities: the 1964 borough elections* (London: Allen and Unwin, 1967)

Vernon, James, 'Border crossings: Cornwall and the English (imagi)nation', in G. Cubitt, ed., *Imagining nations* (Manchester: Manchester University Press, 1998)

Walton, John K., 'The Blackpool landlady revisited', *Manchester Region History Review*, 8 (1994), 23–30

Walton, John K., 'The demand for working-class seaside holidays in Victorian England', *Economic History Review*, 34 (1981), 249–65

Walton, John K., 'Leisure towns in wartime: the impact of the First World War in Blackpool and San Sebastian', *Journal of Contemporary History*, 31 (1996), 603–18

Walton, John K., 'Leisure towns in the aftermath of war: coping with social change and political upheaval in Blackpool and San Sebastian, 1918–23', in F. Walter and R. Hudemann (eds), *Villes et guerres mondiales au XXe siecle* (Paris: L'Harmattan, 1997)

Walton, John K., 'Popular entertainment and public order: the Blackpool Carnivals of 1923–4', *Northern History*, 34 (1998), 170–88

Walton, John K., 'The remaking of a popular resort: Blackpool Tower and the boom of the 1890s', *Local Historian* 24 (1994), 194–205

Walton, John K., 'Seaside resorts and maritime history', *International Journal of Maritime History*, 9 (1997), 125–47

Walton, John K., 'The world's first working-class seaside resort? Blackpool revisited, 1840–1974', *Transactions of the Lancashire and Cheshire Antiquarian Society*, 88 (1992), 1–30

Walton, John K., and O'Neill, C., 'Numbering the holidaymakers: the problems and possibilities of the June census of 1921 for historians of resorts', *Local Historian*, 23 (1993), 205–16

Wild, P., 'Recreation in Rochdale 1900–1940', in Clarke, J., Critcher, Chas, and Johnson, R., eds, *Working class culture* (London: Hutchinson, 1979), 140–60

Yates, N., 'Selling the seaside', *History Today* 38 (1988)

Unpublished theses and papers

Ambrose, R., 'Gay tourism in Blackpool: a geographical study', BA dissertation, Department of Geography, University of Birmingham, 1992

Bertramsen Nye, Helle B., 'Liminality at turn-of-the-century Brighton', unpublished paper, University of Lancaster, 1997

Chase, Laura, 'The creation of place image in inter-war Clacton and Frinton', Ph.D. thesis, University of Essex, 1999

Crouch, D., 'Westgate on Sea 1865–1940', Ph.D. thesis, University of Kent, 1999

Demetriadi, J., English and Welsh seaside resorts 1950–74 with special reference to Blackpool and Margate, 1950–74', Ph.D. thesis, University of Lancaster, 1995

Essafi, N., 'Some aspects of poverty in Blackpool, 1945–60', MA dissertation, University of Lancaster, 1990

Grass, J., 'Morecambe: the people's pleasure', MA dissertation, University of Lancaster, 1972

Jolly, Lisa, 'Blackpool: seaside sex capital?', BA dissertation, University of Central Lancashire, 1999

Messenger, S., 'Youth culture in Blackpool between the wars', MA dissertation, University of Lancaster, 1993

Morgan, N., 'Perceptions, patterns and policies of tourism', Ph.D. thesis, University of Exeter, 1992

Parsons, G.A., 'Property, profit and pollution: conflict in estuarine water management 1800–1915', Ph.D. thesis, University of Lancaster, 1996

Simmill, I., 'The development of an industrial town: Morecambe between the wars', MA dissertation, University of Lancaster, 1993

Stallibrass, H.C., 'The holiday accommodation industry, with special reference to Scarborough, England', Ph.D. thesis, University of London, 1978

Walton, John K., 'The social development of Blackpool, 1788–1914', Ph.D. thesis, University of Lancaster, 1974

Index